KT-462-380

E

PRE-INTERMEDIATE

Ruth Gairns
Stuart Redman

TEACHER'S BOOK

CAMBRIDGE
UNIVERSITY PRESS

CONTENTS

INTRODUCTION

Who this course is for

True to Life is a three-level course designed to take learners from elementary to good intermediate level.

The course is specifically designed for adult learners. Topics have been chosen for their interest and relevance to adults around the world, and activities have been designed to provide adults with the opportunity to talk about their experiences, express opinions, use their knowledge and imagination to solve problems and exchange ideas so as to learn from one another.

True to Life Pre-intermediate is for learners who have covered a basic course such as *True to Life Elementary* or who have a basic working ability at elementary level. It provides approximately 72 hours upwards of classroom activity, depending on the time available and the options used.

Key features

True to Life incorporates the best of current classroom methodology by providing varied teaching materials to meet the needs of different learners and learning styles, but particular attention has been paid to the following:

1 Learner engagement and personalisation

We believe that learning is most effective when learners are actively engaged in tasks which they find motivating and challenging. Moreover, it is essential for learners to have opportunities to see the relevance of new language to their own personal circumstances. We have, therefore, provided a very large number of open-ended and interactive tasks which allow learners to draw on their knowledge of the world and to be creative. These tasks are used not just for fluency work but also in quite controlled activities designed to activate specific language areas (vocabulary, grammar and functions).

2 Speaking and listening

It has been our experience that adult learners lay great emphasis on oral/aural practice in the classroom, often because it is their only opportunity to obtain such practice. We have, therefore, decided to limit the amount of reading material in the Class Book (but increase it in the Personal Study Workbook) so that we can devote more time and space to speaking and listening. Users should find that opportunities for speaking practice are present in most stages of the lessons.

3 Recycling

We have decided to employ the 'little and often' approach to revision. Instead of sporadic chunks, we have devoted one page in every unit to revision. This section is called *Review and development*; it gives learners a chance to review material while it is still relatively fresh in their minds, and ensures that material from every unit is formally recycled on two separate occasions, excluding the tests in the Teacher's Book. For example:

Unit 10

Lesson 1	*Lesson 2*	*Lesson 3*	*Lesson 4*
input	input	input	Review and development of Units 8 and 9

Unit 11

Lesson 1	*Lesson 2*	*Lesson 3*	*Lesson 4*
input	input	input	Review and development of Units 9 and 10

4 Flexibility

It is important that learners know what they are learning and can see a clear path through the material. It is also important, though, that teachers can adapt material to suit the needs of their particular class. We have provided for this with the inclusion of further activities in the Teacher's Book (called Options), and some of these contain worksheets which may be photocopied. This, then, gives teachers a clear framework in the Class Book, but with additional resources to draw upon in the Teacher's Book for extra flexibility.

5 Vocabulary

In *True To Life*, vocabulary is not treated as a separate section because it forms an intrinsic and fundamental part of every unit, and a wide range of vocabulary activities is included throughout the three levels. Moreover, great importance is attached in these activities to spoken practice of newly presented lexical items, so learners have the opportunity to use new words and phrases in utterances of their own creation.

In the Class Book and, even more so, in the Personal Study Workbook, vocabulary learning skills are introduced and developed, as are activities which make learners more aware of important aspects of word grammar. These include lexical storage and record keeping, contextual guesswork, word building, collocation, and so on.

6 The Personal Study Workbook

This aims to be as engaging on an individual basis as the Class Book is on a group basis. Personalisation is, therefore, carried through to the Personal Study Workbook, which provides a range of activities, both structured and open-ended, designed to motivate learners to continue their learning outside the classroom. Special features include:

Visual dictionary: thirteen pages of illustrations for learners to label. That is, a personal dictionary which is easy to compile, and genuinely self-access with the aid of a bilingual dictionary.

Speaking partners: The single thing most learners want to practise outside the classroom is speaking; unfortunately it is often the most difficult to organise. We have, therefore, introduced the concept of 'speaking partners' in Unit 1 of the Class Book, and then included it throughout the Personal Study Workbook. Speaking partners invites learners to find a partner who they meet (or phone) on a regular basis outside the classroom, and practise speaking English with using ideas and activities suggested in the Workbook.

Components and course organisation

At each level, the course consists of the following:
Class Book and Class Cassette Set
Personal Study Workbook and Personal Study Cassette
    or CD
Teacher's Book

The Class Book and Class Cassette Set

The Class Book contains 24 units, each one providing three to four hours of classroom activity. Each unit is divided into four lessons and each lesson is designed to take 45 to 60 minutes. Teachers are, of course, free to explore the material in different ways (indeed we have indicated ways of doing this in the following teacher's notes), but each lesson has been designed as a self-contained, logical sequence of varied activities, which can be used as they stand.

The first three lessons contain the main language input. This consists of:
– a clear grammatical syllabus
– an emphasis on lexical development
– key functional exponents
– listening and reading practice
– speaking and writing activities.

The final section of each unit provides review and development activities based on the two previous units; e.g. the final section of Unit 4 revises Units 2 and 3; the final section of Unit 5 revises Units 3 and 4.

At the back of Class Book there is:
– a Grammar Reference section
– the tapescript of selected recordings for the Class Book
– a list of irregular verbs
– the phonetic alphabet.

The listening material on the Class Cassette Set is very varied – scripted, semi-scripted and unscripted – and a particular feature is the regular inclusion of dual-level listening texts. These provide two versions of a listening passage, one longer and more challenging than the other. This feature allows teachers to select the listening material that best meets the needs of their particular learners, but it also gives more scope for exploitation. In some cases, the content of the listening in each version is different, so teachers may start with the easier listening and then move on to the more difficult one; in other cases where the content is the same but more challenging, the teacher could (if facilities permit) split the group and give a different listening to different

learners. And there is nothing to stop a teacher doing version 1 at one point in the course, and then returning to do version 2, days, weeks or even months later.

The Personal Study Workbook and Personal Study Cassette or CD

The Personal Study Workbook runs parallel to the Class Book, providing 24 units which contain further practice and consolidation of the material in the Class Book.

The exercises at the beginning of each unit concentrate on consolidating grammar and vocabulary; later exercises focus on skills development, with a space at the end of each unit for the learners to record their problems and progress in English.

The Personal Study Cassette or CD provides further material for listening practice, and there is a tapescript at the back of the Workbook along with an answer key for most of the exercises.

An additional feature is the visual dictionary, which provides thirteen pages of illustrations at the back of the book for learners to compile their own personal dictionary. The material is linked to the units in the Class Book, so learners complete it at regular intervals during the course.

The Teacher's Book

This offers teachers a way through the activities presented, but also provides a wide range of ideas that will enable them to approach and extend the activities in different ways. Some of these include worksheets which may be photocopied and distributed in class.

In addition, the Teacher's Book provides:
– guidance on potential language difficulties
– a complete answer key to the exercises in the Class Book.
– four photocopiable formal tests, each test covering six units of the Class Book
– tapescripts of the Class Book recordings which may be photocopied and given to learners.

GETTING STARTED

CONTENTS

Language focus: present continuous for 'around now'
present continuous vs. present simple
use of *should*: a. to express the 'correct' way to do something,
b. to give advice
adverbs of degree, e.g. *a bit, quite, very*

Vocabulary: office equipment
describing how we work and study, e.g. *concentrate,*
sit at a desk, in silence
adjectives describing personality, e.g. *tidy/untidy*

Skills: Speaking: work/study habits
people's characters
temporary activities
arranging speaking partners
Reading: famous writers and their work habits
Listening: people describing their work habits
people talking about temporary activities
discussing speaking partners

PERSONAL STUDY HABITS

Introduction

Some opening activities are suggested below if this is your first lesson with the learners. The first exercise in the Class Book, however, is a warm-up to get the learners active and involved in the theme of the lesson. The questionnaire (Exercise 2) is a reading and vocabulary activity reinforcing the use of the present simple for habits. It is then used as the basis for personalised speaking practice. Learners make use of the information obtained to identify their own and other people's working characteristics, and learn some new vocabulary for describing personality. Having learnt this vocabulary and used the questionnaire, they should be able to listen with increased confidence to native speakers doing the same activity.

(There are easy and difficult versions of this activity: see page 2.)

Getting to know each other

Is this your first lesson with the class? If so, before you start the exercises in the Class Book, you probably need to greet the class, get them to greet each other and learn each other's names. There may also be administrative tasks that your institution requires you to carry out, or you may wish to tell the class something about yourself to encourage them to talk about themselves or to ask questions.

Option 1

Here is one activity for initial greetings. If you know the names of your learners in advance, write out a list of their names, and make a photocopy for each one and distribute it. (If you don't have access to a photocopier, write the names on the board and ask the learners to copy them.)

Tell the learners to find out who the people are on their list, and then to find out one more interesting fact about them and write it next to their name. Demonstrate this first with one or two people in front of the class. Then ask them to mingle and find out the information. Conduct class feedback asking the learners to give information about others in the class.

Option 2

Here is another activity for learners to get to know each other. If you are working with a multilingual group you will need copies of Worksheet 1A, which you will find on page 124. Give each member of the group a copy, put them in pairs of different nationalities, and get them to fill in their partner's name and country on their own questionnaire. Then tell them to fill in the rest of the questionnaire without asking their partner. Encourage them to guess anything they don't know and stress that there is no shame in not knowing the answers. When they have finished, they tell each other their answers and add to the information.

With a monolingual group, use Worksheet 1B. Give each member of the group a copy; tell the learners to find a partner they don't know, then tell them to interview that partner to complete their questionnaire. When they have finished, one person can tell another person about their partner.

Suggested steps

1

You could ask several of the questions before the learners open their books. Then tell them to open their books and write their answers individually. When they have finished, put them in groups to compare answers.

2

Make it clear that they can answer the questionnaire about either work or study, and that it may be more appropriate for some learners to talk about their habits in the workplace (not at home).

Allow time for the learners to read through the questionnaire and look up new words or phrases in a dictionary. Help with explanations where necessary. If your learners do not have access to dictionaries, you may find it quicker and easier to pre-teach items you anticipate will be new, e.g. *lie on the floor*, *a mess*, *scratch your head*, etc. They can then complete the questionnaire individually, although you may be called upon to help those who want to write their own answers in (d).

Put the learners in pairs to discuss answers and monitor their language while they talk. At the end, conduct a quick feedback and point out good examples of language use along with important errors and correction.

3

Pre-teach/check the adjectives and highlight the use of the degree adverbs at the same time (see the Language Point below). Pairs can then discuss their answers.

Language Point: a bit, quite, very

Make it clear to the learners that *a bit*, *quite* and *very* can be used to qualify negative adjectives, but positive adjectives can only be qualified by *quite* and *very*. For example, *very hot* can be a positive or negative remark (it depends how you say it), but *a bit hot* can only be a negative remark.

4 ▢▢ ▢▢

There are two versions of the listening activity, one more difficult than the other. This feature is included throughout the course, and in many cases the main difference between the two recordings is that the easier one has been partly scripted whereas the second recording is completely improvised. Clearly, you are the best person to help the learners decide which one to listen to, although you may decide to do both; the easier one to build confidence and the more difficult one to

provide additional exposure to natural language. In subsequent activities where there are two recordings, you may decide – if you have the facilities – to split the group and let the learners choose which they would prefer to do.

The tapescripts are on page 153.

Answer key

Version 1
1. b   2. a   3. a   4. a   5. a   6. b   7. b   8. b   9. b
10. a
Version 2
1. d (kitchen)   2. d (at a table)   3. a   4. b   5. a   6. b
7. c   8. b   9. b   10. b

If you are using the Personal Study Workbook alongside the Class Book, you may wish to do specific exercises as you proceed through a unit in the Class Book. We have provided suggested exercises for this purpose, and they are signalled at the end of the notes for each lesson from the Class Book. At this point we would recommend:

Personal Study Workbook

5: Understanding this book
6: Correct the text

```
┌─────────────────────────────────────┐
│            QUICK NOTES               │
│  This went well:                     │
│  ..................................  │
│  ..................................  │
│                                      │
│  This didn't quite work:             │
│  ..................................  │
│  ..................................  │
│                                      │
│  Things to think about:              │
│  ..................................  │
│  ..................................  │
└─────────────────────────────────────┘
```

Introduction

The activities present and practise one use of *should* – the correct way to do something – in a natural context, and teach the vocabulary in the texts in a way which creates meaningful oral practice. The personalisation at the end provides further practice and leads into an analysis of the present simple and present continuous, using sentences from the texts.

Suggested steps

1

This can be done in small groups or as a whole class discussion. If you have any books by the authors you should take them to class. (Both authors write popular fiction and have written a number of bestsellers. Jeffrey Archer is a well-known Conservative and is a prominent public figure.)

2

Put the learners in pairs to work on the new vocabulary in Exercise 2. They can help each other and use dictionaries, and you can then check and clarify the meanings at the end.

3

Make sure they cover the text they are *not* reading.

4

After reading, show the learners that the objects on the desk need to be assigned to either Jeffrey's or Sally's desk. Focus on the examples, using *should*, and then elicit one or two more examples, insisting on the use of *should* in the answers. Put the learners in pairs for the rest of the activity and monitor to make sure they use *should*. At the end, you could draw two desks on the board and have the learners tell you where exactly to put the different objects. You may also wish to point out that *should* is used to indicate the correct way to do something or the correct position for something; in our experience the meaning usually becomes clear through the process of doing the activity.

Answer key

The following should be on Jeffrey's desk:
the 7 felt-tipped pens
the pencils
the electric pencil sharpener
the telephone
the family photo
the small clock

The following should be on Sally's desk:
the typewriter
the notepad
the packet of cigarettes
the ashtray
the coffee mugs

5

You could demonstrate by telling the learners how your own workplace is organised.

Option

You could explain how your workplace is organised through a picture dictation, i.e. you describe the contents of your desk and your learners draw it. They could do a similar activity in pairs.

6

The tense review is a quick check on the difference between the two present tenses, using examples from the text. Follow the instructions in the Class Book. The next lesson consolidates this grammar point.

Answer key

1. Present simple: it describes a fact which is thought to be fairly permanent.
2. Present simple: this describes habitual action.
3. Present continuous: this describes something happening around now (not necessarily now at this moment) and which is temporary.
4. Present continuous: this describes something also happening around now and temporary.

Personal Study Workbook

3: There's a mistake – it should be …
4: On my desk
7: Writers and their work routines
9: Visual dictionary

QUICK NOTES

This went well:

....

....

This didn't quite work:

....

....

Things to think about:

....

....

Introduction

The aim of this lesson is to provide practice in the use of the present continuous for temporary activities. This practice is followed by an activity which checks the learners' understanding of the difference between the two present tenses. The lesson begins with an activity to establish the use of the present continuous for temporary activities, with an extensive listening activity to develop listening skills and consolidate the grammar point.

Suggested steps

1

Follow the instructions in the Class Book. Do the first example together; elicit a sentence in the present continuous and put it on the board. Make it clear that you don't want literal sentences here, e.g. *The person is putting money in a pig*, but statements about the temporary activities which are in Exercise 3 (in this example it would be *The person is saving up for something*). Then ask the learners to complete the exercise together.

Answer key (Clockwise from the left)

1. The man is learning to drive.
2. The person is saving up for something.
3. The woman is revising/studying.
4. The man is making something.
5. The man is looking in a newspaper.
6. The man is having an interview.

2 ▭

Play the recording, and then put the learners in pairs to compare their answers. Play the recording again if necessary, before checking answers with the whole class. The tapescript is on page 153.

Answer key

	Exam/test	Feelings
First woman:	'A' levels	feels very nervous
Man:	Open University degree	hard work but fun
Second woman:	driving test	hates it

3

The recording has already provided a model for the speaking activity, but you may wish to demonstrate it once more with several learners. Encourage them to answer naturally and fully where possible.

4

Follow the instructions in the Class Book. Use a couple of examples from the learners' own books to demonstrate it, using the board. Generate as many examples from the learners as possible.

5

Follow the instructions in the Class Book. If you wish, do one example with the group first.

Answer key

1. d   2. g   3. h   4. a   5. i   6. b   7. j   8. f   9. c   10. e

6

This has been included so that the learners become familiar with the Grammar Reference at this early stage in the course; and we hope that as a result of the activity they will return to this section of the book throughout the course and make effective use of it.

Give the learners time to study the reference section and talk about the question in pairs. Then discuss the answers with the whole group.

Option

We have not chosen to practise the use of the present continuous to describe what is happening 'now at this moment' (we assume the learners will be very familiar with this use), but you could revise it with a brief speaking activity if you wish. Ask the class to sit in groups of four or five, in small circles. They must then watch each other carefully and take it in turns to say what one particular person is doing. For example, *Stefan is tapping his foot* or *Christine is smiling*, etc.

Personal Study Workbook

1: He's making a movie
2: I come from Stockholm

QUICK NOTES

This went well:

....
....

This didn't quite work:

....
....

Things to think about:

....
....

Introduction

The last lesson of each unit is normally devoted to the review and development of previous units. However, in this first unit the aim of the lesson is to establish the idea of speaking partners. Learners constantly ask their teachers, *How can I improve my speaking ability outside class?* We recognise this is difficult, particularly in a monolingual environment, but this lesson aims to confront the problem and create opportunities for the learners to work together outside class. We do not expect 100% success, but even if a handful of them adopt this idea, they should derive enormous benefit from it. In many cases the learners attend language classes partly for social reasons, and we are trying to make use of this.

Suggested steps

1

If you are teaching in a monolingual context, use the situation in the book to establish the aims of the lesson, or personalise it using learners in your class. In a multilingual context, you can still begin with the situation in the book, and when your learners have discussed the problems for Juan and Ana, they can then talk about the problems they have in an English-speaking country and compare the two.

At the end of the activity, conduct feedback and write the problems the learners suggest on the board.

2 ▭

Play the recording, then get your learners to compare their answers. While they are doing this, monitor their discussion and play the recording a second or third time if it is obvious that they are having difficulties. Offer the option of looking at the tapescript on the second or third listening. The tapescript is on page 153.

Bring the class together and focus on the use of *should* for advice, highlighting the form. Elicit examples from the class of advice to Juan and Ana, using *should*.

Answer key

Problems	Solutions
1. They didn't know what to talk about.	They talk about work, lessons, free time. The teacher can help as well.
2. They felt stupid.	It was OK after a while; and they speak in a mixture of English and Spanish.
3. Meeting regularly.	They established a routine. They speak on the phone if they can't meet.
4. You can get bored.	They invite other people and make it a social occasion.

3

The questions elicit concrete and down-to-earth data, which will be important in establishing a successful, long-term strategy for oral practice.

Follow the procedure in the book, and be prepared to help them to make contacts and arrangements. You know your class best, and therefore you can suggest ways which will improve the chances of success of the idea. For instance, in some cases meeting in a bar will go down well; in others, a business group having lunch together once or twice a week may be more suitable or more practical.

We should stress that speaking partners is not restricted to pairs, and can work well in small groups.

In the next class, follow up the first speaking partners activities in the Personal Study Workbook to encourage and offer further advice.

Personal Study Workbook

8: Speaking partners
10: Reflections

Reflections is a space for the learners to reflect on their own problems and progress in English. This could take the form of a diary in which the learners describe their feelings about their progress; or it could be more of a record in which they make their own notes on words they have learnt, mistakes they have made, grammar points to remember, etc. You could allow some class time in the early stages of the course for the learners to complete this section, and this can be a useful way for you to evaluate your learners' progress and difficulties. They could show it to you if they wish, but we don't feel you should insist on seeing it. Some teachers may wish to use this space to encourage an individualised written dialogue with their learners.

QUICK NOTES

This went well:

....

....

This didn't quite work:

....

....

Things to think about:

....

....

ASKING QUESTIONS

CONTENTS

Language focus: how to form questions in English: *yes/no*; *wh-* questions;
indirect questions; negative interrogatives
past simple revision
link words: *because, because of, so*
polite refusals: *I'd rather not (answer that)*

Vocabulary: describing important biographical information,
e.g. *I was born / I grew up in ...*
common questions to be learnt as phrases,
e.g. *what's it like? what type/kind of ...?*

Skills: Speaking: questions you can ask in different cultures
describing your own background
asking questions

     Listening: someone describing their background
     Reading: quiz
a jumbled biography to develop cohesion
     Writing: questions

ASKING PERSONAL QUESTIONS

Introduction

This unit presents a range of questions relating to biographical information. Learners are encouraged to think not only about form, but also about cultural appropriateness. In this lesson in particular, learners should have the right not to answer a question if they don't wish to. The instructions in Exercise 2 draw attention to the different ways in which learners can discover the meaning of new words. Throughout the course, we would recommend that you encourage your learners to exploit all of these different methods (and not just rely on you). Once again, we are using personalisation as a way into the lesson and a way to create further practice at the end.

Suggested steps

Option

You may wish to begin the lesson by asking the learners to talk about their speaking partners exercise from the Personal Study Workbook, Unit 1.

1

Ask the learners several personal but non-threatening questions, and encourage them to ask you some questions. This could be an appropriate point at which to teach: *I'd rather not answer that* or *I'd rather not say* (*I'd rather = I'd prefer*). Then continue the exercise in the Class Book.

2

Make clear that the aim of the first part is to check understanding/pronunciation of the vocabulary in the questions, and *not* to answer the questions. When you and they are satisfied that the vocabulary is clear, tell them to group the questions under the three headings, but warn them that several questions may fit two headings. When they have finished, tell them to add one more question for each group.

Conduct feedback to check answers and make sure the learners say the sentences in the feedback, and not just the numbers. Elicit their own additional questions and discuss them as a class. Correct if necessary.

Answer key

Money: 1; 2; 10; 12; 13
Relationships: 3; 4; 8; 9; 11; 14; 15
You: 5; 6; 7; 8

Possible additional questions
Money: How much did your car cost?
Relationships: Do you often have arguments with your
     partner?
You: Are you ambitious?

3

Do a few examples with the class before they work in groups. At this point you could check that they understand *rude* and *shocking*. It is not our intention that learners should put the questions into indirect speech in this activity (i.e. it is acceptable to say, 'It's rude to ask,

"How much do you earn?" ').

Monitor the groups and collect language points for feedback at the end. For example, you could note examples of good or inaccurate English and write these on the board for learners to comment on. Make sure you also have a class feedback on their ideas.

4

Follow the instructions in the Class Book. Remind the learners not to ask questions if they already know the answers: there should be plenty of questions there that they will not know the answers to. You should also remind them not to ask questions which they themselves said were inappropriate in the previous exercise.

This exercise is equally suitable for monolingual and multilingual groups, but the questions are likely to be different in the two contexts. In this way learners can ask each other genuinely communicative questions.

Personal Study Workbook

4: Catch the pronoun
5: Stress and rhythm
7: Jokes

QUICK NOTES

This went well:

....
....

This didn't quite work:

....
....

Things to think about:

....
....

HOW MUCH DO YOU KNOW?

Introduction

Learners at this level can usually ask questions to fulfil their basic needs, but they may be inaccurate. There are also certain questions in English which learners often confuse, e.g. *would you like/do you like*; *how much/how many*. This quiz is, therefore, provided as a way of revising question forms, and collects together a range of predictable problems involving form and meaning.

We are again drawing the learners' attention to the Grammar Reference at the back of the Class Book, since awareness of these notes can encourage learner independence. The final activity provides further practice of questions.

Suggested steps

1

With any form of problem-solving activity, there are some learners who prefer to work individually before comparing answers, and it is probably counter-productive to force them to work with a partner initially. This is an ideal opportunity for you to monitor and give individual attention to your learners.

As soon as the learners have finished, encourage them to use the Grammar Reference on pages 158 and 159 to find the answers to the first three questions. (This will give those who finish quickly an extra task to do.) Use the feedback to clarify any further errors of form and meaning.

Option

You could devise a scoring scheme for this quiz, and organise the class into teams. These teams would confer on their answers before feedback.

For example:
Question 1: 3 marks total
Question 2: 2 marks
Question 3: 2 marks (quite a difficult one)
Question 4: half a mark for each question: 3 marks total
Question 5: 2 marks
Question 6: 2 marks
Question 7: 2 marks
Question 8: 2 marks
Maximum score = 18 marks

Answer key

1. Where do you live?
   What does *cheat* mean?
   How often did you go there?
2. Why don't you visit them?
   Why didn't she leave?
3. The word order is wrong. The correct answer is: Do you know where the station is? This is because you can't have two interrogatives in one sentence.
4. *Possible answers:* How much money/food/water? How many apples/books/people?
5. *What's she like?*
   She's very nice / tall and slim / a bit strange, etc.
   What does she like?
   She likes classical music / ice cream / painting, etc.
6. sort; kind
7. *Would* you like to go to a concert tonight? (*Would you like* for a specific invitation; *Do you like* for a general enquiry.)
8. *How do you do?* is only used for the first introduction to someone and is quite formal. After that we say *How are you?* when we meet them.

2

Follow the instructions in the Class Book. Do the first
one together first, referring the learners to the picture.
Do the second example if necessary before they work
either individually or with a partner.

Answer key

Possible answers
1. Would you like a biscuit?
2. What does *awful* mean?
3. What kind of computer is it?
4. Do you know where the bank is?
5. Why didn't you tell me?
6. How much did it cost?
7. How many people were there?
8. How are you?
9. What's their new flat like?
10. How often do you see them?

Option 1

If the learners find this exercise quite easy, you could ask
them to write their own answers in pairs, and then pass
these to another pair who write appropriate questions.
They then pass them back to the original pair to check
the questions.

Option 2

Worksheet 2 on page 125 offers an alternative way of
testing the learners' knowledge of question forms. This
is based on error analysis, i.e. there is a mistake in many
of the questions, and the learners have to correct them.
Follow the instructions on the worksheet.

Answer key

Worksheet 2
1. How long does it take from London?
2. How often do the trains run in the morning?
3. correct
4. Which train is quicker – the 9.00 or the 11.00?
5. correct
6. Do you know where platform 5 is?
7. correct
8. Does the 9.00 train stop at Amiens?
9. correct
10. How much does a return cost? *or* How much is a
    return?

Personal Study Workbook

2: What, where and how often?
6: Kangaroos

ASKING ABOUT PERSONAL HISTORIES

Introduction

A reading and listening text is used to present and
consolidate the vocabulary describing biographical
information, but also to revise the past simple in all its
forms. The reading text has been jumbled in order to
focus on aspects of cohesion in written text (e.g. the role
of conjunctions and adverbials in connecting text), and
for this reason the first exercise highlights important link
words. The learners practise the grammar and
vocabulary in a personalised activity at the end.

Suggested steps

1

Begin by directing the learners towards the examples.
Monolingual groups may wish to translate these link
words into their own language, and this is probably a
good way for you to check they have understood the
concepts.

Answer key

Because of is followed by a noun phrase, e.g. *because of the
weather.*
Because introduces a subordinate clause, e.g. *because it was
raining.*

2

Follow the instructions in the Class Book. In the
feedback there will be a range of possible answers.

Answer key

Possible answers
I lost my job because I was late every day.
I lost my job because of my boss.
I lost my job, so I had to sell my car.
It was difficult to get another job because the economic
    situation was very bad.
It was difficult to get another job because of my age.
It was difficult to get another job, so I decided to go
    abroad.

3

Help any learners who seem to be having particular difficulty. In the feedback, highlight (perhaps on the board) important vocabulary collocations, e.g. *leave school* and *get a job*.

Answer key

1. I was born in a small village,
2. but we moved to Bristol when I was three
3. and that is where I grew up.
4. At school I didn't do very well
5. and I failed most of my exams,
6. so I left at the first opportunity.
7. Unfortunately I couldn't find a job in England,
8. so I decided to go abroad
9. and I got a job in a safari park near Nairobi.
10. When I came back to England a year later
11. I managed to get a job in a zoo near London
12. because of my experience in Kenya.

Option

You could ask the learners to memorise the story about Paul. If you have written the sentences on the board in the correct order, give them 3–4 minutes to memorise the whole thing. They will be very challenged by this activity, but our experience is that learners can do it and find it enjoyable and satisfying. They also get a great deal of concentrated exposure to the language. After the 4 minutes is up, clean the board or remove some sections, and tell them to say the story with a partner.

4 ▢▢ ▣▣

There are two versions of the listening, one more difficult than the other. Choose the most appropriate one for your class.

The learners could compare their answers to the questions before discussing the relationship between Paul and the woman on the recording. The tapescripts are on page 153.

Answer key

1. In Africa.
2. In Africa.
3. Very well.
4. Yes.
5. When she was 18.
6. She went to university.
7. Agriculture.
8. Africa.
9. England.
10. Bristol.

The woman is Paul's mother.

5

Demonstrate by telling the learners to ask you questions about your past. If appropriate, use the phrase *I'd rather not say* as a way of revising this expression. Correct any errors of form in the questions. The learners can then interview each other. Monitor the pairs and provide feedback at the end.

Option

The learners could write a summary about their partner once they have the key information. The summaries are then given to you to read aloud, omitting the name. They have to guess who you are talking about.

Personal Study Workbook

1: Jumbled questions
3: Opposites and contrasts
8: An autobiography
9: Speaking partners

QUICK NOTES

This went well:

....

....

This didn't quite work:

....

....

Things to think about:

....

....

Introduction

As this page is devoted to revision, we would suggest that you let the learners focus on particular exercises here. Their decisions could be linked to the problems they noted in their Personal Study Workbook. You could help them to form their own groups to collaborate on these activities. Alternatively, you may decide yourself that certain exercises are useful for everyone.

1 ▭

This exercise provides some controlled practice of the present continuous for events captured at the moment of speaking in a photograph, and in the second part there is a listening activity to consolidate the present continuous. Pre-teach/check *advertisement* and *to advertise*.

Answer key

1. What the people are doing: A woman is holding a cup and smiling.
   What they are advertising: a smokers' toothpaste
2. What the people are doing: A girl is standing in front of / leaving a house. A piano is falling from one of the windows.
   What they are advertising: shock-absorbant shoe soles (*trainers* would do)
3. What the people are doing: A man and woman are walking through a park, with a bicycle each.
   What they are advertising: bicycles
4. What the people are doing: A woman is holding a bunch of flowers and crying.
   What they are advertising: a service for sending flowers
5. What the people are doing: A man is sitting in the garden, sleeping under a newspaper.
   What they are advertising: a doorbell extension

2

When verbs commonly collocate with particular nouns, e.g. *waste time/money*, it is important to highlight and teach them as they are often different in other languages. Follow the instructions in the Class Book. When the learners have completed the first part, they could test each other.

Example: A: *homework?*
             B: *do homework.*

Answer key

1. do   2. play   3. bite   4. cheat   5. complain   6. vote
7. lie   8. make   9. waste   10. throw away

3 ▭

This exercise type occurs at regular intervals throughout the course. In addition to revising large chunks of vocabulary, it provides intensive listening practice leading to further speaking practice. Pause and/or repeat the recording as necessary.

The learners could make a note of any vocabulary they hadn't remembered in the Reflections section of the Personal Study Workbook. The tapescript is at the back of the Class Book and also here on page 154.

Answer key

1. Yes.   2. Yes.   3. No.   4. No.   5. Yes.   6. No.
7. No.   8. No.   9. No.   10. Yes.   11. No.   12. Yes.
13. Yes.   14. No.   15. No.

QUICK NOTES

This went well:

....

....

This didn't quite work:

....

....

Things to think about:

....

....

STREETLIFE

CONTENTS

Language focus: expressing possibility and probability
revision of *there is/are; some/any*
giving directions
indirect questions

Vocabulary: buildings and monuments
roads and traffic

Skills: Speaking: giving directions
describing your local area
discussing situations in the street
Listening: understanding directions
dialogues in the street
Reading: street questions in different cultures
jumbled directions
Writing: a description of a place

PICTURE THE SCENE

Introduction

The first exercise presents the vocabulary necessary for the subsequent speaking activity in which the learners use their knowledge and imagination to speculate about different places. In so doing, they use the language of probability and possibility in a natural way. In the final activity, the newly presented language is transferred to a context which is relevant to the learners.

Suggested steps

1

Follow the instructions in the Class Book. You could put the learners in groups to pool their knowledge or let them work on their own. Tell them *not* to write the words on the pictures at this stage or the later peer testing activity won't work. Conduct feedback.

Answer key

2

When you go over the answers you could mark the stress on the words on the board and provide oral controlled practice before the learners test each other in pairs.

Answer key

/stætʃuː/; /faʊntən/; /kɑːsəl/; /mɒsk/; /kəθiːdrəl/; /fæktəri/

high-rise building
road sign
souvenir shop
pedestrian crossing
parking meter
pavement café
litter bin
traffic lights
underground station

Option

For further practice of the vocabulary, ask the learners to look through the list again and write down the things they see on their way home from class. Having done that, they must put the things in the order in which they see them.

3

You could begin by giving one or two examples about the places in the pictures, using language from the box, e.g. *There's probably a castle in Budapest. There probably aren't any parking meters in Parati.* To check your learners' understanding of these words, you could ask them the approximate percentage possibility of each expression. Elicit further examples from the learners and correct any errors before they work on the activity with a partner.

Language Points

1. Notice that the position of *probably* is different in negative and positive sentences.
2. Plural nouns are preceded by *some* in the positive form and *any* in the negative.

When most of the class have finished the activity, elicit their ideas, correcting grammar where necessary, and then go through the answers.

Answer key

Budapest: You would find all the things except a mosque.
Parati: You would find the following things: statue, fountain, cathedral, road sign, souvenir shop, pavement café, litter bin.

4

Describe a local scene yourself without saying where it is, while the learners listen and guess the answer. Alternatively, you could write a short model for them to read and guess. Be prepared to help them with vocabulary when they write their descriptions. Follow the rest of the instructions. They might like to display their written work on a wall poster.

Personal Study Workbook

2: It might be Chinese
5: Unusual maps

```
QUICK NOTES

This went well:

.............................................

.............................................

This didn't quite work:

.............................................

.............................................

Things to think about:

.............................................

.............................................
```

Introduction

The initial activity is a warm-up for the theme of the lesson, and the problem-solving task in Exercise 3 aims to engage the learners in a somewhat well-trodden path. Much of the language here will be recognised by the learners, so they should be able to organise the directions. In our experience, the difficulty is in using the expressions accurately, and there are certain phrases which learners at this level rarely use, e.g. *keep going*; *the first turning*; *until you get to …*; the controlled practice of this is therefore an important stage. The two version listening allows you to select the most suitable material for consolidation.

In the final activity, the learners have the opportunity to use what they have learnt to talk about their local environment.

Suggested steps

Language Points

1. Prepositions are a common problem here, e.g. *opposite ~~to~~*, *near ~~from~~*, *turn ~~on the~~ left*; (see the Visual dictionary on page 120 of the Personal Study Workbook).
2. Use of the definite article: *the* is not normally used before a road or street name, unless the name of the road is its destination.

   Examples: *Take the Cambridge road.* (the road which goes to Cambridge)
   The shop is in Cambridge Road. (that is the name of the road)

1

This warm-up may throw up some interesting anecdotes, and you might ask certain learners to retell their stories to the whole class in a feedback.

Option

Some groups of learners may find Worksheet 3 on page 125 an interesting alternative to this warm-up. If you are using it, you may need to pre-teach one or two items of vocabulary, e.g. *compass*, *stars*.

As a warm-up you could ask the whole class to point to where they think north is. Or ask the learners to stand up with a partner; one closes their eyes and the other turns them round a few times. The first person then has to point to where they think the board is, without opening their eyes.

Show the learners how to use the scoring column on the right of the questionnaire by doing the first two examples yourself. Then follow the instructions on the worksheet.

Unit 3 STREETLIFE

2

This focuses the learners on the map and clarifies a potential source of confusion.

Answer key

'ST' can mean 'Saint' (St Albans) or 'Street' (Normandy St).

3

Follow the instructions in the Class Book. The meanings of certain words and phrases, e.g. *roundabout*, should become clear through the completion of the task. You may wish to highlight these on the board in a feedback stage.

Before the learners memorise the directions in pairs, do some pronunciation practice of the phrases with the whole class.

Answer key

1. come out of Abbey Station
2. go up Holywell Hill until you get to the High St
3. go straight on, past the town hall
4. keep going until you come to a roundabout
5. turn left at the roundabout
6. take the second turning on the right into Normandy Rd
7. the hospital is at the end of the road on the left-hand side

Option

Before you move on to Exercise 4, you could obviously do more extensive practice of directions using the map. Learners can ask each other the way to other landmarks, either across the class or in pairs.

4 ▭▭ ▩▩

Select the appropriate version of the listening for your group, or divide the class and give one version to some learners and the other to the rest, if you have those facilities. The tapescripts are on page 155.

Answer key

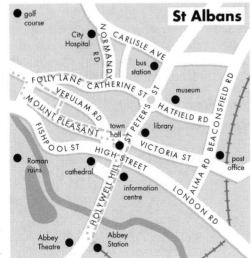

5

This is an important consolidation stage in which the learners create their own written record of the directions. You will need to monitor and conduct feedback on what they consider to be important. Alternatively, you could do this exercise as a class activity using the board, and allow time for the learners to copy.

Option 1

As an alternative to Exercise 5, use Exercise 1 (Take the first road on the left) from Unit 3 of the Personal Study Workbook.

Option 2

Trust your partner. Demonstrate this activity first with one member of the group. Tell them to shut their eyes (or blindfold them), and give them directions around the room, ensuring that they don't bump into furniture.

Example: *OK, take four steps forward, turn left, take five steps towards me*, etc.

Encourage the rest of the class to give the directions. Then put the learners in pairs to do the same activity, extending it out of the class if this is feasible.

6

Emphasise to the learners that the quality of their drawing is not an issue, and that the map should not be very extensive.

It is clear that the learners will require additional language in this exercise, which may be impossible to anticipate since it is a communicative activity. Be prepared to assist where necessary, and let the learners make prudent use of bilingual dictionaries. During the activity, monitor and note down any errors of communication, and deal with them at the end rather than interrupt the learners in full flow. You may wish to bring in maps of your local area.

Option

Learners work in pairs and write directions from the building they are in now to a specific place in the town, without giving the destination. They then swap their directions with another pair who work out what the destination is.

Personal Study Workbook

1: Take the first road on the left
6: A bad sense of direction
7: Postcards
9: Visual dictionary

STREET-WISE?

Introduction

In this lesson we extend the theme to include cross-cultural issues to do with streetlife, and the lesson provides a range of skills work including controlled and free speaking activities, reading and listening. There is also a focus on indirect questions which were introduced in the previous unit and are now practised more extensively.

Suggested steps

1

Follow the instructions in the Class Book, but make sure your learners don't look at the photos accompanying Exercise 3. Conduct feedback at the end.

2

Again, follow the instructions in the Class Book, and after the pair comparison elicit some of the differences. If you are actually teaching in or around Rio, ask the learners to read and underline anything they have not experienced, or anything they didn't put in their list.

3

Look at the pictures and see if the learners can think of one or two further questions for picture 1. At this stage, the learners should write their own questions and they don't have to write indirect questions.

Monitor while they are working in pairs, improving accuracy as appropriate. In feedback, elicit example questions from the class. There is certainly potential for humour in this activity as they compare their ideas.

4 🔲

Play the recording. Pause and replay it where necessary to allow the learners time to write out any questions they haven't already written. This dictation is important if you are going to focus on indirect questions. Elicit the questions and write them on the board. You may wish to focus on some of the answers too. The tapescript is on page 155.

Answer key

1. Excuse me, do you know where the nearest paper shop is?
2. Excuse me, can you tell me where the post office is?
3. Excuse me, how do I get to the cathedral from here?
4. Do you know what time this shop opens?
5. Excuse me, have you got the time, please?
6. Is this your car, sir?

5

In the first part, elicit answers from the class.

Answer key

We use the indirect form here because the direct form can sound rather abrupt and assumes that the listener knows the answer. The indirect form, therefore, tends to sound a bit more polite.

The second part of Exercise 5 provides fairly mechanical practice because in our experience, learners often make mistakes with this form even when they 'know' it. You will need to highlight the word order in indirect questions.

You could do the examples as a class drill before they work in pairs on both pair activities. Monitor and correct.

6

This is intended as a freer speaking activity, and you may wish to give the learners time to act out their dialogues in front of the class at the end. Alternatively, you could leave this activity until the beginning of the next lesson, where it would also give an opportunity for revision.

Option

You could ask the learners to work in pairs and mime a short sketch of strangers in the street, one of whom is asking a question. They then perform their sketch, and the rest of the class have to work out what is being said.

Personal Study Workbook

3: Picture dictation
4: Dialogues
8: Speaking partners

QUICK NOTES

This went well:

....

....

This didn't quite work:

....

....

Things to think about:

....

....

REVIEW AND DEVELOPMENT

REVIEW OF UNIT 1

1

Follow the instructions in the Class Book.

Answer key

tidy – untidy
serious – easygoing
organised – disorganised
sensible – silly
efficient – inefficient

2

Follow the instructions in the Class Book. For the final part of the activity, with their partner, they could write one sentence each about themselves which is true. It is then possible to practise the third person.

Example: *Kyoko usually does her homework in the library but at the moment she's working at home because the house is empty.*

You could also encourage your learners to write humorous examples.

Answer key

Possible answers

1. I usually study in the library but at the moment, I'm studying at home because the library burnt down.
2. Generally I read an English book every month but at the moment I'm not reading anything at all because some friends are staying with me.
3. I normally go to the gym twice a week but at the moment I'm going every night because I'm running in a marathon next month.
4. Normally I only do housework at the weekend but at the moment I'm doing it every day because my mother is ill.
5. I usually drive to work but at the moment I'm taking the bus because my car is at the garage.
6. Generally I practise the piano twice a week but at the moment I'm practising five hours a day because I've got a concert soon.

REVIEW OF UNIT 2

1

Follow the instructions in the Class Book. If it is successful, you could repeat the exercise at regular intervals throughout the course with different questions or phrases; it can be a simple but effective way of revising important language.

In the second activity, pairs can compare their answers with other pairs and choose the five most important questions overall.

2 ▭

This type of activity is important in order to help learners to understand connected speech. For most learners it is less important to be able to reproduce these accurately than to understand them when used by others.

Play the examples on the recording and focus the learners' attention on the *pronunciation* of the contractions in the first examples and the weak forms in the second examples.

Do the dictation and check the answers, using the board.

Do some class and individual drilling as necessary before learners go on to part B in pairs.

Answer key

1. What's your name?
2. Where are you from?
3. Where do you live?
4. What do you do?
5. Do you enjoy it?
6. Why are you studying English?
7. How do you get to school?
8. What have you got in your pocket?

QUICK NOTES

This went well:

....

....

This didn't quite work:

....

....

Things to think about:

....

....

CREATIVITY

CONTENTS

Language focus:	present perfect for finished states and events without a time reference; contrasted with past simple infinitive of purpose, e.g. *you can use it to kill flies* suggestions, apologies and refusals
Vocabulary:	creative acts, e.g. *paint, invent* speech acts, e.g. *suggest, refuse*

Skills:	Speaking:	doing and discussing creative tests improvising situations talking about previous achievements
	Listening:	improvised story endings dictated questions and answers creative improvisations
	Reading:	creativity tests
	Writing:	story endings

CREATIVITY TESTS

Introduction

This is largely a fluency-oriented lesson in which the learners have the opportunity to use their imagination in both speaking and writing activities. The first creative test practises the infinitive of purpose, and the learners also listen to native speakers doing one of the tasks. Following the creativity tests learners discuss and evaluate the tasks.

Suggested steps

1

To motivate the learners for the following activities, do the first one together with the group. Pre-teach the word *brick* and ask what they are normally used for (to build houses, walls, etc.). Then tell them they are going to think of different / 'not normal' uses for a brick, and give them one of the examples from the Class Book. Write this on the board, highlighting the form (infinitive of purpose), and then ask them for other uses for a brick. From this activity you could also teach the words *creative* and *creativity* to illustrate the theme of the lesson.

Language Point: infinitive of purpose

Although not a difficult structure syntactically, the infinitive of purpose does seem to be a source of error. This is probably to do with the learners' L1.

Common errors include:

~~I came to class for learn English.~~
~~I came to class for to learn English.~~

Highlight the form and illustrate the meaning clearly: *to do* here means *for this reason*.

Refer the learners to the rest of the creative tests and ask them to scan read them. Deal with any problems of understanding before they find a partner and choose their three tests. You should give them about 20–30 minutes for this activity.

Alternatively, you may wish to select certain of the activities yourself if you feel that some are more suitable for your class than others. It would also be feasible to have all the learners work on one of the tests, do feedback on it, then work in groups again on another, have feedback, and so on. It is not necessary to work through all of the tests systematically.

Note: The tests create a need for language which is necessarily unpredictable, so be prepared to monitor and help in different ways. Also try to ensure that learners have access to monolingual and/or bilingual dictionaries. While you monitor, see which tests produce the most interesting answers, so that at the end you could ask those learners to tell the class what they did.

Answer key

Possible answers

Test 1 Unusual Uses

a knife: to open a tin of paint, as a screwdriver, to stir paint, to open a letter.

a newspaper: to kill flies, as an umbrella when it is raining, to clean mud off your shoes, as a blanket if it is cold.

Test 2 Patterns

1. Tunnels in a mountain, closed eyes, two bald men behind a wall, car headlights.
2. Thin trees seen from above, cats' eyes, coat hooks, a fork seen from the end.

Test 3 Word Associations

Light (opposite *dark*); light (opposite *heavy*); a light (you can switch on); a light (for a cigarette); to light (a fire/cigarette).

Back (opposite *front*); back (part of your body); to back (drive in reverse); to back (support somebody); to go/come back (to return).

Test 4: Story Endings

(See also the listening material in Exercise 3.)

Strange ending: Moira touched the man's arm and he disappeared because he was a ghost.

Sad ending: The men attacked her and then ran away with the money.

Happy ending: She said, 'Oh, I thought I had lost it!' And he said, 'I found it in the cupboard under the sink.'

Test 5: Lateral Thinking

Put something heavy in the bowl to displace the water.

Use a straw and blow the water out or drink it.

Boil the water until it evaporates.

Freeze the water and take it out.

2

For the discussion, reorganise the learners into groups. Some groups will generate a great deal of discussion, but others may not have much to say. If that is the case with your class, you could use an exercise from the Personal Study Workbook, e.g. Exercise 4 (Creative word search).

Option

An imaginative class might like to use the tests as models and create other examples of tests to try out on each other. They might, for instance, think of other objects to test each other on for Test 1.

3 🔲 🔳

Use the listening activity if your learners have done Test 4: Story Endings. The tapescripts are on page 155.

Answer key

Version 1

1. a sad ending – £75 was stolen
2. a happy ending – a surprise birthday party

Version 2

1. a strange ending – the electricity man thinks Moira is his mother
2. a happy ending – the electricity men gave Joe and Moira some money

Personal Study Workbook

4: Creative word search
7: Creative visualisation
8: Creative uses
9: Speaking partners

```
QUICK NOTES

This went well:
..................................................
..................................................

This didn't quite work:
..................................................
..................................................

Things to think about:
..................................................
..................................................
```

YOUR CREATIVE EXPERIENCES

Introduction

In this lesson, the learners personalise their creative experiences. The first exercise provides them with the vocabulary to talk about creative acts; and the present perfect and past simple enable them to talk about their own previous creative achievements, with or without a specific time frame. The grammatical concepts are approached contrastively, since the two tenses are very commonly confused.

Suggested steps

1

Use the visuals on the page and your own explanations to clarify the meaning of any new items. Check the learners' pronunciation.

Do the first two questions as a class before groupwork, and encourage discussion (i.e. learners giving reasons or personal anecdotes).

2 ▭

Use the sentences on the recording as a dictation, and bear in mind that these may be new forms for the learners, so don't expect them to be perfect.

After they have written the conversations with D and E, you could encourage the learners to discuss their answers to the question about the tense. Ask the learners for their explanations, and correct/clarify where necessary.

With a monolingual group, you could suggest that they translate the questions and answers into their own language to distinguish the concepts. (This can be done even with mixed nationality groups, though it is not easy for a teacher to monitor a range of translations. However, two or more learners with the same language can compare their translations.)

Answer key

See the tapescript on page 156.
D and E use the past simple. See the Language Point below.

> **Language Point:**
> **Have you ever (written a poem)?**
>
> The present perfect is used here to ask about or describe a past experience in the life of a living person, without any specific time reference. Normally if we talk about when or where something took place, we use the past simple.
>
> *Ever* is used to reinforce the notion of 'any time in your life'.

3

Before you begin, you may wish to check that the learners know the past participles of the verbs they need to use. In our experience, they usually know how to form regular past participles, but you may need to remind them about this. Remember that there is a list of common irregular verbs at the back of the Class Book.

Elicit questions from the learners and correct any errors, particularly with past participles. At the same time, give some genuine and interesting answers to the questions they ask you, using the past simple and present perfect as appropriate.

4

When you are satisfied that the learners have a preliminary grasp of the form and concept, move on to the personalised activity. At the end, conduct a feedback in which learners tell the class about other people's experiences. Use this opportunity to clarify the 3rd person form if necessary.

Option

For further practice you could write three things on the board that you have done, two of which are true and one which is false:

Examples: *I've met Paul McCartney.*
I've walked across England.
I've written a book about the weather.

Tell the class that the information in one of these sentences is false, and give them a few minutes in groups to think up questions to ask you to help them decide which sentences are true. Bring the class together and let them ask their questions, making up any answers you don't know. Let them vote on their choice of incorrect information. Then they can write their own true or false sentences, and do a similar activity in groups.

Personal Study Workbook

1: Missing letters
2: Dictation

QUICK NOTES

This went well:

....

....

This didn't quite work:

....

....

Things to think about:

....

....

CREATIVE IMPROVISATION

Introduction

In addition to listening practice, the lesson provides a focus on specific functions – apologising, refusing and suggesting – and the opportunity for some creative improvisation by the learners.

Suggested steps

1

Follow the instructions in the Class Book. You may wish to do some work on intonation in the first activity before listening to the recording, e.g. the wide voice range in the greetings; the query in *Late?*; the emphatic use of *did* in the affirmative form.

2 ▭

Play the recording and elicit answers.

Answer key

At the end of the first dialogue, Mark and Lucy have dinner together. At the end of the second, Mark leaves.

3 ⊂⊃

Play the recording again, and let the learners compare their answers with a partner. After the feedback, you could also ask the class which improvisation they preferred, and why. The tapescript is on page 156.

Answer key

Mark makes a suggestion.	1
Lucy is angry.	2
Mark apologises.	1
Lucy is in a panic.	2
Mark sounds a bit negative.	2
Mark refuses to help.	2
Mark is embarrassed.	1
Lucy is pleased to see Mark.	1

4

This introduces more ways of suggesting, refusing and apologising. Follow the instructions in the Class Book and then go through the answers.

Answer key

apologies:
I'm terribly sorry.
Sorry to keep you waiting.
suggestions:
How about going out for a meal?
Perhaps we could have dinner together.
Why don't we meet some other time?
refusals:
I'm sorry, but that's just not possible.
I'm sorry, I can't.
I'd love to, but I'm afraid I can't.

You could provide some quick practice of these phrases. Use the suggestions and apologies to elicit suitable replies from the group; or use stimuli that should then produce refusals in the answer.

Example: A: *Could you lend me any money?*
B: *I'm sorry, I can't.*
The learners can do the same thing in pairs.

5

You can either allow the pairs to think about and discuss their improvisation before they actually do Exercise 5; or you can throw them in at the deep end, i.e. just tell them to do it. Monitor carefully and help where necessary. Ask certain pairs to perform their improvisation for others. From your comments and feedback, the pairs may then be able to improve on this first effort when they improvise the dialogue in the next exercise.

6 ⊂⊃

Put the learners back into pairs for this final improvisation, and when they have finished play the improvised version of the second dialogue on the recording. The tapescript is on page 156.

Personal Study Workbook

3: Expressing personal feelings
5: Weak forms and word stress
6: Wake up your brain's creative side!

```
QUICK NOTES

This went well:
..............................................................
..............................................................

This didn't quite work:
..............................................................
..............................................................

Things to think about:
..............................................................
..............................................................
```

REVIEW AND DEVELOPMENT

REVIEW OF UNIT 2

1

Follow the instructions in the Class Book and highlight the rising intonation in the example:

Are you ready?

If necessary, do other examples, and get the learners to mimic your intonation.

When they have finished the exercise, they can practise the questions and responses orally in pairs. Get them to answer without looking at the book, or if they prefer, create their own answers.

Answer key

A
1. Are you coming?
2. Have you got a light?
3. Do you want a coffee?
4. Would you like a cigarette?
5. Did you have a good journey?
6. Have you ever been there?
7. Is it/this yours?
8. Did you get what you wanted?
9. Have you finished?
10. Are you tired?

B
1 i   2 a   3 f   4 d   5 c   6 g   7 h   8 e   9 b   10 j

2

We are grateful to Philip Dale for this activity.

Explain the aim (to brainstorm questions) and elicit a few sample questions, as in the Class Book. Give the learners time to write their questions together. Fifteen questions may seem a lot initially, but once they get going, it can be done. If they are having difficulties, reduce the number to ten. Monitor their questions while they are writing, point out errors and see if they can correct them.

Bring the class together. Tell them they mustn't repeat a question that someone else has asked, and if you like, set up a point scoring system (e.g. 2 marks for a correct question, 1 mark for an incorrect question which they correct). Answer their questions honestly, and keep up a good pace. Learners can then ask each other the questions about their own shoes.

This type of activity works well with a range of topics (the teacher's hair, family, pets, etc.).

REVIEW OF UNIT 3

1 ▭

Follow the instructions in the Class Book. You could encourage the learners to think up some questions of their own to ask each other.

2

Follow the instructions in the Class Book. This type of exercise can be used to revise a wide range of topic areas.

QUICK NOTES

This went well:

....

....

This didn't quite work:

....

....

Things to think about:

....

....

YOU AND YOUR BODY

CONTENTS

Language focus: frequency adverbs and revision of present simple for habits
       reflexive pronouns
       instructions
       adverbs of degree

Vocabulary: parts of the body
       verbs of movement
       time expressions, e.g. *twice a week, every other day*
       health and fitness

Skills: Speaking: giving instructions, e.g. *bend your knees*
                         body stories
                         discussing health issues
                         looking after yourself (questionnaire)
       Listening: body stories
                         mathematical body quiz
       Reading: DIY surgery

KNOW YOUR OWN BODY

Introduction

The first activity focuses on vocabulary in the box which we anticipate will be new, although the practice stage allows the learners to choose the items they wish to concentrate on. The listening is intended as a humorous activity to check understanding of the lexis in Exercise 1. With the presentation of verbs of movement, the learners then have the vocabulary to engage in a more extended practice activity involving parts of the body and body movements.

Suggested steps

1

Before using the book, ask the learners to think of three parts of the body that they don't know in English, but would like to know. Then tell them to look at the picture in the book and the box of words to see if they can find the things they want to know. Then follow the instructions in the Class Book and let them use dictionaries.

In feedback, check that the learners can pronounce the words correctly. Particular problems might be *thumb* (silent 'b'), *knee* (silent 'k'), and the vowel sounds in *stomach, tongue* and *breast*.

In the practice stage the learners can obviously focus on the words that are new or particularly important to them.

Answer key

1. heel	8. thumb
2. toe	9. wrist
3. knee	10. skin
4. hip	11. lip
5. waist	12. tongue
6. elbow	13. chin
7. nail	

2 ▭

Pause the recording after each question in the mathematical quiz so that the pairs can discuss and decide on their answers.

Option

For further practice, the pairs could then write their own mathematical quiz and try it out on other pairs.

Answer key

1. 6   2. 12   3. 16   4. 40   5. 8   6. 4   7. 15   8. 20

3

You could use mime to illustrate the meaning of the four verbs in the first question, and then ask your learners if they could do these things to their legs. This will give them the idea, and they can then complete the rest of the activity in pairs, using dictionaries and each other to help with new words. At this point you can monitor and help if necessary. Check their answers and clarify any problems they may have.

Answer key

1. d   2. b   3. b   4. a   5. b   6. c

4

Demonstrate with another learner, and then get the rest of the group to stand up to do the exercise.

Option

Take in two music cassettes (one fast, one slow). Learners work in groups with a cassette and write a series of instructions for a fitness routine, based on their music. They rehearse it, then perform it for the class.

Personal Study Workbook

4: I shut my head
7: Body factfile
8: Visual dictionary

QUICK NOTES

This went well:

....

....

This didn't quite work:

....

....

Things to think about:

....

....

LOOKING AFTER YOURSELF

Introduction

The basis of this lesson is personalisation, and our aim is to provide a memorable context for the target language through both the questionnaire and the listening about body stories. We have tried to keep the material interesting without becoming too personal, but we are aware of the sensitive nature of the topic and we have therefore included an alternative questionnaire (Worksheet 5) if you would prefer to omit the material in the book. It covers similar areas of language to the Class Book material.

Suggested steps

The notes below apply equally to the questionnaire in the book or to Worksheet 5, which you will find on page 126.

1

One or two time expressions in the box may be new, e.g. *whenever I feel like it*, and some will not be part of the learners' productive vocabulary, e.g. *hardly ever*, but the learners will be familiar with most of the expressions in the box, so they should be able to complete the exercise quite easily. When you check the answers you can clarify the meaning of any new expressions.

Answer key

1. the day before yesterday; a few days/weeks/months ago
2. quite often; hardly ever; twice a year; whenever I feel like it; every day; never; once a week/month/year; every other day; occasionally
3. half an hour; a couple of minutes; a few seconds

2

Use the exercise in the Class Book or use Worksheet 5 (on page 126) instead. In both cases, give the learners time to read through the questionnaire and ask questions about any vocabulary they don't understand. Tell them to note down their answers.

3

Insist that your learners ask full questions to practise the target language, and repeat that they do not have to answer questions if they do not want to.

4

Be prepared to supply necessary vocabulary and censor any questions you think may offend other members of the class.

5 ▭▭ ▭▭

You could introduce the listening by telling the class your own body story – if possible using a similar framework to the stories on the recording (i.e. part of body, what happened, result). Then ask the learners to recode the story, using the headings in the table in the book.

Play the appropriate recording, and put the learners in pairs to check their answers. If you feel they have missed quite a lot of information, you could repeat the recording before conducting a class feedback. The tapescripts are on page 157.

Answer key

Version 1

Speaker	Part of body	What happened	Result
1	ankle	fell over while roller skating	hospital; broken ankle in plaster for six weeks
2	wrist	playing the flute; chair moved and she fell off stage	hurt her wrist; couldn't play flute for a long time

Version 2

Speaker	Part of body	What happened	Result
1	chin	bit a tin can and cut his chin	hospital; still has a scar
2	arm	fell off her horse	broke her arm and now cannot straighten it

Finish with the class telling their own stories and if possible record the best ones. It goes without saying that this topic should be handled with sensitivity, and that the learners must not feel coerced into telling stories they don't want to. For this reason we have suggested they could talk about a body story of someone they know.

Personal Study Workbook

3: How often do you …?
5: Bathtub pleasure
6: When I was in Spain
9: Speaking partners

QUICK NOTES

This went well:

....

....

This didn't quite work:

....

....

Things to think about:

....

....

DIY SURGERY

Introduction

The rather shocking text forms the centrepiece of the lesson, and while some learners may find it morbid, we anticipate that they will read it with great interest and will find the text (and therefore the target language) memorable. The initial vocabulary activity prepares the learners for the text by pre-teaching important items, and the final activity expands on the use of reflexive pronouns in the text through a matching exercise and personalised practice.

Note: It goes without saying that if you think your learners will react badly to this text, you should omit it.

Suggested steps

1

Follow the instructions in the Class Book and clarify any problems of meaning.

Answer key

The odd one out is *population* because all the other words are connected with health and medicine.

2

Teach the word *DIY (Do-it-yourself)*. Ask the learners what kind of DIY things people usually do. After eliciting several examples, you might suggest, 'How about operating on yourself?'. Then ask them to read the text. Follow with a whole class reaction and discussion, using the questions in the book.

Language Point: very, really, absolutely

Very is used to qualify degree adjectives; *absolutely* is only used to qualify extreme adjectives. Compare:

very surprised absolutely horrified
very hot/cold absolutely boiling/freezing
very big/small absolutely enormous/tiny

Really has the advantage that it can qualify degree and extreme adjectives, e.g. *really big/enormous.*

3

You could contrast object pronouns and reflexive pronouns through simple mime, e.g. *I bandaged her / I bandaged myself.* Then work through the other examples with the class. You could elicit examples of the forms from the learners, and put them on the board rather than using the book.

Tell the learners to complete the matching exercise. They can use dictionaries if they wish. Conduct feedback with the class, then put them in groups to personalise the sentences. Make sure that they say the sentences for practice.

Language Point: reflexive pronouns

We do not use these pronouns in English for actions that we normally carry out ourselves, e.g. *wash/shave/dress*, etc.

They are, however, used for specific emphasis with the verbs above, e.g. *My little girl is learning to dress herself.*

In many languages, reflexive pronouns would be used in all examples with these verbs.

4

The learners could stay in the same groups to discuss the questions. If there are local and/or topical health issues relevant to the class, it would be appropriate to use them alongside or in place of the questions in the book. During this free stage, avoid correcting the learners as this may inhibit discussion. You may wish to make a note of communicative problems you hear, and go over these afterwards, as well as praising the learners where they communicated effectively.

Personal Study Workbook

1: Break, broke, broken
2: Enjoy yourself

```
┌─────────────────────────────────────────┐
│              QUICK NOTES                 │
│                                          │
│  This went well:                         │
│  ......................................  │
│  ......................................  │
│                                          │
│  This didn't quite work:                 │
│  ......................................  │
│  ......................................  │
│                                          │
│  Things to think about:                  │
│  ......................................  │
│  ......................................  │
└─────────────────────────────────────────┘
```

REVIEW AND DEVELOPMENT

REVIEW OF UNIT 3

1

Follow the instructions in the Class Book.

Answer key

town hall   parking meter   traffic lights   railway station
litter bin   post office   bus stop   ring road
office block   pedestrian crossing   shopping centre
car park   department store   golf course

> ### Language Point: compound nouns
>
> Compounding is a particularly common type of word formation in English, and learners need to be aware of it, especially if this process does not happen frequently in their mother tongue.
>
> Compound nouns can be one word (e.g. supermarket), two words (e.g. town hall) or hyphenated (e.g. air-conditioning), but this last form is much more common with compound adjectives (e.g. good-humoured).
>
> Unfortunately there are no rules governing the form a compound takes, so learners will have to use dictionaries to check if they are unsure.

2 ▭

Follow the instructions in the Class Book.

Answer key

town hall, pedestrian crossing

3

Talk the class through the initial part of the activity, then get them to do the matching exercise, either alone or in pairs.

Answer key

1. f   2. d, h   3. b, c   4. a, e, g

Do some controlled oral practice of the phrases, then in Part B encourage the learners to think up questions that will elicit different answers. After the mingling activity, you could ask some pairs to act out their conversations for the rest of the class.

Option

This is a different type of activity to revise directions. Begin by giving classroom directions to one of the learners, who should have his or her eyes open.

Example: *OK, Norbert, stand up and take three steps forward. Now, turn left, and carry on. Stop! Now, turn right and walk to the wall.*

Tell Norbert to go back to his place and then give him the same set of directions, only this time tell him to close his eyes. Encourage the rest of the class to help give the directions, and make sure that Norbert keeps his eyes closed. (Provide a blindfold if necessary.)

Put the learners in pairs and they can do the same activity, swapping roles at a suitable point.

We would like to thank Françoise Cormon for the idea behind this activity.

REVIEW OF UNIT 4

1

The learners could brainstorm this activity in groups. They will probably need dictionaries or help from you with vocabulary. You could add a competitive element by setting a time limit and awarding points for the number of correct items.

Answer key

Possible answers
a cup; a glass; a ball; a can; a coin; a bowl; the sun; the moon; an electric fan; fruits: an orange, a melon, etc.; a wheel; a tyre; a mirror; a face; a globe/the world. You will probably be able to accept many other suggestions from the class.

2

Begin by asking the class, *Have you ever sung a song in the street?* and elicit replies. Then refer them to the examples in the book, and ask them to provide some more questions, working alone or in pairs. Monitor and correct errors.

Practise the mini-dialogues in the book, and check that the learners remember why the present perfect and past simple are used (i.e. general question about an experience in one's life versus an event at a stated time in the past). Then get them to have similar conversations, using the questions they have thought up.

An alternative is to ask each person to memorise one of their questions and do a mingling activity. The learners count the number of people who have done whatever they are asking, and in feedback at the end, they say, for example, 'Three people in the class have said "I love you" to a stranger in the street. David said it when he was at a carnival.'

QUICK NOTES

This went well:

....

....

This didn't quite work:

....

....

Things to think about:

....

....

LEARNING – PAST AND PRESENT

CONTENTS

Language focus: present perfect to describe a finished action in an
                unfinished time period in contrast with past simple
        use of *should* for expressing opinions
        so and *such*
        before and *after* + *-ing*
        spelling rule: doubling consonants

Vocabulary: adjectives to describe schools and education
        classroom habits and learning strategies,
        e.g. *work in groups, sit in silence, look something up*

Skills: Speaking: secondary schools and adult learning
                  discussing ways of learning
                  discussing the best age to learn things
      Listening: an adult language class
      Reading: grammar and spelling rules

AN ADULT LANGUAGE CLASS

Introduction

The main aim of this lesson is for learners to discuss their experiences of secondary school learning and indirectly to compare this with their current situation as adult learners. The topic is relevant to them and you may discover interesting and revealing information about your learners' attitudes to their learning, past and present. The first activity provides some of the lexis needed to describe their past learning situations, and the recording acts both as extensive listening practice and as a springboard for discussion; it also contains vocabulary which learners will probably need to draw up their list of features of adult classes.

Suggested steps

1

You could begin by telling the learners to look at the photos and discuss what kinds of situation are represented. Then do the first example in the exercise together. The learners can work individually or in groups, using dictionaries where necessary.

Answer key

progressive – traditional
old – modern
good – poor
useful – useless
nice – unpleasant
easygoing – strict
interesting – boring
hardworking – lazy
wide – limited

Conduct feedback, checking that the learners can pronounce the words correctly with the stress in the right place. If necessary, do some repetition practice before they describe their secondary schools. If the learners are all from the same place, group them so that they are not all talking about the same school.

Option 1

Game: Pelmanism
Photocopy Worksheet 6 on page 126 to make one game per group (for example, if you have three groups of five learners, make three photocopies).

Cut up all the squares to make a game with 20 words in each pack.

Give each group a set of words, and tell them to put the pieces of paper face down.

Learner 1 turns up a word, shows it to the others and turns up one other word. If the two words are opposites (e.g. *progressive* and *traditional*) the learner wins the pair. If they aren't opposites, he or she turns them face down again in the same position. Everyone has to try to remember where all the words are in order to win pairs when it is their turn.

The winner is the person with the highest number of pairs when all the cards have been taken.

You can adapt this game for a number of groupings: words of similar meaning, words of opposite meaning, words and pictures, words and definitions.

Option 2

Before the learners work in groups to describe memories of secondary school using the framework in Exercise 1, you could describe your own secondary school as a model. You could also invite them to ask you questions about it.

2 ▭

Before the group listens to the recording, ask them to draw a grid on a piece of paper with two columns: things they like about the woman's class and things they don't like. When they have extracted the necessary information (and you may choose to play the recording several times), let them compare their answers with a partner.

There are obviously no set answers to this listening task: the aim is for learners to listen and express their opinions. You will of course need to help them if they are not able to understand, for example, by replaying certain phrases intensively if they have difficulty with them, or by telling them to listen with the tapescript on the second or third listening. The tapescript is on page 173 of the Class Book.

3

Elicit one or two examples from the class, then put them in groups to continue their lists. While they are discussing the topic, you will need to circulate and, if necessary, help with vocabulary. Monitor and note any particular language points which occur. You could then go over these points after the groups have given feedback to each other on their lists.

4

Introduce one or two new items from the tapescript to the class before the learners work in pairs. Dictionaries would be useful for this exercise, and you may wish to take the opportunity to discuss with the class how they will keep a record of new items: translation, synonyms and opposites, a definition in English, an example sentence, etc.

Answer key

to do a course
to be strict
evening school
to behave
to call someone by their first name / surname
to talk to someone like an equal
to do homework
to sit at desks
to sit on chairs in a circle/semi-circle
to work in groups
to sit in silence
to put your hand up
to shout out
set texts, course books
economic vocabulary
a good atmosphere
to waste time
to explain things

Other useful items you may wish to feed in in the final part of Exercise 4 include:

to revise, to learn by heart, to do an exam, to fail/pass an exam, university degree, qualifications, certificate, grade, mark, head teacher, principal, director of studies.

Personal Study Workbook

2: Words with more than one meaning
5: Learning to juggle
6: Who'd be a juggler?

```
┌─────────────────────────────────────────┐
│              QUICK NOTES                  │
│  This went well:                          │
│  ........................................ │
│  ........................................ │
│                                           │
│  This didn't quite work:                  │
│  ........................................ │
│  ........................................ │
│                                           │
│  Things to think about:                   │
│  ........................................ │
│  ........................................ │
└─────────────────────────────────────────┘
```

WAYS OF LEARNING

Introduction

Rather than simply talk about different learning methods in the abstract, this lesson enables the group to learn some grammar and spelling rules through different methods, test themselves on what they have learnt and then reflect on these methods.

Suggested steps

1

We suggest a short time limit for the first part of the question, as the aim here is simply to engage the learners in the subject, but not to exhaust it; there is a longer discussion after the experiment.

Before the learners embark on the three exercises, explain that they are going to experiment with different ways of learning grammar and spelling rules. You could either let the learners work through Exercises A, B and C at their own pace, or do the exercises one at a time, with feedback where necessary. With Exercise C, you should ask the learners simply whether they think they have understood the rule; if not, tell them to read it again. To explain it, in this instance, would destroy the object of the exercise.

> **Language Point**
>
> Another useful spelling rule for verbs is that the final 'e' is omitted when you add *ing* or *ed*.
>
> Examples:
> *write – writing; make – making; hope – hoping; decide – decided* (not *decideed*)
>
> This is not true for verbs ending in 'ee'.
>
> Examples:
> *see – seeing; agree – agreeing*

Answer key

A
If a verb follows directly after prepositions (including *before* and *after*), it must be an *-ing* form.

C
So is followed by an adjective; *such* is followed by an adjective and a noun. If the noun is singular and countable, you will also need an indefinite article directly after *such*.

2

When all the learners have completed the three exercises, put them in pairs to test themselves.

Answer key

Possible answers
1. It was so crowded that he couldn't get into the party.
   There were such a lot of people that he couldn't get into the party.
   There were so many people that he couldn't get into the party.
   The music was so loud that he decided to complain.
2. It was such a nice day that he went to the beach.
   The weather was so nice that he went to the beach.
   It was so sunny that he went to the beach.

1. After turning off the light, the man left the house.
   Before leaving the house, he turned off the light.
2. After buying some flowers, he went to the bank.
   Before going to the bank, he bought some flowers.

| stopped | starting | winning | meeting |
| looked | robbed | crying | climbed |

3

In this discussion activity, ask the learners to think of examples wherever possible. This will help to focus and structure the discussion. They can quote examples from language learning or life in general. At the end, get groups to tell other members of the class the most interesting points that came out of their discussion.

Option

Some groups may like to extend the whole discussion about learning to other topics, and you could suggest that they spend a little time at home preparing to teach a skill to other learners in the class in English. For example, how to draw, how to do a dance step, how to make something, how to fold paper, how to tell the time by the stars, how to read palms. With the right atmosphere, such peer-led content learning should be not only motivating and interesting, but excellent for skills development.

If members of the group were willing, you could organise a rota over the next few lessons for different individuals to teach their skill to the class in the first ten minutes.

Personal Study Workbook

3: It's such an easy exercise
4: How to pronounce the letter *u*
8: *Writing, writting* or *writeing*?

> ### QUICK NOTES
>
> This went well:
>
> ....
> ....
>
> This didn't quite work:
>
> ....
> ....
>
> Things to think about:
>
> ....
> ....

Introduction

The lesson looks at another aspect of the contrast between the present perfect and past simple: a finished action in an unfinished time period and a finished action in a finished time period, e.g. *I've written to them this week* (unfinished) and *I wrote to them last week* (finished).

Because of the structure of the lesson, it is necessary to begin with a different activity so that the learners have something to talk about in the later stages of the lesson where they use the present perfect – hence the discussion activity on the best age for learning different things.

Suggested steps

1

You may wish to pre-teach new vocabulary yourself, using the visuals if appropriate. Otherwise, follow the instructions in the Class Book. *Most people* can be interpreted as *most people I know* or *most people in my country*.

Option

Before the learners work in groups, they could think of two or three similar things that need to be learnt and ask the others in their group what they think the best age is.

Examples: *learn to ride a bike*
learn to fly
learn to take things easy

Monitor while discussion is taking place so that you can invite individuals to put forward different opinions in a brief feedback stage.

2

Most of the vocabulary will be known, but you may wish to highlight the use of *do* with *exercises* and *make* with *mistakes*. (This point is revised in Unit 8, Review and development, page 56.)

If the learners are unfamiliar with the past participles of some of the verbs, you could run through these quickly before they do Exercise 3, or you could refer them to the irregular verb list on page 175. At this stage, avoid discussion on the use of the present perfect, as this would pre-empt the deductive activity in Exercise 5.

3

Encourage the learners to make as many examples as possible using the prompts, and elicit a few from the class before they work in pairs. Be prepared to correct errors of form with the tense.

4

Follow the instructions in the Class Book. You may wish to encourage the learners to write some sentences down for both Exercise 3 and 4.

5

The learners are given a choice of method here: either to discover the rule for themselves or to look it up. You could pair up learners who chose different methods so that they can compare their ideas.

Answer key

We use the present perfect in Exercise 3 because we are talking about actions happening during a time which is not yet finished; the lesson is still happening.

Example: (So far in this lesson) *I've learnt three new words.* The lesson isn't over, so I could learn some more.

We use the past simple in Exercise 4 because we are talking about actions happening in a time period which has finished.

Example: (In the last lesson) *I learnt 10 words.*

6

Give your own realistic examples to introduce this exercise – anything which is familiar to your learners. You could ask the learners to write some example sentences so that you can monitor and correct them. Refer them to the list of irregular verbs on page 175.

Personal Study Workbook

1: *I've seen* or *I saw?*
7: What can you do?
9: Speaking partners

QUICK NOTES

This went well:

....

....

This didn't quite work:

....

....

Things to think about:

....

....

REVIEW OF UNIT 4

1

Follow the instructions in the Class Book. Before the oral practice in the second part of the exercise, you could begin by doing some group repetition work to highlight the wide voice range on Jean and Rob's greetings; the emphasis on *you* in *What are you doing here?* and on *terribly* in *I'm terribly sorry.*

You could also vary the activity by telling the groups to change three or four things in the dialogue (for instance, instead of an invitation to lunch, perhaps Rob had arranged to take the children out). Learners could then perform their dialogues for each other and identify the changes.

Answer key

1. Dave greets Rob after Jean does.
2. No.
3. Jean.
4. They are all pleased to see each other.
5. Everyone is embarrassed, but probably Dave more than anyone.
6. Rob makes a suggestion (twice, in fact).
7. Rob refuses to stay for the party.
8. Yes.
9. Yes, with Dave.

2

This activity recycles both vocabulary and the use of the present perfect and past simple. Begin by telling the learners to ask you some of the questions, and answer them fully. If you answer *yes* to any of them, encourage them to ask you more, and point out that subsequent questions will almost certainly be in the past simple form.

> ### Language Point: the present perfect
>
> The present perfect is used here for eliciting general information about an unspecified time in the past. Once the general information is given, further information usually becomes part of a narrative, hence the use of the past simple (or other narrative tenses). The time may still be unknown.
>
> Example: A: *Have you ever broken your leg?*
> B: *Yes, I have, actually.*
> A: *How?*
> B: *It was a riding accident – my horse threw me at a fence …*

When you are sure the learners understand the vocabulary and the idea of the activity, encourage them to circulate. During the mingling activity, monitor and help where necessary.

It goes without saying that learners should not be forced to divulge anything too personal or sensitive. You may wish to make that clear at the start, and remind them of the phrase they have used in earlier units: *I'd rather not say.*

In feedback, encourage the most interesting anecdotes to emerge. If appropriate, allow time for a correction slot on any difficulties which emerged with the use of the present perfect.

REVIEW OF UNIT 5

1 ▭

This exercise type occurs at regular intervals throughout the course. In addition to revising large chunks of vocabulary, it provides intensive listening practice leading to further speaking practice (the tapescript is at the back of the Class Book).

The learners could make a note of any vocabulary they hadn't remembered in the *Reflections* section of the Personal Study Workbook.

Answer key

1. No. 2. Yes. 3. Yes. 4. Yes. 5. No. 6. Yes.
7. No. 8. No. 9. No. 10. Yes. 11. Yes. 12. No.

2

Follow the instructions in the Class Book. This exercise can be done individually or in pairs.

Answer key

1. burnt herself
2. looked after themselves
3. cut myself
4. introduced ourselves
5. hurt yourself
6. looked at himself
7. weighed myself
8. helped ourselves

```
┌─────────────────────────────────────────┐
│              QUICK NOTES                 │
│  This went well:                         │
│  ....................................... │
│  ....................................... │
│  This didn't quite work:                 │
│  ....................................... │
│  ....................................... │
│  Things to think about:                  │
│  ....................................... │
│  ....................................... │
└─────────────────────────────────────────┘
```

LETTERS THAT TELL A STORY

CONTENTS

Language focus:	comparative and superlative adjectives *have to, need to, don't have to, don't need to*	
Vocabulary:	types of text (informal letter, essay, etc.) professions personal characteristics (wordbuilding)	
Skills:	Speaking:	comparing handwriting styles qualities required in a job discussion on handwriting analysis
	Listening:	dictation a short story about letters
	Reading:	a collage of text types a newspaper text on graphology
	Writing:	spelling

HANDWRITING STYLES

Introduction

The dictation at the start of the lesson has two aims: to provide listening and writing practice, and also to give a basis for discussion about handwriting at the end of the lesson. Reading and identifying different text types leads into a brief personalisation stage before moving on to focus on comparatives and superlatives, at the end of which the learners are asked to provide the rules governing their formation.

Suggested steps

1

So that your learners don't guess that they will be discussing their own handwriting, it is probably best not to direct them to open their Class Books until you are ready to do Exercise 2.

Either play the dictation, pausing and repeating as necessary, or read the text aloud yourself. Give the learners an opportunity to compare their spelling before you write (or ask one of them to write) the text on the board or OHT. There are a number of weak forms in the dictation (personal pronouns and articles) which learners might have difficulty with.

2

Deal with any problems of lexis as they arise, or tell your learners to use dictionaries. You may wish to focus on the pronunciation of certain items here: the sounds in *message* /mesidʒ/ and *recipe* /resəpi/ and the stress in these items:

recipe, essay, diary, envelope.

Answer key

a telephone message

3

The learners could match the texts and items with a partner.

Answer key

A an addressed envelope
B a recipe
C an essay
D a diary entry
E an informal letter
F an immigration form
G a formal letter
H a job application

They could then do the personalisation with the same partner and another pair. If you feel it would be useful, remind your learners about the use of the present perfect here, which was dealt with in the previous unit, i.e. a finished action in unfinished time.

4

Our assumption here is that comparative forms will be familiar, but probably not used very accurately. Begin by dealing with any vocabulary before the learners do the exercise: *neat* and *uniform* might cause problems. In feedback, ask your learners to make full sentences to practise comparatives (and do the same when you come to Exercise 5). There is obviously room for differences of opinion in this exercise and this is perfectly understandable, unless it becomes apparent that a vocabulary item has been misunderstood.

5

Do this in a similar way to Exercise 4, checking that the learners understand that *worst* is the opposite of *best*.

6

This is a checking stage. Encourage the learners to look back at the examples in Exercises 4 and 5 to deduce rules for comparatives and superlatives if this seems appropriate. You may wish to elicit the rules at the end and write them on the board for the learners to copy.

Answer key

See Grammar Reference page 162.

Option

You could go back to the approach used in Unit 6 where the learners chose whether to deduce the rule or to look it up, and then compare their answers.

7

You may want to direct the group's attention back to comparatives and superlatives in Exercises 4 and 5 – but they do not need to restrict themselves to these adjectives. Careful grouping of learners may be required to avoid any problems of sensitivity.

Option

Worksheet 7 on page 127 is an alternative to the final speaking activity in this lesson. Learners can discuss the questions in groups and report back any interesting findings at the end. Exercise 5 in the Personal Study Workbook would also be suitable to use with this worksheet.

Personal Study Workbook

1: Lexical pairs
2: A leopard is faster than a camel
4: Text types
7: Spelling rules

WHAT YOUR WRITING REVEALS

Introduction

The wordbuilding activity provides lexical input that learners will use at various stages of the lesson: in the practice of modal verbs in Exercise 2 and in the text on handwriting analysis which is the central theme of the lesson. At the end, the learners discuss the pros and cons of the topic.

Suggested steps

1

Follow the instructions in the Class Book. In feedback, check that the learners are able to say the words with the correct stress. (Incorrect word stress on *reliable* is a common difficulty.)

Language Point: word stress

A simple rule exists for nouns ending in -*tion* and -*ity*: the stress falls on the syllable before these suffixes.

Examples: *imagination, promotion*
popularity, sensitivity

Answer key

Adjective	Noun
reliable	reliability
honest	honesty
imaginative	imagination
popular	popularity
sensitive	sensitivity
self-confident	self-confidence
artistic	art
intelligent	intelligence

2

You could introduce the expressions with reference to the jobs or professions of your learners. For example, you have a learner who is a nurse. Ask the group what qualities are necessary for a nurse.

A nurse *needs to be* / *has to be* *reliable, sensitive,* etc.

A nurse doesn't *need to be* / *have to be* *artistic.*

You could do some controlled practice using one or two of the professions before the learners work in groups, and check that they understand all the professions vocabulary.

3

Introduce the text by asking the learners if they think there is a connection between personality and handwriting (which may have arisen in the discussion in the previous lesson). Pre-teach the word *graphology*. Tell the learners to read the text and answer the true/false questions; then they can compare with a partner and you can conduct class feedback to check the answers.

Answer key

1. True 2. True 3. False 4. False 5. True

4

For the discussion, you could instruct groups to answer the questions in any order according to interest. You could also encourage them to draw on their own experience.

Option

You could ask the learners to work with a partner and extend the list of questions, extending the theme if necessary, for subsequent discussion in groups.

Personal Study Workbook

3: Prefixes
5: What do your letters say?
8: Speaking partners

QUICK NOTES

This went well:

....

This didn't quite work:

....

Things to think about:

....

OTHER PEOPLE'S LETTERS

Introduction

This is a skills lesson based around a short story which is related to the general theme of writing; in this case, writing letters. The introductory activity is designed to promote discussion around the topic, and the second exercise pre-teaches essential vocabulary contained in the short story on the recording. Following comprehension tasks on the story, learners work on spelling and punctuation before writing their own letter.

Suggested steps

1

If you have a personal experience yourself of opening someone's mail, this would be the ideal way to start the lesson. Then learners can exchange ideas, but the discussion needs to be brief, otherwise the lesson will become too long.

2

The words in the circle represent key vocabulary in the short story, so it is important that the learners understand the words, although there will be later opportunities to practise some of the vocabulary. Allow them to use dictionaries to help, and clarify any problems when they appear to have finished.

3

Apart from anything else, the learners need to be very familiar with the names of the characters as this will greatly assist their understanding of the story. Encourage any explanations of the letters at this stage, but cut the discussion short if anyone appears to have guessed the actual story (it may spoil it for others). Choose the appropriate version of the listening for your class. The tapescript is on page 158.

Option 1

If you are familiar with the story, or know the tapescript well, you could tell the story yourself. This can be more involving than a recording, and gives your learners the opportunity to ask you questions as you proceed if they don't understand.

Option 2

A language laboratory would be suitable for this listening passage and would allow learners to work at their own pace, and possibly even on the version they preferred to listen to.

4

Put the learners in pairs to complete the sentences and discuss the story.

Answer key

1. handkerchiefs
2. thank him; opened all his mail
3. Clovis Sangrail
4. sent; Clothilde
5. the first; upset
6. he didn't know anyone called Clothilde
7. realised it was a trick
8. not to open his letters again

Conduct a feedback with the class to check the answers.

Option

For further practice, the learners could work in pairs to retell the story to each other, one beginning and the other taking over after the first letter.

5

Follow the instructions in the Class Book.

Answer key

> 16, Kensington Gardens,
> London W8
> 14th March, 1911

Dear Bertie,

I'm just writing to thank you for the wonderful handkerchiefs that I received in this morning's mail. You always find the prettiest gifts and you know how much I adore beautiful things. I sincerely hope you will come and visit me soon and then I can thank you in person.

With best wishes,

6

Follow the instructions in the Class Book. You may want to highlight the layout of the address and date and greetings in the letter in Exercise 5 before the learners write their own letters. When the pairs have finished, ask them to give their letters to the pair they wrote to.

Personal Study Workbook

6: Learning to write

```
QUICK NOTES

This went well:
.......................................................
.......................................................

This didn't quite work:
.......................................................
.......................................................

Things to think about:
.......................................................
.......................................................
```

REVIEW AND DEVELOPMENT

REVIEW OF UNIT 5

1

Follow the instructions in the Class Book. Pre-teach *diameter*. It might be useful to have tape measures or string, but only used with the greatest discretion, naturally. If this exercise is in any way taboo, avoid it.

Answer key

1. leg and foot
2. eyes
3. ankle
4. wrist to elbow
5. should be teeth
6. thumbnail
7. waist
8. could be either

Be prepared for your learners to prove otherwise! This exercise is intended for fun revision.

2 ⊡

If necessary, show the learners physically by saying /ð/ and /θ/: one is voiced and the other voiceless. Avoid putting a vowel sound afterwards as this makes it more difficult to hear the difference. Getting learners to make the two sounds and put their hands on their throats to feel the vibration with /ð/ is sometimes helpful. You may also need to point out the position of the tongue.

If learners are having difficulty deciding in which column to put the words, you could say them aloud so that they work from an oral model.

Answer key

Column 1 /θ/	Column 2 /ð/
bath	there
breath	breathe
teeth	another
thumb	themselves
throat	without

Use the recording to check the answers and conduct some controlled oral practice.

3

Before beginning the exercise, check that the learners understand any new items of vocabulary such as *sew* and *camcorder* (a portable video camera). Then ask them to complete the table.

Before the groupwork, you could tell them to ask you about yourself.

Example: *Can you play poker?*
Yes, my brothers taught me when I was younger.
Can you cook?
Yes. I taught myself, and my father taught me to make some dishes too.

REVIEW OF UNIT 6

1

Follow the instructions in the Class Book. This can be used as a class exercise or by a small group within the class. Check that the learners have answered appropriately according to the tenses used. The tapescript is at the back of the Class Book.

2

Follow the instructions in the Class Book. The learners could check their answers themselves, then take turns to test each other.

Answer key

Present participles

putting	meeting	feeling	setting	coming
planning	sailing	dropping	starting	climbing
robbing	hitting	biting	cleaning	winning
writing	saying	swimming	using	stopping

Past participles

put	met	felt	set	come
planned	sailed	dropped	started	climbed
robbed	hit	bitten	cleaned	won
written	said	swum	used	stopped

3

Do the first example together, and see if the learners can provide any alternative explanations for the first one. Then follow the instructions in the Class Book.

Answer key

Possible answers

1. Because I was so busy / I had such a lot of things to do.
2. Because I left the house so late / I had such a heavy suitcase.
3. Because there were so many people / such a lot of people.
4. Because I had such a bad headache / because it was so boring.
5. Because they were so difficult / because I had such a difficult journey home.
6. Because there was such a long queue for the buses / the buses were so crowded.

```
QUICK NOTES

This went well:
.................................................
.................................................

This didn't quite work:
.................................................
.................................................

Things to think about:
.................................................
.................................................
```

8

TAKE IT OR LEAVE IT

```
                        CONTENTS

Language focus:    going to and might for future plans
                   will for spontaneous decisions
                   present continuous for future arrangements

Vocabulary:        shopping expressions
                   names of shops
                   phrasal verbs
                   services and forms of payment

Skills:   Speaking:   shopping dialogues
                      discussing how you pay for things
                      talking about things you are planning to buy
                      discussing the relative cost of things
          Listening:  how people pay for things in Britain and
                          America
                      responding to statements (using will)
          Reading:    quiz: ways of talking about the future
                      jumbled order of events: shopping scenario
```

BUYING SOMETHING TO WEAR

Introduction

In this lesson the learners begin with a vocabulary/phrasal verb activity, ordering the steps in buying an item of clothing. They then learn and practise useful functional expressions and vocabulary for shopping situations. After a speaking activity, they focus on the use of *will* for spontaneous decisions and practise in a controlled activity using written and aural prompts.

Suggested steps

Option

You could begin the lesson by telling your learners about an item of clothing you bought recently, and describing the steps you went through – where you bought it, etc. This would give them some natural exposure to the language which comes up in Exercise 1.

Alternatively, you could ask the learners to talk to each other about the clothes they are wearing; where they bought them, when they bought them, how often they wear them, etc. Begin by doing a quick model of this yourself, describing your own clothes.

1

Focus the learners' attention on the photographs, and try to elicit what is happening if you have not done one of the optional activities above. Then look at the statements, and follow the instructions in the Class Book, doing the first two steps together before the learners work alone or in pairs. Encourage them to use dictionaries where necessary, or if you prefer, pre-teach a couple of expressions such as *item of clothing, receipt, refund* and the phrasal verbs.

Conduct feedback with the class, providing controlled oral practice of the items (especially the pronunciation of *receipt*), and highlight the prepositions in particular. It can be useful to elicit and write the correct order on the board or OHT for clarity.

Option

Once they have the steps in the correct order, the learners could memorise them, either in class or for homework. If you have written them on the board, you could progressively erase parts of the steps, and let the learners test each other in pairs. Such processes often contain useful lexis and the memorisation is contextualised and meaningful; learners often find this challenging and useful. Similar processes include: steps in eating out in a restaurant; buying a car; having a cold; driving to school or work; getting married, etc.

Answer key

1. You look for an item of clothing you want.
2. You try it on.
3. You take it off and try another one on.
4. You decide to buy it.
5. You pay for it.
6. You get a receipt.
7. You take it home and discover a problem with it.
8. You take it back.
9. You ask for a refund.
10. You show your assistant your receipt.
11. You get your money back.

Numbers 9 and 10 could be reversed.

2

Follow the instructions in the Class Book. Again, either pre-teach *to fit* and *changing room*, or let the learners deduce these or use dictionaries. In the feedback, provide controlled oral practice of the phrases as you go through the answers.

Answer key

Here's my receipt. (You show your assistant your receipt.)

Excuse me, where's the changing room? (You try it on.)

I'll take it. (You decide to buy it.)

Do you take American Express? (You pay for it.)

Oh, no, there's something wrong with it. (You take it home and discover a problem with it.)

Excuse me, I'm looking for a sweater. (You look for an item of clothing you want.)

Could I have my money back, please? (You ask for a refund.)

I'm afraid it doesn't fit. (You take it off and try another one on.)

Here's your receipt. (You get a receipt.)

I bought this here last week and I'm afraid ... (You take it back.)

Thank you. (You get your money back.)

3

Before they begin, encourage the learners to decide what they are buying, and what is wrong with it.

Option

Props (i.e. bringing in items of clothing) are always a motivating factor and can liven up role plays. You may also want the learners to do one of the following:

- act their conversation for the rest of the class
- record it on cassette or video for playback
- write out their conversation for writing practice, perhaps on a word processor, if these are available.

While the learners are doing the activity, monitor and help where necessary and note down any particular difficulties you wish to deal with at the end of the activity with the class.

4

Highlight the use of *will* for spontaneous decision, using the picture and dialogue. You could even act this scene out with learners and demonstrate that the decision to answer the door is made at that moment, and not pre-planned.

Practise the pronunciation of *I'll*, if necessary contrasting:

I answer it.
I'll answer it.

Do the examples together, and as many of the prompts in the exercise as is necessary. The learners can then work in pairs, doing the prompt/answers as mini-dialogues.

Answer key

Possible answers
1. OK, I'll turn off the heater.
   OK, I'll open the window.
2. OK, I'll wash them.
   OK, I'll get some clean ones.
3. OK, I'll answer it.
4. OK, I'll put the light on.
   OK, I'll open the curtains/blinds.
5. OK, I'll (go and) buy some.
   OK, I'll have tea.
6. OK, I'll turn it up.

5 ▭

Encourage the class to shout out their decisions using *will*. A variety of responses may be acceptable – including humorous ones.

Answer key

Possible answers
1. OK, I'll open the window / turn the heater off / open the door / break a window.
2. OK, I'll turn it down/off.
3. OK, I'll buy a new one / repair it.
4. OK, I'll take a bus/train / I'll walk.
5. OK, I'll buy some / make some / eat rice.
6. OK, I'll sing her to sleep / go and look after her / give her something to eat.

Personal Study Workbook

2: Could you ring me back?
3: Paraphrasing
7: Skeleton story

SHOPPING PLANS

Introduction

In the previous lesson, the learners focused on the use of *will* for spontaneous decisions. In the first part of this lesson, they practise the use of *going to* for plans and intentions, and *might* for speculations about the future through a personalised activity. They also learn shop vocabulary. In the second part of the lesson, there is a quiz which brings together the use of *will* and *going to* and introduces the use of the present continuous for plans and arrangements. Learners crystallise their understanding of this challenging area of grammar in a gap-fill activity on rules.

Suggested steps

Option 1

You could begin by telling the class about some shopping you are going to do in the next few days. This would introduce the topic in a personalised and concrete way. You might do this as a free dictation: you tell the learners in a natural way the things you are going to buy in different places, and they write out your shopping list.

Option 2

Follow the instructions on Worksheet 8 on page 127. This is a pair or small group activity.

1

Follow the instructions in the Class Book. If the learners are having difficulties, they can look at the list of shops in the grid below. In feedback, focus on and practise word stress, and pronunciation of *jeweller's*, *chemist's*, etc.

Answer key

1. jeweller's
2. supermarket
3. chemist's
4. department store
5. electrical shop
6. greengrocer's
7. street market
8. clothes shop

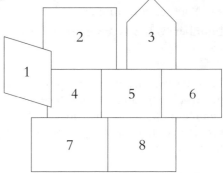

> ### *Language Point: 's*
>
> The *'s* genitive is often used with shops:
>
> *I'm looking for a chemist's.*
> *She's gone to the newsagent's.*
>
> It means *the chemist's/newsagent's shop*.
>
> It is not necessary to say *shop* if you use the genitive form. Other examples include *the baker's*, *the butcher's* and *the florist's*.
>
> These items often include the consonant clusters *st's* or *nt's* which require special attention.

2

First clarify that *I'm going to do it* means that you decided in the past, and that you are expressing a plan or intention. *Might* expresses possibility in verb form (i.e. it is possible, but not certain).

Show by your own examples how to complete the table, and add one or two shops at the end (under *anywhere else you like*) to demonstrate that they should include other shopping plans. Then ask the learners to do the same for themselves. Highlight the form of *be going to do* and *might do* on the board, or in the dialogue. Practise the controlled dialogue together as a class, then do the same dialogue with a learner, encouraging them to substitute information from their table. Then get two learners to do the dialogue, again using real information, before they all work in pairs. Change the pairs after a few minutes to maximise practice. Conduct feedback, with different pairs either doing their dialogue in front of the group, or with individuals reporting back what they discovered about their partner. Correct any errors of form or meaning with *going to* or *might*.

3

Follow the instructions in the Class Book. Do the first question together, then let the learners work together or work alone, then compare answers.

Answer key

1. c 2. b 3. c 4. c 5. b 6. a

Note that in questions 4 and 6 the correct answer is in the present continuous. This use of the tense is taught in *True to Life* Elementary Class Book, but learners should be able to work out the correct answer by a process of elimination. In any case, it will be important to reinforce the concept by using Exercise 4.

4

Tell the learners to work individually or with a partner. Follow the instructions in the Class Book. If necessary, provide further examples to test or clarify. Exercise 1 in the Personal Study Workbook could be used here if you feel the learners need more focus on this area.

Answer key

1. We use *going to* (*do*) to talk about plans and intentions, when we have decided in the past about an action in the future.

   Example: *I'm going to work hard next year.*

   (I thought about it in the past and made a decision before now.)

2. We use *will* when we decide something at the moment of speaking, not before.

   Example: A: *Would you like a drink?*
   　　　　　 B: *Yes, please, I'll have a coffee.*

3. We use the present continuous to talk about plans and arrangements we have made in advance with other people.

   Example: *I'm having lunch with Jenny tomorrow.*

   (I phoned her yesterday and we made the arrangements.)

Personal Study Workbook

1: Are you busy this evening?
4: Sounds similar
8: Speaking partners

```
┌─────────────────────────────────────────┐
│              QUICK NOTES                  │
│  This went well:                          │
│  ....................................... │
│  ....................................... │
│  This didn't quite work:                  │
│  ....................................... │
│  ....................................... │
│  Things to think about:                   │
│  ....................................... │
│  ....................................... │
└─────────────────────────────────────────┘
```

PAYING FOR THINGS

Introduction

In this lesson, the learners have the opportunity to discuss both how they pay for things and the cost and value of services and goods. The emphasis is on speaking, with some lexical input and a cross–cultural listening activity.

Suggested steps

1

Begin by focusing on the meaning of the words in the list. If some items are not appropriate to your class, add your own, or ask the learners to think of more items themselves.

Other possibilities:

music cassettes　stationery　furniture
electrical equipment　newspapers and magazines

Highlight the prepositions *in cash*, *by cheque*, etc., and check that the learners understand *direct debit* and *debit card*. Then put them in pairs for the discussion.

2 ▭

Play the recording and follow the instructions in the Class Book.

Answer key

	American speaker	*British speaker*
supermarket shopping	cash	debit card
petrol for your car	credit card	credit card
new clothes	credit card	cheque
daily/weekly transport	cash	cash
an airline ticket	credit card	credit card
car insurance	direct debit	cheque
stamps	cash	cash
a restaurant meal	cash/credit card	credit card
a phone bill	direct debit	cheque

3

Check that the learners understand the vocabulary and can pronounce the items before they begin the discussion. In multilingual groups, there should be some differences; clearly less so in monolingual groups, although they may not all agree. While the learners are working in groups, monitor and note any difficulties of communication for later feedback.

4

Do one or two examples as a class to demonstrate the activity.

Examples/suggestions:

soap: personal hygiene is important for the health of a nation and free soap would encourage cleanliness.
local phone calls: this would be good for local businesses.

Make it clear that they do not have to find a justification for everything being free (the instruction says 'can you think of one good reason?'). They may well feel, for example, that there is no justification for free tobacco! Allow plenty of time for discussion. Allocate different parts of the list to different groups. (For example, some groups begin at the bottom of the list.) Monitor and collect examples of language learners use, correct or incorrect.

In feedback at the end, encourage open discussion, and allow time for feedback on any important language points which have emerged.

Personal Study Workbook

5: Shopping in London
6: Listen and answer
9: Visual dictionary

QUICK NOTES

This went well:

....
....

This didn't quite work:

....
....

Things to think about:

....
....

REVIEW OF UNIT 6

1

Follow the instructions in the Class Book.

Answer key

progressive
modern
poor
limited/narrow
useful
interesting
pleasant
easygoing
hardworking

2

For this activity, encourage the learners first to keep a clear written record of phrases with *do* or *make*. You may wish to take in the written work to correct and hand back.

Answer key

do: an exercise, an exam, homework, a course, one's best
make: a noise, friends, a mistake, a mess, progress

REVIEW OF UNIT 7

1 ⊂⊃

You can either use the recording or dictate the sentences yourself. The activity could also be done in a language laboratory or listening centre which would give learners more flexibility to listen as often as they wished. In feedback, you could highlight once again the rules of spelling for doubling consonants which were dealt with in Units 6 and 7.

Answer key

1. I'm writing to their boss.
2. I mustn't lose the address.
3. We planned the meeting last Tuesday.
4. I always forget how to spell *quite*.
5. Whose handwriting is the easiest to read?
6. It's wetter and warmer than yesterday.
7. He's bigger than me.
8. Which suitcase is heavier?
9. She's sitting down over there.
10. I'm putting on weight, but she's much thinner.

2

This is firstly a recognition activity for superlatives. Ask the learners to read the questions and to say if there are any they don't understand. Give them a few moments to note their answers. Impress upon them that they aren't expected to know all the answers, and that they should guess if they don't. Conduct a mingling activity, where the learners try to find out information from each other. They will have to do a number of things such as looking at each other's handwriting, asking about jobs, etc. When they have collected information, elicit sentences from the class using superlatives:

Examples: *Maria Helena has the longest hair.*
I think Jules has the most difficult job. He's a doctor.

3

This is a brainstorming activity based on the theme of Unit 7. You may wish to set a time limit of two or three minutes to work alone, then five minutes to compare in groups. The learners will need dictionaries.

At the end, you could compile the lists jointly on the board.

Answer key

Possible answers

Usually typed
company report; business letter or any kind of formal letter; university thesis; legal document; job application

Usually handwritten
letter to friend or family; diary entry; English homework; message to someone in your house; birthday or greetings card; cheque; form

Both
menu; some notices; addressed envelope; recipe

```
QUICK NOTES

This went well:

..........................................................

..........................................................

This didn't quite work:

..........................................................

..........................................................

Things to think about:

..........................................................

..........................................................
```

9

FOOD AND DRINK

CONTENTS

Language focus: present simple passive
must/have to for obligation
mustn't for prohibition
don't have to for lack of obligation/necessity
should/shouldn't for advisability
functional expressions to use in restaurants

Vocabulary: food and drink
verbs: *cook, serve, peel, keep, produce*, etc.

Skills: Speaking: cultural norms at the dining table and
when visiting people
what to say in restaurants
Listening: cross-cultural restaurant norms
Reading: quizzes, menus
text about customs at the dinner table

DRINKS AROUND THE WORLD

Introduction

In this lesson, the learners begin with a warm-up on the theme of the lesson, then proceed to a general knowledge questionnaire which includes examples of the main teaching point, the present simple passive. After confirming their answers to the questionnaire, they focus on the form and use of the passive and practise it in a controlled activity.

Suggested steps

Option

For many adult learners where alcohol is not a contentious issue, Worksheet 9 on page 128 may be a useful and stimulating option. It can be used in place of *Drinks around the world* in Unit 9, but does not focus on the present simple passive. In place of that, it includes a discussion on alcohol. Follow the instructions on the worksheet.

Answer key

Worksheet 9 Wine quiz
1. True.
2. True.
3. True.
4. False. Some wine gets better if you keep it, but most wine is best drunk within 1–2 years of the vintage.
5. True, although room temperature should be 18–19°C, and not the kind of temperature you find in most centrally heated rooms, i.e. 21–22°.

6. False. Some wine is better if it is opened in advance, but it is not true for most wine and certainly not always true.
7. True.
8. False. There are certainly some recipes for fish with red wine in Portuguese and French cooking.
9. False. Some wine keeps in good condition for several days, but it is generally not true.
10. False.

1

You could begin the warm-up by demonstrating it yourself, i.e. telling the class what you have drunk and why. Encourage them to ask you questions. Needless to say, if any learners are particularly sensitive about alcohol, you could omit discussion on the last two drinks. Then ask the learners to tell a partner, or perhaps mingle and tell a few other people.

2

Before the quiz, you may wish to pre-teach a few items: *to store, a worm* (use an illustration), and *meatballs*. Alternatively, the learners could look up important new items while doing the quiz, as there are not many and they should be motivated to find out.

Quickly get some feedback from the group on their answers, and tell them the correct answers to the quiz. Make sure they correct any mistakes in the statements, and check at the end by writing them on the board.

Answer key

Six of the statements are true, and four are false. The ones which are false are :

Question 1: Kenya isn't the largest producer of coffee in the world; Brazil is.

Question 5: In Britain, most people drink tea with milk.

Question 7: Nobody (except the manufacturer) really knows what Cola is made from, though the ingredients are thought to include extract of cola nut and cocoa.

Question 10: Irish coffee does have cream and whiskey, but it doesn't have beer in it.

3

Focus the learners' attention on the form and use of the present simple passive. You could use your own examples of the form which will be more culturally familiar.

Show the learners that they can complete the sentences in any way they like, as long as they are logical. Do a couple of examples together before they work in pairs.

Answer key

Possible answers

Coffee is produced in Brazil, Colombia, etc.
                    for export.
                    in large/small quantities in …

Cola is sold in bottles and cans.
              all over the world.
              in supermarkets, newsagent's, etc.

Cognac is sometimes drunk after a meal.
                           when people have had a
                               shock.
                           with milk before going to
                               bed.

Rice is grown in Japan.

Yoghurt is made from milk.

Coffee is drunk all over the world.

Tea is exported in large boxes.

Champagne is served at special parties and ceremonies.
           is served very cold.
           is served in tall glasses.

Tea is grown in India, Sri Lanka, etc.
     is grown for export.
     is grown in hot countries.

Mineral water is produced in many countries.

Accept any logical sentences in the second part of the practice exercise. While the learners are writing out their sentences, monitor and help / correct errors. You may wish to have a quick feedback after the mingling activity to provide oral practice and correct further errors.

Option

The learners could invent their own questions in the *Drinks around the World* quiz to test each other. These do not need to be cross-cultural questions in a monolingual environment; they could be local.

Personal Study Workbook

1: Correct my mistakes

5: Tourist guides

QUICK NOTES

This went well:

....

....

This didn't quite work:

....

....

Things to think about:

....

....

FOOD AND DRINK: DOS AND DON'TS

Introduction

In this lesson, the learners look at modal verbs expressing obligation, necessity and prohibition in the context of food and drink. The first exercise is designed to check understanding of these verbs which are often a source of conceptual confusion. The practice activity in Exercise 2 further checks understanding. The reading is intended as a springboard for discussion about cultural factors in eating, and provides freer practice of the modal verbs.

Suggested steps

1

You could begin by writing a few true/untrue sentences on the board appropriate to your group for discussion. Otherwise, begin by asking the class if they can think of any rules to do with food and drink – what you have to wash, what you mustn't eat, etc. Keep this brief but just enough to stimulate interest in the topic.

Ask the learners if there is any vocabulary in the first exercise that they don't know. Elicit the first example sentence (*You have to/must pay for a meal in a restaurant*) before the learners match the sentence halves alone or in pairs. If they seem to be doing this well, tell them to go on to match the explanations and sentences.

Answer key

You have to/must pay for a meal in a restaurant. (It is necessary or an obligation to do this.)

You should go on a diet if you are overweight. (It is a good idea to do it.)

You don't have to wash melon before you eat it. (You can do it if you want, but it's not necessary.)

You shouldn't eat apples which aren't ripe. (It isn't a good idea to do it.)

You mustn't eat seafood which isn't fresh. (It is wrong or dangerous, or sometimes not permitted. It could make you very ill.)

Language Point: (don't) have to, must(n't) and should(n't)

1. *Have to* is sometimes confused with *have* both in form and pronunciation. Make it clear that the auxiliary verb *do* is required in the negative and interrogative.
2. Learners may well confuse *don't have to* and *mustn't*. In the affirmative form, they know that *must* and *have to* are similar in meaning. However, in the negative *don't have to* means *it isn't necessary* and *mustn't* means *it is prohibited*.
3. Learners often overuse *must* as they come across it early on when learning the language. Point out that *have to* is more common amongst native speakers.
4. *Should* and *shouldn't* cover a range of meanings from advice (e.g. *you should go and see a doctor*) to strong moral obligation (e.g. *you should never hit children*).

When going over the answers, clarify any difficulties and stress the difference between *mustn't* and *don't have to* in particular. You should certainly consider translation as a way of ironing out difficulties here, particularly with monolingual groups. You could also check understanding by asking questions:

Example: *You don't have to wash melon before eating it.*
Question: *Is it necessary to wash a melon? Can you decide/choose?*

You mustn't eat seafood which isn't fresh.
Question: *Is it OK to eat it? Is it dangerous?*

2

Begin as a class doing the first few examples together. Make sure that if the learners say the sentences are not true, they correct them, as this provides practice in the forms.

Although the examples have clear answers from our point of view, we have occasionally found cultural differences amongst our learners. For this reason, be prepared to accept answers which learners can justify; at the same time, be wary of conceptual confusion. Let the learners use dictionaries, or check that they understand *to peel* and *to keep*.

Answer key

1. True.
2. False. You shouldn't/mustn't drink wine. (This depends how strongly you feel about it.)
3. False. You have to cook them. (Though in a very few countries, you might not.)
4. False. You don't have to cook them.
5. True. Green potatoes can be poisonous.
6. False. You should / have to wash it.
7. False. You don't have to. (Some people say you have to peel them.)
8. False. You should / have to keep yoghurt in a cool place.

3

Check that the learners understand *to refuse* and *dessert* and can pronounce these words correctly. Then ask them to read the text.

4

When they have finished, deal briefly with any problems with vocabulary, then ask them to give a few reactions to Dorinda, using the sentence beginnings. Once they understand what to do, ask them to continue in groups using the phrases as much as possible.

The activity aims to stimulate discussion. With a multilingual group, there should be a considerable number of differences of cultural behaviour to discuss; with a monolingual group, there may be more homogeneity. However, regional differences, the generation gap and social grouping may well provide differences in perspective.

Some learners may be interested to know the cultural norms in Britain, though this is not the primary aim of the activity. If they want some information, here are some guidelines:

In the first place, most of Dorinda's behaviour could be acceptable, as long as she is very close to the family, indeed considered 'one of the family' and if the behaviour described is acceptable to them all. However, it would normally be considered 'unacceptable' in Britain for a visitor to do the following:

– take off their shoes at the door (unless the family is Muslim)
– say 'enjoy your meal' (but the host/hostess might say something similar)
– help themselves uninvited to food, ask for wine, smoke at the table, begin eating before everyone else, or eat with their fingers (unless it is obviously 'finger food').

For some people, leaving your knife and fork on the table and breaking bread into your soup is unacceptable.

It might be considered strange, but not rude to do the following:

arrive early, bring a dessert without making a prior arrangement, refuse food without giving a reason, say nothing about the food. It is normal to allow a few minutes at least to elapse before leaving, following your announcement.

It would be considered acceptable to bring wine, ring the following day and say you enjoyed your meal, and even to ask for the recipe.

While groups are discussing the text, circulate and make a note of interesting points, or errors to deal with in a feedback activity at the end.

Option

Learners could write up their ideas on Exercise 4 for homework.

2: Dialogue completion
3: Verbs with two objects
7: Sequencing events
8: Speaking partners

QUICK NOTES

This went well:

....

....

This didn't quite work:

....

....

Things to think about:

....

....

EATING OUT

Introduction

This lesson introduces words and expressions that will be useful in restaurant situations, and through the quiz also highlights appropriate and inappropriate language. A listening activity then explains cultural and linguistic norms in different parts of the English-speaking world. The menu provides an opportunity to learn new vocabulary and personalise it, before finishing with the restaurant role play to consolidate language from the lesson and the unit.

Suggested steps

1

Too much pre-teaching would spoil the point of the quiz, but you may wish to check that your learners understand *book a table* and *order a meal*. Remind them that more than one answer is possible for each question before they begin.

> **Language Points**
> 1. *Have you any seats left?* is a question you could ask in a theatre or cinema.
> 2. *Card* is a false friend for many learners.
> 3. *Can* is possible instead of *could* in Question 7 with little difference in meaning.

Conduct a brief feedback on the answers to the quiz but don't confirm any at this stage.

2 ▭

Play the recording so that the learners can check their answers. With a multinational group you may also want to discuss the different ways of doing things in their countries.

Answer key

1. b (You don't ask for seats, and c is a bit rude.)
2. b (a is possible but unlikely, and c is rude.)
3. b (a is rude and c is wrong.)
4. a or b (c is wrong.)
5. a or c (b sounds a bit rude.)
6. b is correct in Britain, but c is correct in America. (a is wrong.)
7. b is correct in Britain, and c is correct in America. (a is wrong.)

3

Give the learners time to look through the menu, using dictionaries and the pictures to identify new vocabulary. They can do this individually or in pairs. Provide controlled practice to check pronunciation. Common sound problems include *soup* (cf. *soap*), *raw*, *cabbage*, *honey*, *pineapple* and the collapsed syllable in *strawberry*.

Following this, put them in groups to discuss whether the menu items appear in their own countries. With a multilingual group it is clearly more interesting to mix the nationalities as much as possible.

Option

With a multilingual group you may wish to extend Exercise 3 by getting the learners to produce a 'typical' menu from their own country. They can then discuss the menus in groups, and you may select one or two to present their menus to the rest of the class.

4

This is obviously more fun if you can rearrange the furniture to approximate a restaurant. Photocopy the role cards on page 141. Divide the group into waiters/waitresses and customers, and give each learner one of these role cards to read and learn before they begin (customers will be assigned 1, 2, or 3). Put them in different parts of the room to discuss any new vocabulary. Organise the waiters/waitresses first, as they have more to read. Omit role card 3 if your learners are sensitive about alcohol.

After the learners have had time to digest the information on their role cards, put them in their groups to act out the situation. As it unfolds you can obviously keep it moving and prompt more interaction if necessary, e.g. suggest quietly to one of the diners that they want more bread, wish to go to the toilet (but don't know where it is), would like a second bottle of wine (but not the same as the first), etc. Also make sure the waiters/waitresses are kept busy. Tell them to check that the diners are happy with their meal, etc. At the same time, try to be as discreet as possible and note down important mistakes and good examples of language use.

Conduct a feedback. Go over mistakes and point out where the learners were performing well. (Too often feedback sessions only consist of correcting errors, but positive feedback is also important for learner motivation and reassurance.)

Personal Study Workbook

4: Food
6: What's on the menu?
9: Visual dictionary

```
┌─────────────────────────────────────────┐
│              QUICK NOTES                 │
│                                          │
│   This went well:                        │
│   ......................................  │
│   ......................................  │
│                                          │
│   This didn't quite work:                │
│   ......................................  │
│   ......................................  │
│                                          │
│   Things to think about:                 │
│   ......................................  │
│   ......................................  │
└─────────────────────────────────────────┘
```

REVIEW AND DEVELOPMENT

REVIEW OF UNIT 7

1 ⬚⬚

Work through the examples with the group; if your learners are familiar with syllables, go straight to the practice activity. Check their answers before they move on to the second activity in which they mark the stress.

Answer key

A
message (2)   diary (can be 2 or 3)   punctuation (4)
thousand (2)   cheque (1)   envelope (3)   reliability (6)
recipe (3)

B

1st syllable	2nd syllable	3rd syllable
politics	intelligent	sensitivity
architect	reliable	politician
character	imaginative	personnel
necessary	advertisement	popularity
advertising	analysis	application
sensitive	computer	

For controlled practice, you could let the learners do a 'mumble drill': they practise saying the words quietly to themselves at their own pace, and you monitor and correct as necessary. In this way, they can all practise at the same time without disturbing each other.

2

Follow the instructions in the Class Book. You may decide to do one or two examples with the class before putting them in pairs or groups to complete the rest of the task. Conduct a feedback at the end.

Answer key

Possible answers
1. You can do it with one hand easily.
2. You can do it with one hand with great difficulty.
3. You need two hands.
4. You can do it with one hand with difficulty.
5. You can do it with one hand with difficulty.
6. You can do it with one hand with difficulty.
7. You can do it with one hand with difficulty.
8. You can do it with one hand with difficulty.
9. You can do it with one hand easily.
10. You can do it with one hand easily.

REVIEW OF UNIT 8

1

Give your learners a couple of minutes to complete the table. While they are doing that, move round and monitor their answers to make sure they are doing it correctly.

Before they mingle in groups, you may wish to try it once yourself with a strong member of the group. Ask the person if they have any plans for this week, and if they have positive answers, follow up with additional questions in order to make it appear a more natural conversation. Then go on to ask about plans for this year. When you have finished, let them do the same in groups. Once again you can move round and monitor their answers.

2

With a multilingual group it will obviously be more interesting to mix the nationalities. If you are working with a group from the same country and town, ask them to be as specific as possible in their answers, as this may promote discussion about particular shops they all know or experiences they have had.

```
┌─────────────────────────────────────────┐
│              QUICK NOTES                 │
│                                          │
│   This went well:                        │
│   ......................................  │
│   ......................................  │
│                                          │
│   This didn't quite work:                │
│   ......................................  │
│   ......................................  │
│                                          │
│   Things to think about:                 │
│   ......................................  │
│   ......................................  │
└─────────────────────────────────────────┘
```

Unit 9 FOOD AND DRINK

10

FEELINGS:
THE GOOD, THE BAD AND THE UGLY

CONTENTS

Language focus: verbs with *-ing* form or infinitive
suggestions using *could*, e.g. *they could get some nice
pictures for the walls*
expressing feelings: *it makes me (angry)*
I get (angry) when ...

Vocabulary: verbs and idioms of liking and hating;
other verbs, e.g. *hope, decide, imagine, want,
promise, avoid*
emotions
verb + noun collocations, e.g. *start a car, tell a story*

Skills: Speaking: expressing personal feelings
how to overcome a bad mood
suggesting how to improve an office
Listening: a poem
how to beat a bad mood
Reading: inferring the content of a poem
Writing: sentence completion

SAY HOW YOU FEEL

Introduction

The lesson begins with a personalised activity and then concentrates on verbs and phrases followed by an *-ing* form or infinitive. The important role of dictionaries in showing such grammatical information is highlighted here, and the lesson moves through controlled practice to a freer, more personalised activity at the end.

Suggested steps

1

Begin by demonstrating the first activity yourself, i.e. tell your learners how you feel about doing the things in the list. Encourage them to ask follow-up questions and elaborate a little on the topics:

Example: YOU: *I don't like getting calls late at night. Someone phoned me at 12 last night and woke me up.*

LEARNER: *Did you get up? Do you often get calls at night?*

Then ask the learners to tell each other about the topics in the list. You probably need to clarify *I don't mind*, but at this stage it is not necessary for the learners to use the language taught in Exercise 2. It is acceptable for them to say *I like* or *I don't like* or *I hate* or *it's OK*, since this is a warm-up to the theme. Conduct a brief feedback after the mingling activity.

Option

Worksheet 10 (on page 129)
There is potential for a good deal of interaction on the topics in the warm-up activity, so we have included a worksheet which develops and expands on the warm-up and can be used in place of it. Follow the instructions on the worksheet, making sure that the group understands any new vocabulary before they start writing.

2

You could either pre-teach a few items before the matching exercise, or encourage the learners to use dictionaries: *regret* and *can't stand* are likely to be new.

For this activity, a certain amount of subjectivity is to be expected; the matching exercise is meant to stimulate use of the forms and not to have fixed answers. At the end, conduct a class feedback for an exchange of opinions.

Answer key

Possible answers

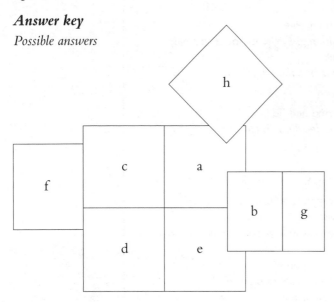

3

Try to elicit the correct answer from the class and then highlight the difference on the board.

Answer key

Want and *would like* are followed by the infinitive; the others are followed by the *-ing* form.

> ### Language Point: like and would like
>
> Learners often confuse the forms after *like* and *would like*:
>
> *Like* when it is not conditional can take either the infinitive or *-ing* form in British English, although there is a very slight difference in meaning:
>
> *I like to meet new people when I travel,* is a little more theoretical than *I like meeting new people when I travel.* The distinction is not one that need concern your learners at this stage.
>
> *Would like,* however, is always followed by the infinitive. For example, *I'd like to meet Mrs Johns.*

Option

If you know your class well, and they have a good relationship with each other, they could suggest sentence endings about themselves or other members of the class, using the verbs/phrases underlined in Exercise 2. This would give personalised practice. Alternatively, you could give them some sentences of your own about your learners to see if they can guess who it might be.

Example: *I hate doing homework.*
          Oh, that's probably Riita.

Study the dictionary entries together and look up the first verb in Exercise 4 as a class. The dictionaries you and your learners have available may well be very different from the samples in the Class Book, so you will need to adapt your approach to take account of the way your dictionary highlights verb patterns.

4

The learners could share the task of looking up the words between them in small groups. You could write up the constructions on the board at the end to provide a clear written model. Check that they understand the meaning of the items.

Answer key

Verb + infinitive: refuse, expect, decide, hope, promise, offer.
Verb + *-ing* form: give up, imagine, avoid, finish.

Option

This might be a good opportunity to reflect on the way your learners record vocabulary. In the first and second lessons, verb patterns and verb/noun collocations are dealt with; for many learners, systematic recording of structures and patterns such as these is useful.

5

Give the learners time to work alone while you monitor and iron out difficulties. Then ask them to compare and discuss their sentences in groups. Encourage them to expand on their sentences, demonstrating in front of the group with one of your learners:

LEARNER: *I hope to build a house next year.*
YOU: *Really? Where? How? etc.*

Personal Study Workbook

3: What did they say?
4: Sounds missing

> ### QUICK NOTES
>
> This went well:
>
> ....
>
> ....
>
> This didn't quite work:
>
> ....
>
> ....
>
> Things to think about:
>
> ....
>
> ....

Introduction

The poem at the beginning of the lesson aims to provide an opportunity for learners to look beyond the words and make inferences. It is also intended as a springboard for personalised discussion. In the second part of the lesson, some of the collocations in the poem are studied, developed and practised.

Suggested steps

1 📖

You could begin by telling the group some of the things that make you happy and encourage them to ask you questions about these things. Your own photographs could help to make this a very engaging activity. In fact, you could set this up in the previous lesson and ask the learners to bring in photos of things that make them happy.

Ask the learners to look at the pictures and the poem and follow the instructions in the Class Book. Let them compare their answers and/or use dictionaries to check vocabulary. Conduct a quick feedback on the exercise.

Either play the recording while the learners follow the poem in their books, or read it aloud yourself.

2

Work through the first two examples together, making it clear that the learners have to justify their ideas using the poem. Check that they understand the vocabulary in the questions, then let them work together.

Answer key

1. We don't know. She talks about children, but we don't know if they are hers.
2. Yes. She talks about the dog which probably means her dog.
3. Yes. She talks about communion and God.
4. Yes. She likes walking in the country and gardening, but most of her hobbies are indoor ones.
5. Yes. She talks about liqueur coffee, but that doesn't mean she drinks very much!
6. No. She talks about log fires and the problems of starting a car in winter.
7. Yes. She talks about the satisfaction of helping a patient to get better. She also mentions the look on a mother's face when she sees her baby for the first time, so perhaps that is part of her job satisfaction.
8. Yes. She probably spends a lot of time alone, walking, reading, listening to music, relaxing. And she obviously likes her day off.
9. She sounds an optimistic, positive person. The poem shows she is positive about most aspects of her life.

3

This is a personalised speaking activity, and your learners may need a little time to plan their thoughts and check words in the dictionary before they begin. Monitor the pairs and conduct feedback afterwards on what they discussed, and any language difficulties they encountered.

Option

Learners could write similar poems, either in class or for homework, alone or together, for themselves or for a wall poster.

4

Collocations are not new for learners at this level, but by way of introduction, you could show them some common errors of collocation and ask them to correct them, using your own examples (e.g. to make homework). Learners may find dictionaries useful here, as 'strong' collocations are often used in the sentence examples. For example, if you look up *joke*, it is probable that *tell a joke* will be used in at least one of the examples. Unfortunately, dictionaries cannot always be relied upon to include all the common collocations.

Answer key

Errors of collocation:
1. You can have 10 years old.
2. You can start an illness.
3. You can look at a football match.
4. You can tell a speech.
5. You can get a baby.
6. You can watch a photo.
7. You can make a photo.

> **Language Point: verb + noun collocations**
>
> 1. *To have ten years old* and *make a photo* are common translation errors from Romance languages.
> 2. *Look at* and *watch* often overlap in meaning, but it is rare to use *watch* for something which doesn't normally move, e.g. you *look at* a picture and *watch* a film.
> 3. *Tell* and *say* are often confused and where possible it is best to learn certain collocations as in the exercise. *Tell* often conveys the idea of narration. The two verbs are also grammatically different; *tell* is transitive, and *say* is intransitive. This explains the common learner error, *he said me*.

5

Demonstrate first with a member of the group, then put them in pairs. After a few minutes, tell them to swap roles and continue.

6

Follow the instructions in the Class Book.

Personal Study Workbook

2: Using *get*
5: Happiness
6: Do you like blue?
8: Speaking partners

```
QUICK NOTES

This went well:

.............................................

.............................................

This didn't quite work:

.............................................

.............................................

Things to think about:

.............................................

.............................................
```

HOW TO BEAT A BAD MOOD

Introduction

This lesson is largely skills-based, starting with a focus on structural patterns to express feelings, then leading on to speaking, listening, reading and further speaking practice. In the final activity, learners practise giving suggestions using *could*.

Suggested steps

1

To stimulate interest, you could give your own examples of the structures using local and relevant examples. Write these on the board, and highlight the structure *It makes me* (+ adjective) *when ...* and *I get* (+ adjective) *when ...* .

Monitor while the learners are writing their sentences, correcting errors and helping with vocabulary where necessary. Then organise the mingling activity. In feedback, aim to discover the most common problems.

2

Before the learners work in groups, elicit one or two ideas from the class about how the things in the table might help. If the learners find this difficult, make one or two suggestions yourself, but encourage them to personalise and give specific examples of things which help them. If they wish to make notes, they should use a separate sheet of paper as they will need the table in the book to complete the listening activity. You may wish to appoint spokespeople for the subsequent feedback.

After the group work, encourage feedback on the ideas, perhaps using the board to write up their suggestions.

3 🔲🔲

Choose the appropriate version of the listening. The learners will probably need to hear the recording more than once if they are going to take notes. Make sure that they don't try to write everything down; just the key points.

Go over the answers to the listening activity, then give the learners time to give their reactions to the ideas, either as a whole class or in groups.

Option

You could deliver the information yourself in a short talk and not use the recording at all.

Answer key

1. exercise: natural things are better than drugs; exercise makes better use of oxygen.
2. colour: dark colours are depressing; bright colours are better for a bad mood. Red isn't good if you are angry. Neutral colours are best if you are anxious.
3. music: change the music slowly from music which is the same as your bad mood to happier music.
4. food: carbohydrates make you calm and relaxed. Too much tea and coffee makes you anxious.
5. positive thinking: take an interest in other people (think of something funny: version 2)

4

You may wish to pre-teach or check a few items before the learners read the letter, e.g. *to employ*, *bored* and *depressed*, *the (working) environment*. Then let them read the letter and look at the picture.

Answer key

Relationships in the office are bad and the speaker thinks this is because of the office environment itself.

5

Focus the learners' attention on the use of *could* for suggestions and, if you like, get them to repeat the sentences for oral practice. Then elicit one or two more suggestions using *could* before organising the groupwork. Again, you could consider appointing a spokesperson in each small group for feedback. Monitor while the learners discuss in groups. It is not necessary for them to use only the structure suggested, but they should try to include a few examples. At the end, call the groups together and have an exchange of ideas. Give the learners feedback on their language, praising good use of language as well as providing them with some errors to correct.

Option 1

Learners could write a reply to the letter using the ideas discussed in the groupwork.

Option 2

You could have a similar practice activity for suggestions based on a room they all know which requires some improvements.

Personal Study Workbook

1: Make a suggestion
7: Dear Abby …
9: Visual dictionary

```
QUICK NOTES

This went well:
.................................................................
.................................................................

This didn't quite work:
.................................................................
.................................................................

Things to think about:
.................................................................
.................................................................
```

REVIEW AND DEVELOPMENT

REVIEW OF UNIT 8

1

Follow the instructions in the Class Book. Let the learners compare their answers.

Answer key

1. look after   2. fit   3. bookshop   4. lend   5. take off
6. wear   7. take   8. sensitive   9. bill   10. on

2 ▭

Follow the instructions in the Class Book. You could elicit any questions the learners wrote down which were not included on the recording.

REVIEW OF UNIT 9

1

Check first that the learners understand the vocabulary in the list, then set a time limit for the groupwork (say 5 minutes). Monitor while they are working. Watch out in particular for unnatural examples, where *can* or *can't* would be more appropriate (e.g. *you can't peel biscuits*). If necessary, say that they can use *can*.

Some discussion or disagreement may well emerge in the feedback and this is to be encouraged.

2

Follow the instructions in the Class Book. It may be useful to translate the word *keep* if you are working with a monolingual group; it may not have just one equivalent in other languages.

If you like, encourage the learners to add to the list, and ask each other about their additions: e.g. birth certificate, love letters, scissors.

3

Follow the instructions in the Class Book. Learners may need dictionaries for this activity. You could conduct a group feedback on their ideas.

Answer key

Possible answers

1. The company is paying.
2. You are going to the cinema and you haven't got time to go home to eat.
3. For a celebration: someone's birthday or wedding anniversary.
4. You haven't got any food at home.
5. You have got food at home but you are too lazy to cook.
6. You are staying in a hotel, so you have no choice.
7. You are trying to beat a bad mood, so you go out to a restaurant to cheer yourself up.
8. A new restaurant has opened and you want to see what it is like.
9. Someone invites you.
10. The restaurant is offering a special cheap meal.

```
QUICK NOTES

This went well:
.................................................................
.................................................................

This didn't quite work:
.................................................................
.................................................................

Things to think about:
.................................................................
.................................................................
```

11

WEATHER

```
                           CONTENTS

Language focus:    too versus very
                   too + adjective; adjective + enough; enough + noun
                       too much/many + noun
                   adverbs of degree: a lot, quite a lot, a bit, not at all
                   verb patterns: keep something + adjective;
                       stop something + -ing
                   can for known possibility, e.g. it can be noisy

   Vocabulary:     weather
                   consumer goods
                   jobs

        Skills:    Speaking:    how does the weather affect you?
                                how does it affect your job?
                                how does it affect sales of goods?
                                what's your ideal climate?
                   Listening:   people's opinions on the weather
                                supermarket sales and the weather
                   Writing:     your ideal climate
```

IT KEEPS YOU COOL

Introduction

After an initial personalisation in which the learners practise weather vocabulary and then listen to a recording of native speakers giving their opinions on weather conditions, the main focus of the lesson is a number of verb constructions. The context for further practice is an extended activity in which the learners talk about the positive and negative features of seasonal goods/products.

Suggested steps

1 🔲

Ask the learners to tell you about yesterday's weather, today's weather and possibly tomorrow's weather by way of introduction to the theme. Then check that they understand the vocabulary in the questions. Put them in groups or do it as a mingling activity. Conduct a quick feedback.

Play the recording. The learners will need to write down a phrase or sentence for each of the weather conditions. Pause and replay the recording as necessary. Let them compare their answers. The tapescript is on page 161.

Answer key

1. I just want to stay in bed all day.
2. You feel relaxed and happy, especially if you're in good company.
3. I love to be in the countryside – in a town or city, I feel hot, sticky and miserable.
4. I like to stay in bed.
5. I feel as though I've got no energy at all and I just want to drink a lot.
6. I usually feel in a bad mood and anxious.

2

After the students have completed the matching exercise, check their answers and do controlled practice of the pronunciation of the items. Pay particular attention to the correct stress on the compound nouns.

Answer key

A suntan lotion   D a fan
B an umbrella   E winter boots
C central heating   F air conditioning

3

Go through the examples with the class and get them to put the sentences in the appropriate places in the table. If necessary, do a further example to clarify the form and/or concept of the constructions. It may be helpful for the learners to translate these constructions.

Answer key

It keeps you cool in hot weather = air conditioning
(positive)
They stop your feet getting cold = winter boots (positive)
It can mark your clothes = suntan lotion (negative)
They can be very noisy = fans (negative)

4

Follow the instructions in the Class Book for the
pairwork extension.

Answer key

Possible answers
umbrellas + They keep you dry.
         + They stop you getting wet.
         – They can be a nuisance. / You can lose
            them easily.
fans + They keep a room cool.
    + They can be portable.
    + They can be cheap.
    – They can be noisy.
central heating + It keeps you warm.
               – It can be very expensive / difficult to
                  regulate.
suntan lotion + It stops you burning.
          + It keeps your skin soft.
          – It can be very oily. / It can mark your
             clothes.
winter boots + They keep your feet warm/dry.
         + They stop your feet getting cold.
         + They can be fashionable.
         – They can be very ugly/heavy.
air conditioning + It keeps you cool in hot weather.
                 – It stops you sleeping.
                 – It can be very noisy/expensive.

5

Monitor and collect examples of the learners' language in
the groupwork activity and conduct a feedback at the end.

Personal Study Workbook

1: What's it like?
3: Hot and cold countries
4: Learning English keeps me busy

QUICK NOTES

This went well:

....

....

This didn't quite work:

....

....

Things to think about:

....

....

Introduction

After an initial concept check on the difference between
too and *very*, the learners are exposed to the target
structures for this lesson: *too*, *enough*, *too much* and *too
many*. For most learners at this level, *enough* is the only
item likely to be new, but all four items cause problems
of production for most nationalities. For this reason,
there is a focus on the meaning and form of the items in
Exercises 3 and 4. Finally, learners speak about and write
a profile of their ideal climate. Throughout the lesson,
there are also some new items of vocabulary related to
the weather.

Suggested steps

Option

As a warm-up to this lesson (or indeed the other two
lessons in the unit), you could use Worksheet 11 on page
129. Learners can work in small groups to brainstorm as
many ideas as possible within a time limit (say ten
minutes) then share them with the class.

1

Follow the instructions in the Class Book.

2

Check that the learners understand the weather
vocabulary. If they do not know *enough*, you could
provide a quick explanation: for many languages the
synonym *sufficient* is helpful. Let them work in groups to
compare their answers, then conduct a feedback with
the whole class on their opinions. Even within a group
of the same nationality, there are likely to be some
differences of opinion. Encourage the learners to use the
sentences in feedback for practice.

3

Let the learners work in pairs before feedback, then go
on to Exercise 4.

Option

Alternatively, you could begin by teaching the rules for
the use of the target items in Exercise 4, then use
Exercise 3 to check learning.

Answer key

1. correct
2. I was too tired
3. correct
4. too many people
5. correct
6. wasn't hot enough
7. correct
8. correct
9. correct

4

Follow the instructions in the Class Book.

Answer key

too   enough   enough   too much   too many

5

There may be more varied discussion with mixed nationality groups, but even with monolingual groups there should still be some difference of opinion. Begin by teaching the weather vocabulary items, and check the learners' pronunciation. Then give them a time limit for the activity (we suggest a 'flexible' ten minutes, to be extended if the discussion takes off) and appoint a spokesperson for each group. Monitor and assist where necessary; conduct feedback at the end on the content of the discussion and on any relevant language points you noticed during groupwork.

Option

Learners could put their ideas on a wall poster; adult learners often enjoy producing something visual, including artwork, for display. (After all, this kind of activity happens regularly in management training courses.)

Personal Study Workbook

2: Quantity
6: Seasonal Affective Disorder
9: Visual dictionary

QUICK NOTES

This went well:

....

....

This didn't quite work:

....

....

Things to think about:

....

....

....

WEATHER AND THE ECONOMY

Introduction

In this lesson, the learners are asked to discuss the effects of the weather on jobs and sales of goods in shops. They learn and practise vocabulary of professions and consumer goods as well as focusing on phrases such as *a lot* and *not at all*.

Suggested steps

1

You could begin by teaching the word *affect* as it recurs frequently in the lesson. (*The weather affects some sports meetings: when it is very windy, athletes run slower; if the weather is terrible, football matches are cancelled. The weather doesn't affect indoor sports.*)

Focus the learners' attention on the quantifiers; give an example of *not at all* in a sentence, e.g. *I didn't like the film at all*; *I don't use computers at all in my job.*

Check that the learners understand and can pronounce the jobs (*firefighter* is another word for *fireman* or *firewoman*). Go through the first two examples with the class, then let them work individually, with a partner or in small groups on the rest of the task. Monitor and help where necessary. Conduct a feedback, perhaps tabulating some of the answers on the board.

Put your learners into groups for the extension at the end, then conduct feedback.

Answer key

Possible answers

supermarket manager: a lot because they have to order different products for different seasons.

fashion model: a bit because they wear different clothes at different times.

firefighter: quite a lot because there are often more fires in hot, dry weather.

author: not at all.

chemist/pharmacist: a bit because people have different illnesses at different times of the year.

2 ▢

Before you play the recording, refer back to the points the learners made about the supermarket manager to set the scene. Then play the recording (twice if necessary), and go over the answers. The tapescript is on page 161.

Answer key

	Product		When?
	coffee		in wet weather
	tea		in sunny weather
	soft drinks		dramatically when the temperature goes over 15°
Sales of	salad	go up/rise	after the first warm weekend in spring
	bread		as the weather gets colder
	beef sandwiches		in winter
	chicken sandwiches		in summer

Let the learners discuss their reactions to the recording, either as a class or in small groups.

3

Explain new vocabulary items using the illustrations to help you, or let the learners work with dictionaries. Check that they can pronounce the items. Begin by discussing one of the products together, making sure that the learners justify their answers. Do feedback on some of the products at the end.

4

Follow the instructions in the Class Book.

Personal Study Workbook

5: Using the weather to predict the future
7: Advertising slogans
8: Speaking partners

```
QUICK NOTES

This went well:
.................................................................
.................................................................

This didn't quite work:
.................................................................
.................................................................

Things to think about:
.................................................................
.................................................................
```

REVIEW AND DEVELOPMENT

REVIEW OF UNIT 9

1 ▭

Follow the instructions in the Class Book. The answers are on the recording.

2

This is intended as a revision activity as well as a learning strategy, and you can adapt the idea for a wide range of vocabulary areas, which can provide useful warm-up activities.

Answer key

Accept any appropriate answers in 1–3. Possible general words might be: fish, seafood, vegetables, fruit, soft drinks, alcoholic drinks, cooking equipment, ways of cooking, etc.

REVIEW OF UNIT 10

1

There are one or two new items of vocabulary here that appear for the first time, e.g. *pollution*, so check that the learners understand before they answer the questions. Give them a few minutes to prepare their answers, and monitor the discussion. Conduct feedback on the content and language at the end.

2

Follow the instructions in the Class Book. Conduct feedback.

Answer key

1a: enjoy, regret, give up, can't stand, don't mind, avoid, imagine, finish, hate
1b: promise, offer, refuse, decide, would like, want, hope
1c: love, intend
2. enjoy, can't stand, don't mind, love, hate, would like
3. refuse, regret, can't stand, avoid, hate
4. promise, intend, decide, would like, want, imagine, hope
5. intended, regretted, decided, avoided, wanted, hated (minded)

```
QUICK NOTES

This went well:
.................................................................
.................................................................

This didn't quite work:
.................................................................
.................................................................

Things to think about:
.................................................................
.................................................................
```

12

ROMANCE

CONTENTS

Language focus: past continuous and past simple
link words: *when* and *while*
verb + preposition
prepositional phrases

Vocabulary: relationships and romance
physical scenery

Skills: Speaking: romantic occasions
narrating holiday romance anecdotes
role play

   Listening: about Valentine's Day
holiday romance anecdotes

   Reading: beginning of a romantic story
coincidence anecdote

   Writing: Valentine card messages

VALENTINE'S DAY

Introduction

Much of this lesson involves skills work of different types: personalised discussion, listening, reading and writing rhymes. Throughout the lesson there is vocabulary input on relationships and romance and the rhymes provide a focus on syllables and sounds.

Suggested steps

1

Check that the learners understand the vocabulary in the discussion prompts. (*Partner* may need revising from Unit 2; here it is used as a catch-all for a range of romantic relationships, not to be confused with *partner* in the classroom context.) Encourage the learners to think up their own ideas of romantic actions/scenes. There may well be interesting cultural differences here.

Note: Impress on the learners that they are under no obligation whatsoever to talk about themselves (and in certain cases this might be quite inappropriate). However, they should be able to talk about someone they know. It may be helpful to talk about these things yourself, as an example, but don't feel obliged to talk about yourself either!

At the end of the activity, get different groups to report back interesting facts.

Option

At the end of this activity, you could elicit the vocabulary to do with relationships and romance and begin to build up a wall poster of the vocabulary in the unit. Remember to include any useful items which came from the learners themselves.

2 ▭

Check that the learners can pronounce *Valentine's Day*, and let them answer the questions by comparing and mingling. Do not confirm or reject their answers as this would pre-empt the listening activity.

Play the recording several times if necessary, and let them compare their answers in groups. Check their answers. If the learners are having a lot of difficulty, let them follow the passage with the tapescript, which is on page 161 of this Teacher's Book.

Answer key

1. February 14th.
2. People send cards/chocolates/flowers to their loved ones and put messages in the daily newspapers.
3. We don't know the origin but there are several popular theories:
   One of them is about the tragic figure of Saint Valentine. He fell in love with a blind girl, performed a miracle and gave her back her sight, and was then killed by the girl's father.

3

Organise groups for the short discussion. Monitor and provide feedback at the end of the activity.

Option

For monolingual groups, Exercise 3 is likely to be more generative if you ask the learners in groups to invent a list of half a dozen people who should have a special day to themselves.

Examples: *honest politicians' day*
hardworking students' day

4

Show first how in the example the rhythm and rhyme work by saying the rhyme aloud and stressing the rhyming words. Then elicit the missing words in the second rhyme before the learners go on to try the other rhymes in pairs.

Answer key

Possible answers
My love for you will always be true
As I do today
I love you best
Darling valentine / Dearest valentine
Like never before
Is to share it with you

5

You could begin by brainstorming words to do with love on the board. When the learners have written their rhymes (and they don't need to be more than 4 lines long), they could read them to another pair or you could make a wall display of them.

Option 1

If you think Exercise 5 would not be successful with your learners, you could ask them instead to write a love letter together, using the two in the Personal Study Workbook Exercise 6 as a springboard. They might even write replies to these letters.

Option 2

If you wish to develop the theme of greetings cards/festivals, use Worksheet 12 on page 130. Follow the instructions on the worksheet. The final activity can work well if your class write messages to each other (they write, say, three messages each on a piece of paper, you monitor and collect them in, then 'deliver' the messages).

You will find a list of useful greetings for learners to refer to in the Personal Study Workbook, Exercise 8 (Speaking partners).

Answer key

Worksheet 12
1. Anniversary card
2. Birthday card
3. Get well card
4. Christmas card
5. Good luck card
6. Congratulations card
7. Bereavement card
8. Congratulations card

Personal Study Workbook

5: How many words?
6: Love letters
7: A poem

QUICK NOTES

This went well:

....

....

This didn't quite work:

....

....

Things to think about:

....

....

A FIRST MEETING

Introduction

In this lesson, after some initial vocabulary work on scenery, the past simple and continuous are contrasted in the context of a romantic narrative. Learners then have an opportunity to check their grasp of the tenses before going on to the practice activity, retelling the story.

Suggested steps

1

You could begin by asking the learners about romantic fiction. Do they read any? Which authors do they know? What do they think of these kinds of books? Do they enjoy romantic films and TV programmes? The picture in this lesson might be a starting point for the discussion.

Either teach the words yourself, using the visual and your own explanation, or get the learners to use dictionaries. Then do the exercise to check understanding. Adapt the suggested time according to your environment. Check pronunciation through controlled practice as necessary.

2

Follow the instructions in the Class Book. Check the answers, allowing the learners to use their imagination. Accept alternative answers if they are justifiable.

Answer key

Possible answers
1. They are probably boyfriend and girlfriend.
2. Andy is probably going to meet Madeleine's parents for the first time.

3

You could do the first example together as a class, then let the learners work alone before they compare with a partner.

Answer key

1. After *brightly-lit restaurant*.
2. After *they got out of the car*.
3. After *stopped on the bridge and looked back*.
4. After *glanced at him several times but didn't speak*.
5. After *steep hill through the forest*.

4

Refer the learners to the form of the past continuous – you could also put examples on the board, and add a time line to illustrate further the difference between the past simple and past continuous:

1. past simple:

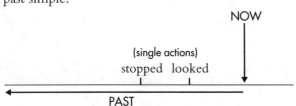

2. past continuous:

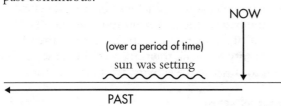

Encourage the learners to make use of the Grammar Reference as a part of learner independence.

Translation/contrast with the learners' L1 would of course be an important consideration in a monolingual setting.

5

This is quite a long lesson, so you could divide up the exercise amongst the class, or ask them to complete it for homework. It could also be done as a competition, with learners forming different teams and getting points for correct answers.

Answer key

1. jumped; put on; looked; was raining
2. was washing; heard; ran; opened; was sitting
3. went; was pouring; came; was shining; went
4. arrived; was filling up; were talking
5. sat down; ordered; were playing; recognised

6

Allow the group the freedom to be creative and amusing. You might wish to brainstorm one or two examples of changes, e.g. the story is now about two famous people or someone in the class; it takes place on an industrial site, etc. Then let the learners make up their own stories with their own changes. When they have completed the planning, rearrange the pairs so that they can retell the story. Monitor and collect examples of language points you wish to give feedback on later. In feedback, you could encourage one or two quick stories to be retold. Then provide feedback on language performance.

Option

You could give the instructions for Exercise 6 in the classroom and ask the learners to think up their own stories for homework. This exercise can also be done in written form; it would take a lot of class time, but for some classes this might be appropriate. Alternatively, the learners could write their stories out of class.

Personal Study Workbook

1: Grammar check
3: Adjective + noun
8: Speaking partners

```
QUICK NOTES
This went well:
..............................................................
..............................................................
This didn't quite work:
..............................................................
..............................................................
Things to think about:
..............................................................
..............................................................
```

Introduction

This lesson continues the theme of romance and begins with listening and speaking activities on holiday romance anecdotes. It then goes on to a reading activity which provides further exposure to the past continuous and past simple from the previous lesson and focuses on link words. The reading is then developed into a role play, before a final exercise which checks prepositions (linked to certain verbs and in prepositional phrases) from the unit.

Suggested steps

1

Begin by telling a holiday romance story about yourself or someone you know in order to demonstrate what to do. Then give the learners a couple of minutes to think of a story to tell each other in small groups. They may need to check words first in monolingual dictionaries.

Option

One way to overcome potential embarrassment is to instruct the learners to tell a story which is either true or false; the listeners in their group having heard it then decide which it is.

2 ▢▢ ▢▢

Choose the appropriate recording and play it to the group. Let the learners compare in pairs before you go over the answers.

Option

If you have the facilities available, you could split the class and let one group listen to the first version in Exercise 2, while the other group listens to the second version. They can then go back into pairs and tell each other about the stories they listened to.

Answer key

Version 1
1. On holiday in Florence, in Italy.
2. He was beautiful – blond with blue eyes.
3. It ends unhappily because the girl discovers Fabrizio with another girl.

Version 2
1. On a bus to New York City.
2. She had blond hair, bright teeth and blue eyes.
3. It ends unhappily because the girl keeps playing the same song and this annoys the boy so much that he has to get off the bus and get another one.

3

Before reading the text, you could set the scene by telling the class they are going to read a true anecdote about three people: Ian, Jane and Elizabeth. Write these names on the board, then follow the instructions in the Class Book.

Answer key

It was not Elizabeth who stood facing Ian, but Jane! It appears that Jane and Elizabeth shared a flat.

4

Ask the learners to read the grammar explanation and then do the task. Translation or the use of monolingual dictionaries is an obvious option here.

Answer key

In the second paragraph, you can use *while* in place of *when* in only one sentence:
When / While Ian was relaxing …

5

You could divide the class into two, half play Jane and half play Ian. Allow them a few minutes to prepare their roles, answering the questions and discussing them with someone playing the same role. If your learners are all male and you feel it would be unsuitable, omit this role play.

If possible, get the learners on their feet to do the role play. Monitor and if appropriate, tell them to swap partners when they have finished and do it again. During the activity, monitor and collect language points for feedback at the end.

Some groups enjoy a final stage where one or two pairs act out their dialogue for the rest of the group.

6

This could be done in pairs as a race – but the activity includes identifying where the verb + preposition or prepositional phrases occurred in the unit.

Answer key

1. to   2. in   3. about   4. on   5. in   6. By   7. at
8. with

Personal Study Workbook

2: Missing words
4: What happened and when?

QUICK NOTES

This went well:

....

....

This didn't quite work:

....

....

Things to think about:

....

....

REVIEW OF UNIT 10

1 🔲

Follow the instructions in the Class Book. For the second part of the activity, divide the learners into pairs, A and B. A reads the questions to B as quickly and clearly as possible, while B listens (with book shut) and answers. Then they can swap.

Answer key

See the tapescript on page 174 of the Class Book.

2

Follow the instructions in the Class Book. In feedback, after groups compare, accept any appropriate answers.

Answer key

Possible answers
You can make: a mess, friends, a mistake, something to eat or drink, a bed, etc.
You can tell: a story, a joke, a lie, the truth, the time
You can't avoid: paying for things (mostly), dying, getting old
You can't imagine: being very old, living in a very different place, etc.
For the next four verbs, learners' own personal examples are required.
Something that keeps you warm: coat, blanket, sweater, central heating, etc.
Something that keeps you dry: umbrella, coat, etc.
Something that keeps you healthy: exercise, a good diet, regular sleep, etc.

REVIEW OF UNIT 11

1

This activity revises weather vocabulary from Unit 11 and the *-ing* form from Unit 10. Follow the instructions in the Class Book, monitoring and correcting as the learners write. Make sure they are producing full sentences as far as possible in order to practise the structures. Encourage them to say why they feel the way they do.

2

Let the learners read the introduction, then look at the first haiku and count the number of syllables in each line together. Then let the learners read the text by Wendy Cope.

Follow the instructions for the gap-fill to be done in pairs.

Answer key

Possible answers
The morning mist lifts
And so once more I can see
the girl in the lake.

A flash of lightning
is soon followed by thunder:
the storm is breaking.

The learners will need some time to do these haiku together. It would also be possible to set this as homework.

Option

You could establish a haiku competition in your class, or even in a school, if you work in one.

```
QUICK NOTES

This went well:
........................................................
........................................................

This didn't quite work:
........................................................
........................................................

Things to think about:
........................................................
........................................................
```

13

IT'S BETTER TO TRAVEL THAN TO ARRIVE

```
                        CONTENTS

Language focus:   plural nouns
                  countable and uncountable nouns
                  requests and enquiries

    Vocabulary:   verb + noun collocations, e.g. to do the packing,
                      to have injections
                  airports and flying; travel arrangements

        Skills:   Speaking:   describing travel preparations and airports
                              discussing travel situations and problems,
                                  e.g. missing luggage
                              airport situations role play
                  Listening:  travel arrangements
                  Reading:    air travel quiz
                  Writing:    a dialogue
```

LET'S GET ORGANISED!

Introduction

The first lesson in this unit deals with the preparatory stages of a long journey. At the beginning, the learners study and reorganise a range of verb + noun collocations. A listening activity gives further exposure to these collocations, and learners then go on to describe their own preparations for a journey. Finally, they focus on nouns which are always plural (in the context of packing for a journey), and practise these in a speaking activity.

Suggested steps

Language Point: travel, trip and journey

It is quite possible that at some point over the three lessons you may feel the need to clarify the differences between these.

On a *journey*, you travel from one place to another. The emphasis is on the actual travelling.

Example: *We had a terrible journey to work this morning.*

A *trip* usually means going on a journey somewhere and coming back.

Example: *She was away on a business trip last week.*

Travel can be a noun or a verb and is the word learners seem to misuse most.

1. *Travel* (noun) is almost always uncountable in current English (i.e. a travel)

   Example: *Air travel is quick and convenient.*

2. *Travel* (verb)

   Examples: *We've travelled all over the world.*
   We never travel by train — it's too slow.

1

Begin the lesson by telling the class what kind of traveller you are, and pre-teach *last-minute* and *long-term planner*. Give examples of what each of these would do in terms of buying tickets, doing the packing, etc. Then let the learners mingle to find someone who is the opposite.

2

Follow the instructions in the Class Book or pre-teach any items you feel will be new. Check that they can pronounce words which commonly cause problems, e.g. *flight, suitcase, injections, insurance, accommodation, valuables,* and highlight the collocations in the table: *to do the packing* (not *to make*), *to take out travel insurance, to book a flight,* etc.

Option

If you feel the learners need to focus more on these collocations, you could do a matching activity: write the verbs on one side of the board and the nouns on the other and ask the learners in pairs to make phrases.

For the second part of the exercise, follow the instructions and elicit a couple of examples from the class of illogical ordering. Then let them discuss the rest in pairs. Monitor and make sure they are using the vocabulary accurately. Conduct feedback on the points they disagreed with in the table, and correct any errors in the use or pronunciation of vocabulary.

3 ◫ ◫◫

Use the appropriate listening activity (version 1 or version 2) as directed: it may be asking too much to tick what the woman did and decide when she did it at the same time. You could encourage the learners to compare their answers after the first listening. Go over the answers together when they have listened sufficiently. The tapescript is on page 162.

Answer key

Note: The two versions are not the same speaker and do not have the same answers.

Version 1
A few weeks before:
made a list; booked a flight; got travel insurance; accommodation was arranged (in the package); checked passport
The day before:
did the packing; bought a guidebook; ordered a taxi
One hour before leaving home:
checked the doors and windows; turned the electricity and gas off

Version 2
Several weeks before:
bought a suitcase and a guidebook; booked flight; took out travel insurance; ordered foreign currency and travellers' cheques; arranged for someone to look after pet; got injections
The day before:
collected foreign currency; did the packing
One hour before leaving home:
gave neighbour box with all her valuables; went round checking doors and windows, etc.

4

Demonstrate what to do by describing the preparations you made yourself for a big journey. Tell the learners where you were going, what preparations you made and when you made them. Clearly you will need to include preparations which are not mentioned in Exercise 2. Then ask the learners to work in small groups to do the same activity. Encourage them to ask each other further questions about the preparations. This activity may well throw up new vocabulary, so be prepared to monitor and assist with this. At the feedback stage, you could focus on some of the vocabulary learners needed and write it on the board.

5

Use the examples to show that certain nouns are always plural. If you are working with a monolingual group for whom there are specific pitfalls on this, choose suitable examples (e.g. in French, the word for *underpants* is *un slip,* an item which is a false friend too in terms of meaning). Work through a couple of examples in the list together, then let the learners work alone or in pairs on the rest of the exercise.

Answer key

Always plural:
jeans; glasses (with the meaning of 'spectacles'); pyjamas; shorts; underpants; pants; scissors; sunglasses; swimming trunks; binoculars; tights

The rest can be singular or plural.

6

Give the learners a couple of minutes to decide what kind of holiday they would like to go on and which items they would take. It can be quite generative to ask them how many of each item they would take; this can introduce a bit of humour. Let them compare their ideas in pairs of different sexes if this is culturally appropriate; if not, compare with the same sex.

Personal Study Workbook

5: Travel tips from the Queen
6: The last minute
8: Speaking partners

```
QUICK NOTES

This went well:
.............................................................
.............................................................

This didn't quite work:
.............................................................
.............................................................

Things to think about:
.............................................................
.............................................................
```

Introduction

The linguistic aims of the lesson are uncountable nouns and airport vocabulary. The quiz at the beginning incorporates a good deal of these two areas and provides a motivating reading and speaking activity. The lesson then goes on to look at uncountable nouns and the way in which they are signalled in dictionaries. Learners then practise these nouns through a writing task.

Suggested steps

1

Follow the instructions in the Class Book. You could give your own answers as a demonstration of what to do. Monitor, and in feedback encourage any learner who has an interesting short anecdote to tell the group.

2

Organise the learners into groups of 3–4 to do the quiz together. If they like team games, you could conduct the quiz as a competition.

Make it clear that the quality of their drawing is not an issue in Part C. There is a certain amount of new lexis in the quiz, and learners will need dictionaries to check new items. If you prefer, pre-teach items such as *luggage*, *baggage*, *equipment*, *security check*, *left luggage lockers* (the last of which do not exist in all airports). When they have agreed, go over the correct answers.

Answer key

Part A
1. True   2. False   3. False   4. True   5. True   6. True
7. False   8. True

Part B
1. No. This is a Car Hire Desk sign.
2. Correct
3. No. This is the Baggage Check In sign.
4. Correct
5. No. This is the Passport Control sign.
6. Correct

Part C
Possible answers

Information   Arrivals   Left luggage/
                                   baggage lockers

3

Focus on the uncountable nouns *weather* and *advice*. If you like, write these sentences on the board. Some teachers find it useful to show the potential errors on the board (for example, by writing *advices* or *an advice*). This can make it more memorable for some learners.

Refer to the dictionary entries, highlighting the way in which countability is marked. If the dictionaries you and your group use are different, adapt the procedure to suit those dictionaries. Then ask the learners to do the task.

Answer key

Countable: journey; suitcase; trip; flight
Uncountable: travel; insurance; information; equipment; luggage; first aid; baggage; air

Monolingual groups can work together on the translation activity and should reach similar conclusions. Multilingual groups also benefit from the exercise and can either work with someone of the same nationality or individually. In fact, different nationalities often enjoy comparing information about their own languages.

4

This provides controlled practice of the vocabulary items with an added twist: writing ten words rather than nine or eleven can be quite challenging – especially if they make mistakes in sentences which means they need to rewrite them. Monitor pairwork closely, correcting errors in sentences so that the learners can rewrite their sentences appropriately. During the monitoring, you could ask some learners to write one of their sentences on the board for everyone to study at the end.

Personal Study Workbook

3: I want some information
7: Lovely to be here
9: Visual dictionary

QUICK NOTES

This went well:

....

....

This didn't quite work:

....

....

Things to think about:

....

....

Introduction

The last lesson of the unit completes the theme of travel with *arrival*. Learners are asked to explore a range of situations which might cause problems if they have to deal with them in English. After evaluating the relative difficulty of these problems and adding to the list, they look at ways of making requests and enquiries, and practise these through dialogue.

Suggested steps

1

Tell the group a real or imagined problem you have had yourself when arriving at a foreign airport, similar to the situations here. Ask them what kind of problems they think you had in dealing with the situation in a foreign language. (Examples: you didn't know the right vocabulary; you didn't know how to ask politely; your explanation to the customs officer was complex and long, which made it stressful; you didn't know the facts or local customs; you couldn't pronounce place names, etc.) This will be very useful preparation for the second part of the exercise.

Look together at the problems and clarify the meaning of *missing* and *nothing to declare*. Then follow the instructions. Conduct feedback on the situations everyone thought of. You could elicit these and write them on the board.

Now ask the learners to rank the four situations plus the two they thought of in terms of how difficult they would be to deal with in English. (For instance, one would expect it to be easier to find the way to the city centre than to deal with the customs problem.)

If you have done the warm-up at the beginning of the lesson, the learners should know what to do.

Option

Instead of asking the learners to speculate on the ease or difficulty of these situations, you could ask them to practise the situations orally without preparation. They then have data on which to base their decisions about the ease or difficulty of the situations. You will also have had an opportunity to assess their linguistic problems and this may influence the importance you attach to the target items later in the lesson.

2

Check that the learners understand the five roles/jobs. If you wish, pre-teach a few items: *(driving) licence, sorry to bother you, to fill in a form, to deliver, straight away, to run (buses)*. Then work through a couple of examples of the task together before the learners complete it individually and/or in pairs.

Answer key

No. of situation	Speaker
1. 1, 2	airline representative, customs officer
2. 1	airline representative
3. 4	car hire representative
4. 3 (4?)	passenger
5. 1, (2?), 3	passenger
6. 1, 4	airline representative, car hire representative
7. 2	customs officer
8. 1	passenger
9. 4	passenger
10. 3	passenger

Accept any other answers that learners can justify! After checking the answers, the learners can practise the questions orally, with invented answers.

Example: A: *Does this belong to you?*
B: *No, it's not mine.*

Monitor their stress and intonation carefully, and then put them into pairs for further practice.

3

Follow the instructions in the Class Book. Encourage the learners to use questions from Exercise 2 in their dialogues. Monitor and correct as appropriate.

Some learners respond well to acting in front of the class; others don't. Use your knowledge of your group to determine this. If you are going to ask the learners to act out their dialogues, arrange the seating accordingly. Give them feedback on their use of English.

Option

To revise a number of multi-word verbs from this and previous units, you could use Worksheet 13 on page 131. Follow the instructions on the worksheet.

Personal Study Workbook

1: Verbs and phrases
2: Before leaving home …
4: Sorry to bother you, but …

```
QUICK NOTES

This went well:
.......................................................
.......................................................

This didn't quite work:
.......................................................
.......................................................

Things to think about:
.......................................................
.......................................................
```

REVIEW OF UNIT 11

1

Although we have provided two possible answers for the example, the learners only have to write one answer for each sentence.

Answer key

Possible answers
1. … was too loud.
2. … was too strong.
3. … wasn't strong enough. / … was too ill.
4. … was too hard/difficult.
5. … wasn't deep enough. / … was too shallow.
6. … wasn't old enough. / … was too young.
7. … were too icy.
8. … was too hard.

2 ⟳

Follow the instructions in the Class Book. You may need to demonstrate the peer testing part of the activity yourself with one of the learners.

The key is in the tapescript on page 163.

REVIEW OF UNIT 12

1

Go through the example with the class; if necessary do the first one together. For oral practice, put the learners into new pairs, A and B – they mustn't look at each other's books. Student A reads any answer he or she has written, and Student B has to complete the sentence appropriately.

Example: A: *I looked out of the window. Someone was stealing a car …*
B: *… so I rang the police immediately.*

Answer key

Possible answers
1. It was pouring with rain …
2. Someone was stealing a car …
3. The postman was walking up the path …
4. A little girl was dropping sweet papers …
5. A man was looking at a map …
6. Someone was sitting on my car …
7. My girlfriend/sister/mother was standing at the door …
8. Someone was looking in …

2

Follow the instructions in the Class Book. Conduct feedback at the end in case the learners have written alternative answers which are also acceptable in the sentences.

Answer key

Learners can check their answers by looking at their partners' exercises.

```
┌─────────────────────────────────────────────┐
│              QUICK NOTES                     │
│                                             │
│  This went well:                            │
│  .........................................  │
│  .........................................  │
│                                             │
│  This didn't quite work:                    │
│  .........................................  │
│  .........................................  │
│                                             │
│  Things to think about:                     │
│  .........................................  │
│  .........................................  │
└─────────────────────────────────────────────┘
```

14

POSSESSIONS

CONTENTS

Language focus: present perfect and past simple: unfinished past use,
e.g. *I've had this watch for 30 years.*
for and *since*
how long + present perfect questions

Vocabulary: possessions
superordinates, e.g. *jewellery*, *pets*
household objects and appliances

Skills: Speaking: personal possessions
inventing explanations
people and their homes

Listening: a correction dictation
description of someone's home

Reading: jumbled newspaper text
description of a home

Writing: description of a home

MY FAVOURITE THINGS

Introduction

In this lesson, the learners begin with a correction dictation about treasured possessions. The text provides a context for study of the present perfect for unfinished time and *for* and *since*. The learners talk about their own possessions using the target language. Finally, they categorise possessions under different superordinates (e.g. *jewellery*, *pets*), which provides further lexical input.

Suggested steps

Option

You could begin by telling the learners about your own most important possession; if possible, bring it in to show them. Include the following information:

– what it is
– where you got it/who gave it to you
– how long you have had it
– what it means to you
– whether you could replace it easily and if not, why not.

This framework should enable you to include examples of the present perfect with *for* and *since*.

You could then retell your account as a dictation, go over it and proceed from Exercise 2, focusing on the grammatical structure.

1 ▭

Give the learners an opportunity to skim read the texts, then follow the instructions. If necessary, pause the recording and replay it.

Answer key

Differences:

Text 1:
father's watch, not grandfather's watch
thirteen years, not thirty years
almost every day, not every day
the Second World War, not the First World War

Text 2:
four hundred, not four thousand
since about 1980, not since 1980
sixteen years, not fifteen years
I'd hate to lose them, not I'd hate to lose any

66

Unit 14 POSSESSIONS

2

Highlight, or ask the learners to underline, examples of the present perfect in the two texts (or your own) to help them think about the concept of the present perfect in this case, and the use of *for* and *since*. If necessary, clarify these by explanation when you go over the answers.

Answer key

Diagram B.

For is followed by expressions of a period of time, e.g. *for thirty years, for two days, for a long time.*

Since is followed by expressions of a point in time, which then links to the present moment, e.g. *since the Second World War, since 1980, since I was at school.*

Highlight the form of the present perfect if necessary. It is not new but may need revising.

Option

To practise *how long* questions, think of something you have done for a period of time (e.g. *I've had a cat for 6 years*). Don't tell the learners what your sentence is, but write *6 years* on the board. Tell them to ask you *how long* questions to find out what you have done for 6 years, e.g. *How long have you been a teacher / had short hair / worn glasses / been married?* Give a clue if necessary. When someone guesses correctly, let them take your place and think of a sentence, or do the activity in pairs.

We would like to thank Ros Canning for this activity.

3

Give the learners time to think about their answers, and encourage dictionary use. Then organise the mingling/peer interviewing activity. Exercise 4 will work best if the list of colleagues' possessions they produce in this exercise has at least six objects; more would be fine. (If your class is very small, say five students, ask them to think of two possessions each.) Make sure they make a written list.

4

Reorganise the class into pairs and follow the instructions. Demonstrate using a couple of examples, e.g. ask them in which categories they would put *earrings* or *scarf*. Monitor the pairwork.

At the end, ask a couple of pairs to tell the class their headings and examples. Then elicit one or two other items they couldn't classify and see if they can think of new headings. Continue the activity in pairs and conduct feedback at the end.

Personal Study Workbook

1: *For* and *since*
2: Past participles
3: Bedside table and bedside lamp

WE HAVEN'T SEEN EACH OTHER FOR YEARS

Introduction

The reading activity at the start of the lesson continues the focus on the present perfect and also provides an opportunity to look at discourse features in text, i.e. what links sentences and paragraphs together. The learners then study further examples of the present perfect and show their understanding of them by inventing explanations for the situations. At the end of the lesson, they practise the negative form of the present perfect in a personalised activity.

Suggested steps

1

Pre-teach *bushy eyebrows* using the photos, then follow the instructions. If necessary, highlight and explain the concept of the negative example of the present perfect here. Then give the learners an opportunity to think of an explanation in pairs or small groups, and let them tell the class. Ask them not to read Exercise 2 at this stage, and don't confirm their guesses about the text.

2

Tell the learners to order the paragraphs; if some of them are having particular difficulty, you may wish to point out certain key linkers: *Since then, However, Bill still remembered* (what?), Gail's first and second appearance in the text, etc.

Answer key

d e b c a

3

After a brief feedback on the previous exercise, move on. Follow the instructions.

Answer key

1. Bill and Buddy haven't seen each other because their mother left the family home with Buddy 67 years ago, and didn't contact the family again. She didn't tell Buddy he had a brother.
2. Bill found Buddy by chance when he went to a bank in Canada and was recognised by Buddy's daughter because of his eyebrows and surname.

4

The learners don't have to invent sentences using the present perfect to explain the situations, but there are opportunities to use it. Let them read the sentences and ask you about any words they don't understand. Look at the examples of possible explanations, and if necessary do the next one together before they work in pairs. Monitor and assist. At the end, let them compare with a new partner, or share their ideas as a group.

Answer key

Possible explanations – accept any other reasonable ones
1. He has lost his licence (i.e. he isn't allowed to drive any more).
   He suddenly lost confidence in driving.
2. The weather hasn't been cold.
   She decided killing animals for their fur was wrong.
3. He has grown a beard.
   He shaves with a razor and shaving foam now.
4. She never goes out.
   She's got no money.
5. He left school very recently.
   He uses a pencil or word processor.
6. She's an invalid.
   She is frightened of the world outside.
7. The rabbit is sick.
   Someone else is feeding it.
8. She's not well.
   Someone has asked her not to play it.

5

Elicit a few sample answers, then give them time to work alone. Monitor and correct written work during this time. Bring the class together and demonstrate the final activity with another person. Then let them do it in pairs.

Option

If you would like further consolidation of this use of the present perfect, you could do Worksheet 14A on page 132. We have not included it in the Class Book because it is not suitable for all groups, but some classes love general knowledge quizzes. You could get the class to do it in pairs, and then mix them so that one learner reads out a sentence from the worksheet, and the new partner must complete it with the correct answers. If successful,

you could divide the class into small groups and they could write their own quiz with gaps.

Answer key

Worksheet 14a
1. 1960; Belgian Congo
2. Martina Navratilova; 9; 1978
3. Brasilia; Rio de Janeiro
4. 13th; Italians
5. the 1920s; Arabic
6. 1967; Japan
7. 1981
8. 1920; Ecuador

Personal Study Workbook

4: Electrical appliances
5: Problems with electrical appliances
6: High-tech appliances

QUICK NOTES

This went well:

....

....

This didn't quite work:

....

....

Things to think about:

....

....

THROUGH THE KEYHOLE

Introduction

This lesson is skills-based, with vocabulary input. The learners read a description of a home and are asked to identify the owner. They then do a similar activity through listening. Some of the vocabulary from these activities is then studied and practised before the learners go on to write their own descriptions of a home.

Suggested steps

Option

You could use Worksheet 14B on page 132 as a warm-up to this lesson. Follow the instructions on the worksheet. Make sure that the learners understand and can pronounce the vocabulary before they begin the activity.

1

Ask the learners to look at the photos and make some guesses about the people: their jobs, ages, interests, the kind of home they live in.

Pre-teach *belong* as in *the house belongs to … .* Then lead into the reading activity as suggested in the Class Book. It is not necessary for the learners to understand all the new vocabulary items; this is a gist reading activity, and they will have the opportunity to work on vocabulary in Exercise 3. Give them time to compare their answers to this exercise in pairs or groups.

There are no set answers to the activity. Different learners will have different opinions – indeed the aim is to encourage some discussion, so in the comparison with a partner, allow this to happen. You may wish to have a general feedback / sharing of ideas on this exercise.

2 ▭

Play the recordings, pausing after the first to give the learners time to think. Replay them as appropriate. You may wish to select a few items of vocabulary to teach from the tapescript. It may be useful in any case for your learners to listen again, following with the tapescript so that they can check some vocabulary items, perhaps with dictionaries.

3

The vocabulary is from the reading and listening exercises in the lesson. If possible, give the learners dictionaries and monitor while they work together.

Answer key

articles of clothing: fur coat; high-heeled shoes; slippers; tracksuit

parts of a house/garden: hall; lounge; drive; fireplace; french windows; balcony

furniture: bedside table; wardrobe; oak desk; armchair; bookcase

electrical appliances: computer; calculator; mobile phone; hi-fi; word processor

Go over the answers, and provide controlled oral practice of the vocabulary. You may need to pay particular attention to word stress on these items. Then move on to the practice activity. Focus on the examples, then let them work in pairs or small groups, working through all the items. This practice is an important stage in helping learners to remember and use the items appropriately.

4

You may wish to put the learners in pairs to write a description together. Refer them to the written text in Exercise 1 as a model (although their own texts could be shorter). If you are intending to spend class time on this activity, monitor and correct the written work as they are doing it; otherwise, it can be started or set in class and finished as a homework task.

The learners will probably be interested to read each other's descriptions of the same picture, so whether you do the writing in class or at home, make space for this exchange to take place at some point.

Personal Study Workbook

7: A description of a home
8: Speaking partners
9: Visual dictionary

REVIEW AND DEVELOPMENT

REVIEW OF UNIT 12

1

Follow the instructions in the Class Book.

Answer key

buy should be *bought*
he were going should be *he was going*
way of do should be *way of doing* or *way to do*
a paper should be *a piece of paper*
while a hawk flew down should be *when a hawk flew down*
took a liver should be *took the liver*
I got should be *I've got*

REVIEW OF UNIT 13

1

Follow the instructions in the Class Book.

Answer key

Possible answers

1. the gas, the electricity, the doors and windows, your tickets and passport
2. your passport, your ticket, your suitcase(s), your hand luggage
3. spirits, tobacco, perfume
4. Could I have some water, please?
   What time are we going to land?
   What is the weather like in (New York)?
5. unfasten your seat belt, collect your hand luggage, put your coat on, stand up
6. Is this where I collect my luggage?
   Where can I get a bus to the centre of town?
   Is there a tourist information office here?

2 ⊂⊃

Follow the instructions in the Class Book, and be careful to point out that the time is 3.00 pm / 15.00 hrs now. Pause the recording as necessary. The tapescript is on page 163.

Answer key

1. yes   2. yes   3. 22   4. yes   5. I don't know   6. no
7. yes   8. no – 13   9. I don't know   10. 3

```
QUICK NOTES

This went well:

..................................................................
..................................................................

This didn't quite work:

..................................................................
..................................................................

Things to think about:

..................................................................
..................................................................
```

15

RULES

CONTENTS

Language focus: zero conditional, e.g. *if you go to the theatre, you can wear what you like*
articles: definite and indefinite,
    e.g. *a woman spoke to me* vs. *the woman spoke to me*
zero article with plural and uncountable nouns in
    general, e.g. *fish is good for you*
rules about geographical features, etc.
past obligation, e.g. *we had (didn't have) to ...*
past permission, e.g. *we could(n't) do this*

Vocabulary: verb + noun collocations, e.g. *break the rules*
geographical features, e.g. *ocean, island*
social behaviour, e.g. *blow your nose, give someone a tip*

Skills: Speaking: discussing social rules
                talking about rule learning
                old school rules and family rules
      Listening: social rules in Britain and Japan
      Reading: questionnaire about rules
                text about articles
      Writing: list of social rules

RULES OF BEHAVIOUR

Introduction

The learners begin with a warm-up on their attitudes to social rules. They then focus on vocabulary in preparation for the text in which they read and discuss social rules about Britain. The target structure (zero conditional) is embedded in this reading activity. After that, they listen to two speakers discussing the questionnaire. Finally, they practise the structure by writing rules about their own country or they personalise the rules they have read.

Suggested steps

1

Give one or two examples of social rules relevant to the context you are teaching in, but if possible avoid the ones in the questionnaire. (For instance, if appropriate, talk about customs for greeting members of the family, or taking gifts to someone's house when you are invited.) Then follow the instructions. If you have followed the suggestion above, the learners should have a clear idea what to do. Monitor and conduct a brief group feedback.

2

Provide dictionaries if possible, and follow the instructions in the Class Book. If you are working in Japan, you will need to be careful about the way you handle *sneeze* or *blow your nose* and you might wish to avoid student demonstration for this!

Answer key

to wear evening dress
to make a call
to give someone a tip
to wait your turn
to call someone 'sir' or 'madam'

After pairwork, go over the answers and then let the learners tell each other which they do more than once a week. (This is a controlled practice activity: make sure they are using the vocabulary.)

Example: *Well, I shake hands with my colleagues every day, and I probably don't tap people on the shoulder more than once a week ...*

> **Language Point: words with multiple meaning**
>
> Several words in this activity have more than one meaning.
>
> Examples:
>
> *tip* means the end of something, e.g. a pencil, and also means a small sum of money given for service.
>
> *shake*: shake hands vs. tremble.
>
> *tap*: to touch lightly vs. a tap in a basin.
>
> *dress*: evening dress = evening clothes for men or women vs. a dress, which only women wear.
>
> *blow*: blow one's nose vs. the wind blows.
>
> *call*: to telephone vs. to address someone.

In this exercise, you may find that the learners think they know the meaning of a word when in fact they know a different meaning from the one in the text. We don't suggest you set out to teach multiple meanings, but be prepared for the problem, particularly if the learners are using dictionaries and don't look carefully at different definitions.

3

Tell the learners to read the questionnaire and ask you if there are any words they don't know, or provide them with dictionaries to check for themselves. Then follow the instructions in the Class Book. Encourage them to guess the answers if they don't know British customs.

In the group activity, encourage plenty of discussion about the rules in Britain, but try to avoid discussion of rules in the learners' own countries at this stage. Do not confirm their answers as these are given in the listening.

4 ▢▢ ▦▦

Select the appropriate version of the listening and make it clear that the learners should note down one speaker's answers. (The woman describes Japanese customs and the man British customs.) It might be wise to have a show of hands to see that there is a reasonable spread of people listening to both speakers.

Note: The information about Japanese customs was provided by a Japanese native speaker, but was re-recorded for technical reasons.

Answer key

1. In Japan, people usually wear smart clothes; in Britain, you can wear what you like.
2. In Japan, you wait your turn; in Britain too, but you can interrupt if it is a real emergency.
3. In Japan, you can sit at someone's table if you ask very politely; true in Britain too.
4/5. In Britain, you can say 'Bless you', but it isn't necessary; in Japan, sneezing and blowing your nose are considered rude.
6. In Japan, they show respect through different levels of politeness in the language they use; in Britain, you don't call someone 'sir' or 'madam' just because they are older.

7. In Japan, people don't usually tip taxi drivers; in Britain, people usually do, but not everyone does.
8. In Japan it is incredibly rude to arrive ten minutes late. In Britain it's normal.
9. In Britain, you go and pay for drinks, then you sit down; in Japan you sit and wait to be served.
10. In Japan, you bow but Japanese people often shake hands with Westerners. In Britain, you shake hands at a formal first meeting.

When the learners have got the answers they need from the recording, let them compare with someone who listened to a different speaker. Only if you feel it is necessary, go over the answers at the end.

5

Refer to the zero conditional structures. This is not normally an area which causes great difficulty for most learners (compared with other conditional clauses) and should not require a great deal of emphasis. However, you may wish to point out the use of simple tenses, modals and imperatives in the main clause. These are used because we are talking about general truths rather than future predictions as would be the case with first conditional sentences. If your learners are in a monolingual situation, do the first activity. Elicit one or two social rules from the class before they work in groups. We suggest they aim for 5–8 rules in each group. Appoint a spokesperson and monitor while they are working. Conduct group feedback on their ideas and on any language points that have arisen.

Option

You could give the learners topic headings if you feel they need more stimulus for this activity

Examples: public transport; theatre and cinema; colleagues at work; in bars and restaurants; being a guest in someone's house; at a party; with members of your family; on special days and holidays.

If your learners are in a multilingual setting, follow the instructions at the end of the exercise. Monitor and conduct feedback on their answers and on any language points you need to raise.

Personal Study Workbook

3: Don't make a mistake
6: Manners for men
7: Expressing opinions

GRAMMAR RULES

Introduction

This lesson approaches the main teaching point, the use of articles, in a direct way: learners read a grammatical explanation and are asked to process it by comparing certain uses of the article with their own language. After practising these through a gap-fill exercise, they move on to a different approach: peer teaching simple rules about article use with geographical features and specific places. These uses are tested through a recorded quiz. The lesson ends with a discussion on learning grammar rules.

Suggested steps

Option

You could use the gap-fill (only) from Exercise 2 diagnostically at the start of the lesson. Let the learners complete it, then read the text in Exercise 1, and go back to make any necessary changes from what they have learnt. This approach can often provide a clearer motivation to read about grammar.

1

You could begin by asking the learners if they know any rules about when to use *a*, *an*, *the* or no article. They will probably know when to use *a* versus *an*, for instance. Then ask them to read the short text on articles and follow the instructions about comparing them with their mother tongue. Allow time for the learners to compare their answers in groups, and conduct feedback on their findings at the end. For some nationalities, there will be little similarity if there are no articles at all in the L1, except for the rule about zero articles for things in general. Clarify if necessary with further examples.

2

Learners can work in pairs, or individually and then compare. Conduct feedback before they go on to the explanation of the story.

Answer key

When I got back to *the* house, there was *a* letter on *the* doorstep addressed to my wife. Normally I don't open *(-)* letters addressed to her, but I recognised *the* handwriting so I decided to read it. Inside there was *a* photograph and *a* cheque for $1,000. I recognised *the* photograph immediately but I was very surprised about *the* money; it's not every day that *(-)* cheques as big as that come through your letterbox.

The learners could work in pairs or small groups to explain the story. This is a fairly short activity, and you could do a quick feedback on their ideas before moving on to the next exercise.

Answer key

Possible explanations

The letter was from the wife's father. The photo was of an old relative, and the man had seen it before because there was a copy on their living-room wall. The relative had died and left the wife a cheque for $1,000.

The envelope was addressed by the wife herself. She had sent a photograph and a self-addressed envelope to a photography competition. The photo was of her husband, and she won the top prize: $1,000.

3

Divide the class in half, and tell one half to read and learn the text on page 98 and the other half to read the text on page 171. As they read their text, they should add one more example to each category to help them process the rules. This is quite an intensive activity and requires considerable concentration. Learners often enjoy a short burst of rote learning; they do not need to be word-perfect, however, as you can let them refer back to their text in the next stage.

During the activity, monitor and check the examples they are adding to their texts, and see if they need any assistance.

Reorganise the learners so that they are in pairs who have read different texts. Instruct those who have read Text A to teach the rules to their partner (who will probably need to write the rules down). Don't let the partner see Text A, but it is OK for the learner who is teaching these rules to refer to it.

When they are ready, the learner who read Text B should teach these rules to their partner.

At the end, have a quick feedback to clarify any problems. Some members of the group may wish to look at the other text to check they have taken down the correct information.

4 📟

This can be done in small groups/teams as a competition. It is probably best to play a question from the recording, pause to allow time for the learners to confer and write down an answer, then go on to the next question, and so on. Replay questions if the learners find they need to hear them more than once.

Impress upon them that correct use of articles (i.e. applying the rules just learnt) will gain them more points.

At the end, go over the answers as a class, awarding points.

Answer key

1. Africa
2. The Balearic Islands (principally Majorca, Ibiza, Minorca)
3. The Red Sea
4. The United Arab Emirates
5. Wall Street
6. The Louvre
7. Central Park
8. Mount Fuji
9. Oil
10. Lake Michigan

Option

Learners often enjoy making up their own class quizzes, and this is a very suitable topic with a useful teaching point. You might need to have an atlas handy to arbitrate in disagreements.

5

Put the learners into small groups and monitor the discussion, collecting examples of good and faulty use of language for feedback at the end.

Personal Study Workbook

1: Places
4: Right or wrong?
5: Good and bad language rules

QUICK NOTES

This went well:

....

....

This didn't quite work:

....

....

Things to think about:

....

....

Introduction

Adult learners are usually far enough away from their schooldays to recall them with interest, and in this lesson they are asked to try to remember their old school rules. The language point (past obligation and permission) is dealt with in this context, both productively and receptively. Finally, the learners consider the rules that existed in their families and which of those family rules they would/do teach to their own children, thus providing further practice in the target language.

Suggested steps

Option

If at all possible, bring in any photos you have from your childhood; perhaps of your family or of your school, schoolfriends, team photo, etc. Such authenticity can be highly involving for learners. If they are in their own countries, they may have photos of their own to bring in to talk about and show the others in the group. Tell them to do so the lesson before.

1

You could begin by revising briefly *have to*, *don't have to* and *mustn't* for present and future obligation/necessity. Write three sentences on the board.

Examples: *They have to leave at 6.00.*
They don't have to take their passports.
They mustn't take much luggage.

Remind the learners of the difference in meaning between *don't have to* and *mustn't* and highlight the forms of these verbs. Then tell the class that they are going to talk about past obligation/permission. Elicit the past forms of the three sentences you wrote: *had to*, *didn't have to* and *couldn't* and add them to the board. (*Weren't allowed to* would also be correct but is rather complex for this level.)

Ask them to look at Exercise 1, and follow the instructions in the Class Book. Monitor and assist/correct where necessary. After they have compared their answers in groups, using full sentences, conduct a class feedback, eliciting answers and correcting where necessary. This is a controlled practice stage, so insist on accuracy and correct any errors.

2

Ask the learners to give you a sentence about the first picture using *had to*, *didn't have to* or *could(n't)*. They will almost certainly arrive at different sentences for each picture. For the first picture, they might write:

In my school we had to sit in rows.
We didn't have to sit in rows.
We could sit where we wanted.

Monitor and correct while they are writing, then ask them to tell a partner. Encourage discussion at this stage; you could demonstrate by telling the class about the school rules you had to obey, using the pictures.

Answer key

Possible sentences will be based around this vocabulary:
1. sit at desks/in rows   2. do sports/gym   3. smoke in school   4. wear uniform   5. do tests/exams

3 ▭

Play the recording, pausing or replaying it as necessary. Go over the answers.

Answer key

Speaker 1 (Rebecca)
She had to wear (a) uniform. She couldn't wear make up or high heels. In the sixth form she didn't have to wear (a) uniform or play sport.

Speaker 2 (Lynn)
She had to cover her textbooks with brown paper. She couldn't use the books without covering them. She had to measure her skirt (not too short or too long). They had to wear hats. They couldn't hold hands in the playground.

Speaker 3 (Gareth)
He had to wear a school cap and take it off when he met a teacher or an older person. They couldn't get on buses before the public.

Option

Give the learners time to discuss in groups any other school rules they had, and their opinions of such rules. Are they necessary? How important is strict discipline?

4

Tell the learners a few rules of your family from your childhood, using the target structures where possible. Rules in this context can be interpreted fairly liberally; family rules are often unspoken. Then put them in groups to brainstorm rules they had to follow as children. (One in each group could write the list.) Monitor and collect language points for feedback.

At an appropriate moment, tell them to do the final activity based on their lists and continue to monitor. At the end, conduct a whole group feedback on their ideas. Then deal with any language points which arose during discussion.

Option

Learners could write their own lists and opinions for homework.

Personal Study Workbook

2: Obligation and permission
8: Speaking partners

QUICK NOTES
This went well:
....
....
This didn't quite work:
....
....
Things to think about:
....
....

REVIEW AND DEVELOPMENT

REVIEW OF UNIT 13

1 ▭

Follow the instructions in the Class Book, demonstrating the activity by pronouncing *knife* and *write*. The learners could compare answers before listening and repeating.

Ask them to work together to make up rules based on the list.

Answer key

A

lis<u>t</u>en	<u>k</u>now	thum<u>b</u>
<u>k</u>nee	lam<u>b</u>	<u>w</u>rist
bom<u>b</u>	forei<u>g</u>n	<u>w</u>rong
cas<u>t</u>le	i<u>s</u>land	whis<u>t</u>le
fas<u>t</u>en	si<u>g</u>n	ai<u>s</u>le

B

'w' is silent in words beginning with 'wr'.
'b' is silent after 'm' at the ends of words.
'g' is silent before 'n' unless there is a syllable break between the two letters as in *signature*.
't' is silent in words ending 'stle'.
't' is silent in verbs ending 'sten'.

2

This exercise revises and extends vocabulary from Unit 13, so the learners may need to use dictionaries. Follow the instructions in the Class Book.

3

Follow the instructions in the Class Book.

Answer key

take out
look after
set off
turned off
check in
sit down
get on
takes off
fill in
stand up
get off
pick up

REVIEW OF UNIT 14

1

Follow the instructions in the Class Book. Check the answers to the first part before the learners complete the sentences in their own way. Monitor and correct during the writing stage.

Answer key

for: a week; three days; ages; two years.
since: last Tuesday; yesterday; last night; August; I was at
    school.

2

Follow the instructions in the Class Book.

Answer key

Possible answers (only one word is necessary in each answer.)
1. watches, earrings, bracelets, etc.
2. a piano, a flute, etc.
3. ten pairs of shoes, four pairs of trousers
4. a parrot
5. a moped, a motorbike
6. a dressing table, an armchair, a chest of drawers
7. a dishwasher, a fridge
8. a tracksuit

```
QUICK NOTES

This went well:

.........................................................
.........................................................

This didn't quite work:

.........................................................
.........................................................

Things to think about:

.........................................................
.........................................................
```

16

KEEPING THE CUSTOMER SATISFIED

```
CONTENTS

Language focus:    will and may/might for prediction
                   if sentences (with will and might)

Vocabulary:        adjectives describing character
                   prefixes and wordbuilding
                   money and business

Skills:    Speaking:    discussing a customer service questionnaire
                        qualities needed to work in different places
                        discussing employment policy (case study)
                        evaluating the consequences of radical
                            decisions
           Listening:   people talking about service in banks,
                            shops and hotels
                        people discussing consequences of radical
                            decisions
           Reading:     a customer questionnaire
                        a case study about employment policy
```

CUSTOMER SERVICE

Introduction

After the warm-up activity introducing the theme of the lesson, a vocabulary exercise introduces key lexical items that appear in the questionnaire about customer service. The questionnaire then provides the input for both discussion and a focus on common prefixes used to form opposites. A listening passage explores the theme of customer service further and acts as a model for the personalised activity at the end of the lesson when learners exchange their own experiences of good and bad service.

Suggested steps

1

Write the saying *The customer is always right* on the board and elicit reactions from the group. Keep it brief as this is only intended to introduce the theme of the lesson and create interest, but do draw out any personal experiences which learners will find of interest.

2

Point out that meaning may not be a matter of black and white, and that the learners may not view some of these words as clearly positive or negative. If so, they can write words in the middle of the box. Let them use dictionaries.

Go through the answers and allow the learners at this point to discuss any possible differences in their interpretation of the words. Correct pronunciation where necessary.

Answer key

positive: helpful, knowledgeable, efficient, smart, businesslike. (*Efficient* and *businesslike* are occasionally used in a negative way to suggest someone is rather cold and unfriendly.)
negative: cold, impolite, ignorant, badly dressed, rude.

3

Before your learners work through the questionnaire, find out which place they are going to use, and organise the pairs (or perhaps groups if there are three or four who are familiar with the same place). Give them five or ten minutes to think about their answers to the questionnaire. Move round and help where necessary.

Let the pairs or groups discuss their answers.

4

Tell your learners to cover the questionnaire, and then direct them to the exercise in their books. Before they complete the task though, you could give them an example of an adjective which takes a prefix to form the opposite, and one that requires a different word to form the opposite.

Example: 1. *happy – unhappy* (or *sad*)
2. *sad – happy*

Learners can check their answers by looking back at the questionnaire.

Answer key

impolite   ignorant   inefficient   cold   well dressed
unfriendly

5 🎧

Choose the appropriate version of the listening and play the recording. Pause the recording if necessary and go over the answers when the learners are satisfied they have answered the questions. The tapescript is on page 165.

Answer key

Version 1

Where?	Good or bad?	In what way?
1. Lanzarote	good	helpful, efficient, friendly to children
2. post office	bad	rude, unfriendly, not interested in the customers
3. swimming pool	good	friendly, polite, very helpful

Version 2

Where?	Good or bad?	In what way?
1. bank in India	good	friendly, efficient, invited customers for tea
2. clothes shop	bad	ignorant, badly dressed, unfriendly and cold
3. hotel in Bath	good	helpful, polite, friendly, smartly dressed; great with children

6

Put the learners into groups for the discussion. They could then exchange answers with another group or you could finish with discussion among the whole class.

Personal Study Workbook

2: Forming opposites
5: Nouns formed with *-ness*

```
QUICK NOTES

This went well:
..............................................
..............................................

This didn't quite work:
..............................................
..............................................

Things to think about:
..............................................
..............................................
```

A CHANGE OF IMAGE

Introduction

The linguistic aim of presenting and practising *will* for prediction is realised through a series of activities in which the learners have to try to predict the potential consequences of decisions taken in different situations. Some of these are set in a business context – this introduces some new business vocabulary – but no specialist knowledge is required. There is a lot of scope for learners to express their own personal opinions, and a listening passage at the end of the lesson is a chance to compare their ideas with a group of English speakers discussing the same situations.

Suggested steps

1

This personalised activity may have added interest if your learners come from different countries where the use of banks may differ. If, for any reason, you feel that the learners may be offended by personal questions about their bank accounts, omit the exercise or discuss the subject in general (without specific reference to themselves).

2

Tell the learners to look at the picture of the bank manager and give their response. Some may immediately comment on his casual dress, while others may think his clothes are quite normal.

Explain the situation and put the example sentences on the board. Highlight the target items *will*, *may/might* and *won't* (*will not*). Elicit a few opinions about the example and insist on correct use of the target structures (see the following Language Point).

Language Point

When we preface a negative statement with the verb *think*, we normally make *think* the negative verb. Thus:

I don't think it'll rain.

or

I don't think it works.

and not

I think it won't rain.

or

I think it doesn't work.

Some languages prefer the second structure, but it does sound very awkward and unnatural to English speakers.

Discuss another example with the class if necessary, and then explain any new items of vocabulary in the remaining consequences for discussion, e.g. *upset*. Give the class several minutes to consider the different consequences, and then put them in groups to discuss their views. Monitor the group discussions and correct where necessary. Conduct a brief feedback so groups can share their views.

3

Again, conduct a brief feedback. By this stage, the learners should be fairly familiar with the target language, and you could just consolidate this familiarity by clarifying that *will* is used in English when we are expressing an opinion about a future situation.

4

Go through the situations to explain any new vocabulary, and let the groups choose which situation they wish to discuss first. If necessary, change the groups so they are with people who want to talk about the same situation.

Option

If your class has a particular interest in the third situation, you could tell them that it is based on a real example, and you could then follow up their discussion with Worksheet 16 on page 133, which is a text about the company and the different changes they made.

When you sense the discussion is beginning to lose momentum, bring the groups together to share their opinions, and if possible, note them on the board (this will help your learners in the final exercise). Use this opportunity as well to give feedback on their use of language and praise/correct where you think it is needed most.

5 ▭

Follow the instructions in the Class Book. This will be easier if you have written down the learners' ideas on the board. Play the recording once or twice and check answers. If you wish you can just ask the learners to listen for the responses to one of the situations; this reduces the memory load.

Answer key

See the tapescript on page 165.

Personal Study Workbook

6: Future trends
7: What does she think?
8: Business letters

QUICK NOTES

This went well:

....

....

This didn't quite work:

....

....

Things to think about:

....

....

A NEW APPROACH

Introduction

The initial correction exercise highlights common opposites, e.g. *go up – go down*, *put up – reduce*, and also provides a series of model conditional sentences. Following controlled activities to check both form and concept, the last part of the lesson gives the learners a chance to use the constructions in the discussion of a case study concerned with employment policy.

Suggested steps

1

Write the example sentence from Exercise 1 on the board and ask your class for any thoughts on the logic of the statement. This should prompt a few suggested changes; write each one down as a separate sentence until you have two or three logical sentences.

Put the class in pairs and tell them to make similar changes to the other sentences. Encourage the use of dictionaries here, and be prepared to monitor and help with vocabulary they may need to make their changes. Let them compare answers with other pairs and then conduct a brief feedback.

Answer key

Possible answers

1. If you *remember* to ring, the client will be delighted. *or* If you forget to ring, the client will be *angry*.
2. If we *put up* our prices, we'll sell less. *or* If we reduce our prices, we'll sell *more*.
3. If we *leave* now, we'll be early for our next appointment. *or* If we don't leave now, we'll be *late* for our next appointment.
4. They may get a pay *rise* if sales go up this year. *or* They may get a pay cut if sales *go down* this year.
5. If our sales go down, we might *lose* a lot of money. *or* If our sales *go up*, we might make a lot of money.
6. We may *get more* customers if our prices are very low. *or* We may lose customers if our prices are very *high*.
7. You'll *keep* your job if you work hard. *or* You'll lose your job if you *don't work* hard.
8. If you get promoted, your salary *will* go up. *or* If you *don't get* promoted, your salary won't go up.

2

Highlight the different forms on the board. As you do so, point out that *may* and *might* are interchangeable. Tell the learners to try to use a range of constructions when they do the sentence completions, and when they have finished, you could elicit some examples from the class to check they have used the target structures correctly.

For the interview stage, demonstrate the dialogue with one or two learners, and then put each learner with a different partner to practise. Make sure they reverse roles so that each partner gets as much practice in answering the questions.

3

Introduce the case study by asking the class about the shop assistants in big stores and supermarkets in their own town. Are they generally young or old, or mixed? Is there a difference in the age of staff depending on the type of shop? Having introduced the theme, get them to read the text. Clarify any problems they may have with understanding, e.g. *tills*, and then put them in groups to discuss the situation. In order to ensure a tangible outcome, you could ask them to write down at least two possible consequences for each course of action. This will provide something concrete for a comparison between the groups.

During the discussion move round and make notes. When you feel they have exhausted the subject, bring the groups together so that they can exchange their views. Finish by giving some language feedback, e.g. praise for effective use of conditionals, correction of important errors, and perhaps a few new items of vocabulary that have emerged during the discussion.

Option

If the topic of the case study stimulates a lot of interest, this could be extended into a small project. Ask the class to divide into pairs or small groups, and give each group a large store in the area. Their task is to go there at the weekend or after school, and note down the number of staff they see and their approximate ages, e.g. teens and early twenties; late twenties, thirties and early forties; late forties and fifties. In the case of very large stores, tell the pairs to choose two or three different departments. If possible, choose different types of shop, e.g. department stores, DIY stores, supermarkets, family grocers, etc.

The data can be used for comparison and discussion in a future lesson, and this encourages learners to get together outside of class and possibly speak more English. With a multilingual class, you should try to ensure that each pair or group does have speakers of different languages.

Personal Study Workbook

1: If it rains …
3: Syllables and word stress
4: Synonyms and opposites in business
9: Speaking partners

```
QUICK NOTES

This went well:
..................................................................
..................................................................

This didn't quite work:
..................................................................
..................................................................

Things to think about:
..................................................................
..................................................................
```

REVIEW AND DEVELOPMENT

REVIEW OF UNIT 14

1

You could begin by talking about several of your own possessions which you have never really used. You could also give the learners a bit of time to think about their answers before they write them down. Put them in groups to compare their answers.

Option

Instead of putting them in small groups to compare their answers, you could make this a mingling activity in which the learners have to talk to everyone and find the most useless possession in the class.

2

Follow the instructions in the Class Book.

Answer key

1. lounge (The others are all things you wear.)
2. parrot (The others are animals with four legs.)
3. rug (The others are pieces of furniture.)
4. fur (The others are musical instruments.)
5. calculator (The others are parts of a house.)
6. skis (The others are all general words which do not refer to a specific thing.)

REVIEW OF UNIT 15

1

You could introduce this activity with some pre-teaching of vocabulary, e.g. *obey, fair, just,* and then make one or two suggestions about good rules or bad rules. For example, is the purpose of rules to be fair or are they present in our society largely to protect people? You could remind your class of the discussion you had earlier in Unit 16 about the new rule introduced by the owner of a bar to ban smoking on certain days.

Put the learners in pairs or groups to think about good rules and bad rules, and to come up with rules for the classroom. When they have finished, conduct a brief feedback. (You may even find that there is a rule which the group would like to implement, or at least try out, in your classroom.)

Answer key

Some possible classroom rules include:
You mustn't speak your first language.
You should sit next to a different person each lesson.
Bring your dictionary to class every lesson.
Don't interrupt when another person is speaking.
Never be frightened to say *I don't understand.*
Use every opportunity to practise new language in the classroom.
Don't laugh at other people's mistakes.

2

Follow the instructions in the Class Book.

Answer key

Possible answers
People who lived two hundred years ago …
– had to travel from town to town by horse or on foot.
– didn't have to insure their houses.
– could own a gun without needing a licence.
– couldn't get free health care. (depending on the country)

People who lived two thousand years ago …
– had to build fires to keep warm.
– didn't have to get qualifications.
– could cut down trees without worrying about the environment.
– couldn't travel about easily.

17

PICTURE THIS!

```
                          CONTENTS

Language focus:   link words: so that, otherwise
                  sequencing: first of all, secondly, etc.
                  look + adjective, look like + noun
                  could (be) for speculation
                  giving advice and warnings

Vocabulary:       photography
                  interiors of rooms

Skills:   Speaking:   evaluating a series of photos
                      giving people advice
                      exchanging experiences of complaints
          Listening:  evaluating good and bad advice when
                          complaining
                      learning facts about a room
          Reading:    a description of a room
                      a text on how to take good photos
          Writing:    describing a room
                      giving advice
```

SAY CHEESE

Introduction

The questions about cameras and camera ownership introduce the theme of the lesson and revise a number of structures from previous lessons. This is followed by a text on taking good photos. Learners use the text for contextual guesswork, and then discuss a range of pictures with reference to the text. Key link words *so that* and *otherwise* are then highlighted and practised through a guided activity, also on the theme of taking pictures. A caption competition based on some of the photos from Exercise 3 provides a light-hearted end to the lesson.

Suggested steps

If you are a camera owner, take it to class and tell your learners how long you have had it, what kind it is, how often you use it, etc. This prepares them for Exercise 1.

1

Allow the learners a few minutes to prepare their answers and then get them to find a partner who has answered the other questions. (If that isn't possible because many more are in one group than the other, put them in threes or small groups.) If you wish, you could model the conversation with one learner before they interview each other.

Option

If your learners show interest in this exchange, you could try Worksheet 17 on page 134 immediately afterwards or at a later stage.

2

The text has some new words whose meaning can be guessed from the context, although your learners may find it difficult to explain the meaning. With monolingual groups you could ask them for translations or a paraphrase in their first language; with multilingual groups remind them that gesture (for *squint* and *pose*) and drawing (for *shadow*) may be the easiest way to convey the meaning.

Answer key

pose = stand in a particular position in order to be painted or photographed
avoid = keep away from (in this context) / try not to use
squint = to look with almost closed eyes (usually because the sun is in your eyes)
shadows = the darkness caused when you block (stop) the light
blurred = unclear (often looking out of focus)

Check the meaning of the new lexical items and then get the learners to explain the six pieces of advice to you; this checks their understanding of the passage.

3

This provides a further test of their understanding of the text, and an opportunity to use some of the new lexis.

Answer key

The good pictures are 1, 3 and 6.
Picture 2. The tree in the background seems to come from the model's head.
Picture 4. The model is not relaxed and the background is unattractive.
Picture 5. The background is unattractive.
Pictures 7 and 8. The model is squinting and has shadows under her chin.

4

Follow the instructions in the Class Book. When you check the answers, pay special attention to the link words *so that* and *otherwise* (see Language Point). Alternatively, you may decide to pre-teach these linkers.

Language Point: so that and otherwise

1. *So that* is used to introduce the purpose of an action.

    Example: *I often buy a magazine* **so that** *I have something to read on the journey.*
    I got up early **so that** *I could have a swim before breakfast.*

    (In sentences in the past tense, *so that* is often followed by *could* or *would*.)

    Purpose is also expressed by *(in order) to*, and the two constructions are often different ways of saying the same thing. Compare:

    I went there **(in order) to** *buy some milk.*
    I went there **so that** *I could buy some milk.*

2. *Otherwise* can be paraphrased as *if not*.

    Example: *You must go now otherwise you'll be late.*
    = *If you don't go now you'll be late.*

    Otherwise is usually followed by *will* with this meaning, but there are other meanings which your learners will encounter in due course.

Answer key

so that
make (him/her) feel
avoid
make sure
they will
shadows
make sure
otherwise
take

5

Do one sentence as a class in order to demonstrate that a number of different answers may be possible. Put the learners in pairs to do the activity and then conduct a feedback at the end.

Answer key

Possible answers
1. so that I can take pictures when I want.
2. otherwise I might lose it / someone might steal it.
3. so that I can take close-ups.
4. otherwise it will get dirty/dusty.
5. otherwise I will lose them.

6

End the lesson with the caption competition. Encourage your learners to think up amusing or silly captions and get them to vote on the best one. If it is successful, you or they could bring further pictures to class for them to repeat the activity.

Answer key

The first caption goes with Picture 2.
The second caption goes with Picture 5.

Personal Study Workbook

1: Logical endings
5: Photo in St James Park
7: Speaking partners

```
QUICK NOTES

This went well:
..................................................
..................................................

This didn't quite work:
..................................................
..................................................

Things to think about:
..................................................
..................................................
```

TAKE MY ADVICE!

Introduction

The first exercise highlights common language used to advise and warn, and subsequent exercises give the learners the chance to practise and consolidate this language through a range of skills activities. The listening passage also introduces a cross-cultural element as learners evaluate the advice given to someone who is going to complain in a shop; this may be very different from country to country. The personalised activity at the end enables learners to exchange their own experiences of complaining.

Suggested steps

1

Follow the instructions in the Class Book.

Answer key

She is probably going to have ballroom dancing lessons.

Option

You could do the first exercise as a process of deduction. Write the first piece of advice on the board and ask your learners to speculate on what the woman is going to do. After a few suggestions, write the second piece of advice on the board and ask for further suggestions or confirmation of earlier opinions. Continue until you have all the advice on the board even if they have all agreed on the likely answer.

The advantage of staging it like this is that you can explain new items as they arise and the learners focus on key phrases as they appear; it is also more fun. An overhead projector is ideal for this type of exploitation.

2

Check they understand the vocabulary in a–d: new items may include *second-hand car dealer, babysitting, pet shop* and *parrot*.

Group the learners according to the situation they choose. Different sized groups do not matter too much, though if a group is very large, you could subdivide it. Then let them write down their completed sentences. Move round the groups and help where necessary.

3

Match each learner with someone who chose a different situation and give them several minutes to compare their answers.

Option

For further practice, pairs could repeat their own version of Exercise 1. In other words, they write advice for a person in a particular situation, and another pair must guess what the situation is.

4 ⬭⬭

Introduce the recording by talking about strategies for complaining. Be brief at this stage, but raise the question of whether it is better to be forceful and aggressive, or quiet and polite. Explain any new vocabulary in the list of ideas before they listen.

Choose the appropriate version of the recording and play it once or twice. The tapescripts are on page 166.

Answer key

Version 1
They're all good ideas according to the speaker.

Version 2
Good ideas:
Take the receipt with you.
Be aggressive.
Demand to see the manager.
Tell them you'll call the police if you don't get your money back.
Try to avoid a busy time.
Bad ideas:
Make a lot of noise.
Take someone else with you.

When you check the answers to the listening, defer any discussion as to whether the speaker's advice is good or not. (Some of it may be, some may not. The decision to be aggressive and make a lot of fuss may be good or bad depending on the culture of the country. In Britain, most people tend to think that aggression is a final resort, and the best strategy is to be firm but polite.)

5

You can begin by telling a personal anecdote of a complaint you have made; this may help the learners to recall their own stories. During the discussion, monitor and collect data for feedback at the end.

Personal Study Workbook

2: Put them in order
3: Word partnerships
6: An informal letter

QUICK NOTES

This went well:

....

....

This didn't quite work:

....

....

Things to think about:

....

....

DESCRIBING PICTURES

Introduction

Pictures are used again as the main stimulus, this time a rather interesting interior of a room which is exploited to introduce and practise *look* + adjective, *look like* + noun, and *could (be)* for speculation. This leads on to more skills work with a listening passage and an extended writing activity, in which learners can consolidate the understanding of the target structures and some new vocabulary.

Suggested steps

1

Begin by pre-teaching key lexis from the text that you anticipate will be new, e.g. *hall/reception area*, *freezer*, *piece of sculpture*, *bare*, *rather* (see Language Points).

> **Language Points: vocabulary and quite and rather**
>
> 1. Entrances
>   There are several different words used to describe the entrance to a building:
>   In a private house it is a *hall*, and the living room, dining room and kitchen usually lead off the hall.
>   In a hotel it is usually called the *reception* (*lobby* in American English).
>   In a cinema or theatre it is usually a *foyer*.
>   In public buildings it may be called the *reception* or just the *entrance*.
>
> 2. *Quite* and *rather*
>   There are quite subtle differences between *quite* and *rather*. At this stage, you can simply explain *rather* as being a bit stronger than *quite*. For example:
>   *Her English is quite good.* (It is very reasonable.)
>   *Her English is rather good.* (It is certainly better than is usual and better than I expected.)

Give the learners time to complete the task and then put them in pairs to discuss their answers. Conduct a quick feedback but don't confirm or reject any of their answers at this stage.

2

Highlight the key phrases after the text. Putting them on the board is preferable as they are all focusing on the same thing. Give further examples and invite examples from the class:

Examples: *This room looks a mess.*
Paolo looks tired.
Naoko looks like her sister.
Hans could be Scandinavian or British to people who don't know that he is Swiss.

Ask the learners to make up more sentences about the pictures as suggested in the Class Book, and monitor and correct where necessary.

Answer key

Possible answers
The woman looks Scandinavian.
The room looks cool/charming/very unusual/clean and tidy.
The floor looks beautiful.
The little boy looks worried.
The woman looks like a teacher/designer, etc.
The room looks like a corridor.
The light in the ceiling looks like a window.
The room could be an office.

The sofa could be a bed.
The fireplace could be false.

3 ▭

Tell the class they can now find out the correct answers to Exercise 1. Play the recording and ask them to note down any new information they learn. Check their answers and then introduce Exercise 4.

Answer key

See the tapescript on page 166.

4

The learners can choose which picture they want to describe, and you may find some of them prefer to work on their own for a writing activity. Tell them to produce a text about the same length as the one in Exercise 1, and encourage them to use vocabulary from that text. The activity will take some time so you will be able to monitor and help individual learners.

Encourage them to show each other what they have written and to comment on it. Then tell them to read the texts which give more information about the places; they are on page 171 in the Class Book.

Personal Study Workbook

4: Wordsearch
8: Visual dictionary

```
QUICK NOTES

This went well:
.........................................................
.........................................................

This didn't quite work:
.........................................................
.........................................................

Things to think about:
.........................................................
.........................................................
```

REVIEW AND DEVELOPMENT

REVIEW OF UNIT 15

1

This exercise revises the use of articles from Unit 15 through the theme of the current unit.

Ask the learners to describe what they can see in the picture, and supply new vocabulary items as they get stuck, e.g. the verb *to water*. This will stimulate interest in the text and also make it easier to understand. Give them five minutes to complete the activity and then put them in pairs or small groups to discuss their answers.

(–) John Rogers   a siege   an embassy   (–) London
the building   (–) office buildings   the embassy   a
colleague   the siege   the   buildings   the photo

2

Most common verbs have a number of different
meanings, although there are some learners who seem
content with just one meaning. This exercise draws
attention to this feature of common verbs, and
translation will highlight for the learner those verbs and
meanings which will require the most attention.

Follow the instructions in the Class Book. If it is not
possible to put a learner with someone who speaks the
same language, it may be possible for learners to work
with someone who speaks a similar language, e.g.
Spanish and Portuguese.

For consolidation, you could also ask the learners to try
to think of English synonyms for the verbs in each
sentence. This will be almost impossible for the different
meanings of *break*, but your learners may be able to
produce the following for *leave* and *see*:

leave
1. departed
2. finished
3. forgot (This is the verb that most learners use when
   they want to express this meaning of leave.
   Unfortunately, in English, we cannot use *forget* if we
   say where something was mislaid/left.)
4. deposited (Most dictionaries explain this meaning as
   let something remain.)

see
9. It is visible with my eyes.
10. visit/meet
11. understand (a very common meaning of *see*)
12. witness

Ask the learners to brainstorm other verbs which are
translated in a number of ways in their language. With
monolingual groups, you may well be able to feed in
some particular examples yourself.

Option

If your learners all speak different languages, you can use
the exercise to develop dictionary skills. Put the learners
in pairs and give each pair, if possible, a good
monolingual dictionary. Ask them to look up the verbs
and find dictionary definitions which correspond with
the meanings in each of the sentences. You can repeat
this type of activity for other common verbs such as *go*,
take and *keep*.

REVIEW OF UNIT 16

1

This exercise is not suitable if your learners do not know
each other, or if you feel that it is rather personal and
may cause embarrassment or offence. With groups who
know each other quite well, the exercise can be great

fun and provide a memorable way to practise the
structure.

Follow the instructions in the Class Book. After the first
part when the learners have completed the sentences and
compared them with a partner, you could ask pairs to
shout out their answers across the class to see how much
agreement there is on the missing names!

Then put them back in pairs or small groups to think up
their own sentences.

2 ▭

Play the recording and pause it after each sentence to
give your learners time to write down their answers. If
necessary play it again. Put them in pairs to compare
their answers. Conduct a brief feedback to check
answers and then draw the learners' attention to the
contractions (of *will*); the pronunciation of the pronouns
him and *her*, in which the 'h' is dropped; the
pronunciation of the weak form of them /ðəm/; and
finally the linking that takes place between a consonant
at the end of one word and the vowel at the beginning
of another, e.g. shut up. It is this feature of
pronunciation which makes it difficult for learners to
distinguish individual words, and which gives them the
feeling that language is just a stream of sound.

Answer key

See the tapescript on page 166.

Play the recording again so that the learners can listen
carefully to these different features.

Introduce the practice activity and demonstrate two or
three exchanges with one of the stronger members of
the class. Repeat with two or three other learners and
listen carefully to see if they are taking account of these
different points. When you are quite happy, put them in
pairs for further practice.

You can repeat this type of activity at regular intervals
with short sentences of your own.

```
QUICK NOTES

This went well:
.........................................................................
.........................................................................

This didn't quite work:
.........................................................................
.........................................................................

Things to think about:
.........................................................................
.........................................................................
```

18

LISTS

CONTENTS

Language focus: requests, suggestions and arrangements
telephoning

Vocabulary: crime
verb + noun collocations
keeping a vocabulary notebook

Skills: Speaking: what lists do people make?
discussing ways of recording vocabulary
practising telephone conversations

Listening: advice on keeping a vocabulary notebook
telephone conversations

Writing: lists
a dialogue
recording vocabulary

WHO MAKES LISTS?

Introduction

The lesson explores an activity that is rarely discussed but often practised: making lists. The main activities concentrate on free speaking, but there is also a short listening exercise and some important lexical input. The final exercise also exploits the theme for vocabulary revision.

Suggested steps

1 ▭

Sometimes it makes a nice change to engage learners in an activity without introducing it or explaining what it's about – the element of mystery grabs their attention. It seems very appropriate for this lesson, so go straight into the listening without any prior explanation.

Option

You can use the recording if you wish, but it is probably more interesting and natural if you give the instructions yourself; you can pause for as long as you like during the instructions, and even provide more examples of lists if you sense they need a bit more help. The tapescript is on page 167.

Allow a few minutes for the groups to compare their answers and talk about the activity, and then explain that making lists is in fact the theme of the lesson.

2

Go through the examples to clarify any new vocabulary, and then give the learners time to complete the task. Put them in small groups to compare and discuss their answers.

3

Do this exercise in two stages. First, get the learners to add up their scores and sort themselves into three groups.

Now ask the groups to discuss the sentences in Exercise 3 in their groups. Move round and monitor the discussion. When they have finished, rearrange the groups so that you have groups consisting of one person from each of the previous groups, if possible. Tell them to discuss the same questions to see if the groups reach similar conclusions.

4

You could put them in groups of three, and then assign each member of a group six previous units to scan for potential lists (i.e. so that they don't all scan the same units). After about 5–10 minutes, they can tell each other about their lists, and then regroup to compare their lists with people who examined the same units. You could make it a competition to see who can find the most. At the end you could refer them to the cartoon and see if they can explain the joke.

Option

You could use Worksheet 18 on page 134 if you have any time left at the end, or as a warm-up to this or any other lesson in the unit.

```
┌─────────────────────────────────────────────┐
│                QUICK NOTES                    │
│                                               │
│   This went well:                             │
│   ........................................    │
│                                               │
│   ........................................    │
│                                               │
│   This didn't quite work:                     │
│   ........................................    │
│                                               │
│   ........................................    │
│                                               │
│   Things to think about:                      │
│   ........................................    │
│                                               │
│   ........................................    │
└─────────────────────────────────────────────┘
```

LISTS IN LANGUAGE LEARNING

Introduction

There are very few learners who do not keep some kind of vocabulary notebook, so clearly most people believe it is a worthwhile pursuit. But how many learners give serious consideration to the way they keep records, and how they can be most effective in learning the vocabulary they scrupulously write down in their books? These issues are addressed in this lesson, and through a listening activity, learners are given advice on keeping a notebook. They then have a chance to put these ideas into practice, and in the process learn a set of new lexical items.

Suggested steps

1

Put the learners in groups and tell them to show each other their vocabulary notes (if they have them) to see how similar they are.

Conduct a brief feedback and write on the board the different systems used, e.g. English words on one side, translations on the other; or English words on one side and English explanations on the other.

2

Direct the learners to the list in their Class Book. Ask them if it is similar to many of their notebooks, and then tell them to work through the list, individually or in pairs, looking up new words in a dictionary. (If they are German speakers, they will have translations, but they should still check in a monolingual dictionary.) Ideally your learners should have access to good monolingual and bilingual dictionaries.

Clarify any problems but don't spend too long on the words at this stage; there are further opportunities for the learners to consolidate their understanding of this vocabulary.

3 ▭

Introduce the possibility that there are other strategies that could be used and then play the recording and tell them to make notes. Replay as necessary. The tapescript is on page 167.

Answer key

2. Write example sentences, especially for words which have special features, e.g. the same form for verb and noun.
3. Write the part of speech: (v), (n), or (adj).
4. Note pronunciation: ideally phonetics, but your own system will do.
5. Organise words into connected groups and leave space to add to them.

Option

For a further speaking activity which will also make the listening task easier, put the learners in groups to predict the content of the listening. In other words, what advice do they think the teacher might give? Bring them back together after their discussion and put their ideas on the board. The listening task will now consist of checking their predictions with the recording; this should be relatively easy if they have anticipated most of the points from the recording.

The strategy of predicting the content of a listening passage can help learners to improve their listening ability, particularly those learners who tend to get over-anxious if they haven't understood every word of a message.

Conduct a quick feedback on the listening and ask the learners if they agree with the advice. Most learners do, in theory, so the real task is putting it into practice. At this stage you could also ask the class if they noted the part of speech and the example sentences (if there were any), when they looked up the new words before the listening.

4

Give them five or ten minutes to reorganise the list, and encourage them to try any other ideas as well, e.g. drawing pictures to illustrate certain items. This can be very helpful as some people have very strong visual memories.

Put them in groups to compare their lists and allow the class as a whole to talk through any issues that may arise. For example, is the implementation of these ideas practical or will it be too time-consuming? How important is detailed vocabulary record keeping? And so on.

5

Emphasise that they are not expected to use all the words in each dialogue – but all the words, if possible, over the two dialogues. How much they develop the dialogues is up to them, but we feel they only need to add about six lines to each one. If they can't include every single item it obviously doesn't matter, but the task of trying to include them all is quite motivating, and obviously a good way to consolidate and test their understanding of the items.

If time permits, they can listen to each other's dialogues and tick off the target vocabulary as they listen. They can also compare their dialogues with these examples:

Answer key

Possible answers

SHOPKEEPER:	… when this man came in and punched me in the stomach.
POLICEMAN:	Was he on his own?
SHOPKEEPER:	Yes, I think so. Anyway, he smashed the glass cabinet and took just about everything apart from a few cheap bits of jewellery.
POLICEMAN:	And what did he look like?
SHOPKEEPER:	I couldn't say. It happened so fast and then he left.
POLICEMAN:	In a car?
SHOPKEEPER:	No, he was on foot. He ran off down the High Street.
POLICEMAN:	And were there any other witnesses?
SHOPKEEPER:	No, I'm afraid not. The shop was empty …

PC BRAITHWAITE:	He ran into the High Street and disappeared among the crowd coming out of the football stadium.
INSPECTOR MAC:	OK, never mind, but did you get a good look at him?
PC BRAITHWAITE:	Yes, he was average height, at least 25 or 30, and he had a beard.
INSPECTOR MAC:	But you didn't recognise him?
PC BRAITHWAITE:	No, I'm afraid not.

Personal Study Workbook

6: Memory aids
8: Language learning

```
QUICK NOTES

This went well:

.............................................
.............................................

This didn't quite work:

.............................................
.............................................

Things to think about:

.............................................
.............................................
```

Introduction

The organising activity at the beginning of the lesson presents and practises important vocabulary items, many of which reappear in later activities. The main focus, however, is on telephone language and important expressions used to make requests, suggestions and arrangements. These are introduced through an activity which requires the learners to deduce the appropriate context for an utterance, and they are then consolidated through listening and a freer speaking activity.

Suggested steps

1

You could pre-teach a few items, but if you do too much, this will give away a lot of information and spoil the enjoyment of the problem-solving activity. We prefer to let learners make use of dictionaries, each other and the context, while the teacher monitors and assists if required.

When the learners have finished, they can compare answers in groups before you conduct a brief feedback and clarify the meaning of any new items, if necessary. Practise the pronunciation of difficult items, e.g. *corkscrew, arrange, delivery schedules*, etc.

Answer key

The learners may have put certain phrases in different groups: accept these if they are justifiable.

Party arrangements
borrow tapes from Jim
organise the catering
tell the neighbours
send out invitations
hire 50 champagne glasses
buy a new corkscrew

Holiday arrangements
get suntan lotion
confirm the flight
leave keys with the neighbours
get my hair cut
see if Mary can feed Felix
buy a new pair of shorts

Work
send fax to D.I.P.
finish report on Greece
write the agenda for Monday
cancel Friday's meeting
arrange meeting with Mrs Howard
check delivery schedules for July

2

Follow the instructions in the Class Book. Alternatively, do it as a class activity, with different members shouting out suggestions. In this case, try to collect at least four additions to the lists.

3

You will need to pre-teach new words and phrases and explain how they are used (see Language Points). Put the learners in pairs to decide which phrases they will need in their chosen situation.

Language Points: functional language

1. Requests. What you say will depend on the nature of the request. Compare:

   Could I borrow your dictionary? (small request)
   with
   Would it be possible for me to borrow your bike this evening? (more substantial request)

2. Saying *no*. Notice the difference in these two common constructions:

   I'm sorry, but I need my bike this evening.
   I'm afraid I need my bike this evening.

3. Suggestions. *How about …?* is used here, but *what about …?* can also be used, with no difference in meaning.

4. Phoning. Notice that we say *Could I speak to Jim?* (American English uses *speak with Jim*.)

---

4 🔲

Play the recording and conduct a feedback. You may also want to highlight one or two phrases from the passage, e.g. *it's no trouble at all*; *let me look* (in my diary). The tapescript is on page 167.

5

Learners will make mistakes in their improvised conversation. Just correct errors with the target phrases from the lesson, and tell the pairs to keep changing the situation so that they can repeat their dialogue several times but with minor changes to maintain interest.

Personal Study Workbook

1: Could you lend me some money?
2: On the telephone
7: A list of facts

QUICK NOTES

This went well:

....
....

This didn't quite work:

....
....

Things to think about:

....
....

REVIEW OF UNIT 16

1

Follow the instructions in the Class Book.

Answer key

1. when   2. If   3. When   4. If   5. If   6. when   7. If   8. When

2

This is likely to be more generative in a multicultural group. Mix the nationalities as much as possible and have a class feedback after the discussion in small groups.

REVIEW OF UNIT 17

1

Follow the instructions in the Class Book.

2

There are several ways you can extend this activity and make it more interactive:

Split the class in half and tell them to complete the sentences in their book. While they are doing this, tell one half of the group that they are going to be very argumentative and want reasons for any advice given. Pair off learners from each half of the class and tell them to role play the situation, with the 'argumentative' half as the ones seeking advice. This should ensure the conversation goes on much longer.

An alternative is to give the learners different instructions. Some of the class can respond to the situation in the book, while others complete the sentences with advice for someone going to a very exclusive dinner party. Put the learners in pairs and tell them to role play their situations, with the person seeking advice to assume no knowledge at all.

QUICK NOTES

This went well:

....
....

This didn't quite work:

....
....

Things to think about:

....
....

19

PUT YOUR TRUST IN OTHERS

CONTENTS

Language focus: *if* sentences with *would* and *might* (second conditional)
offers and requests

Vocabulary: adjectives ending *-ed* and *-ing*
describing speech acts, e.g. *agree, complain*
guessing words in context

Skills: Speaking: talking about the professions we trust
discussing responses to hypothetical situations
improvising situations involving offers and
     requests
how we respond to new neighbours

Listening: people responding to hypothetical situations

Reading: a jumbled text
guessing words in context

APPEARANCES CAN BE DECEPTIVE

Introduction

The warm-up introduces the theme of the lesson
through a free-speaking exercise, but much of the lesson
revolves around a short story, which is initially jumbled
so that the learners have to use reading skills to piece it
together. Having done that, there is a further exercise to
develop the skill of contextual guesswork, and the lesson
finishes with a brief focus on adjectives ending in *-ed* and
-ing, and a personalised speaking activity.

Suggested steps

1

You could write the sentences on the board, and
complete them with examples from the professions on
the right (plus *myself*). Ask the learners if they agree with
your statements. This should provoke a response, which
you can then channel into discussion in small groups.

2

Introduce the jumbled story and give your learners five or
ten minutes to piece it together. As there is a follow-up
exercise on contextual guesswork, however, you should
not allow your learners to use dictionaries during this
first reading. Put them in pairs to discuss answers, and
then check with the whole class. Try not to explain the
meaning of the words which appear in the next exercise.

Answer key

1. b   2. e   3. c   4. g   5. j   6. f   7. a   8. i   9. d
10. h

3

Introduce the topic of contextual guesswork and work
through the examples in the book. It is important to
stress that there are degrees to which you can guess the
meaning of a word from context, but there are also
degrees to which a dictionary definition of a word makes
sense in a particular context. In other words, learners
will generally be most effective if they use the context in
harness with a good dictionary.

Having made this point you can put them in pairs or
small groups to guess the meaning of the selected words
from the story. Tell them to use the context first to
establish if it elucidates the meaning precisely, generally
or not at all. Then they can use their dictionaries to
check and consolidate.

Option

This is for monolingual groups only.

Contextual guesswork is a skill that many people use in
their first language, but some learners do not always
seem to make good use of it in foreign language
learning. If you feel this is true with any learners in your
group, you might try bringing a text in the learners' first
language which contains two or three words that most of
the group will not know. If necessary, you can doctor a
text to include low frequency words. See if your learners
seem any better at guessing the meaning of these new
words, and discuss how they were able, or not able, to
guess the meaning accurately. This might prove an
instructive activity with significance for future learning.

Option

If you want more practice of contextual guesswork, you could do Worksheet 19 on page 135.

4

Explain the difference between *terrified* and *terrifying*. If necessary, add a further example, e.g. *shocked* and *shocking*, and then go round the class eliciting answers to the questions in the book. If you are satisfied that the learners have grasped the difference, check that they understand the meaning of *embarrassing* and *disappointing*, then ask them to complete the sentences about themselves. Move round and monitor to check they are doing it correctly. Put them in groups to discuss their answers, and finish the lesson with a class feedback on the more interesting or unusual answers.

Personal Study Workbook

4: I'm very boring!
5: Urban myths
6: Lexical connections

QUICK NOTES

This went well:

....

....

This didn't quite work:

....

....

Things to think about:

....

....

NEW NEIGHBOURS

Introduction

This lesson presents and practises the second conditional. In the first activity, the learners see the form and use it in a speaking activity. This is then followed by an analysis of both form and meaning in which there is a contrast with the first conditional and a testing exercise. The lesson reverts back to the theme of new neighbours with a further practice activity using the second conditional, and finishes with a cross-cultural discussion on how new neighbours are welcomed by different people and in different cultures.

Suggested steps

Option

If you feel the vocabulary in Exercise 1 deserves more focus with your learners, you could do Exercise 3 (From verb to noun) in the Personal Study Workbook at this stage.

1

Look at the picture of the man and child and ask for responses from the class. For example:
What is the relationship between the two?
What is your impression of the man?

Explain the hypothetical/imaginary situation that this man and his child have moved into the next flat/house. Go through each of the sentences in the box explaining any new vocabulary, and then ask the learners in pairs to discuss how they would react to each offer and request. In our experience, learners quite happily use the construction given them without asking too many questions. But if they do, just tell them that this construction is necessary for this situation, and together you will examine why at the end of the exercise.

2

Put the learners in pairs to answer the four questions, and then check with the whole class. If there are problems with any questions, refer back to the context and sentences in Exercise 1 to explain.

Answer key

1. The past simple.
2. The present/future.
3. *Would* or *wouldn't* + infinitive without *to*.
4. An imaginary situation.

Now ask them to explain the difference between the construction they have been using and the two sentences in the first conditional. If necessary, you can reinforce/test their understanding by asking them why different constructions are possible for the same situation, as in this example:
If I have some free time, I'll help you.
If I had some free time, I'd help you.

The answer is that the speaker in the first sentence sees a real possibility of having some free time, but the speaker in the second sentence thinks it is highly unlikely that he/she will have any free time; in other words the situation is improbable.

3

Test the form and concept and check answers with the class.

Answer key

1. If I <u>see</u> him tomorrow, <u>I'll</u> give him the book.
2. <u>I'd</u> be very surprised if a stranger <u>gave</u> me some money in the street for no reason.
3. If I <u>broke</u> both my legs tomorrow, I <u>might</u> write a book.
4. If I <u>get</u> home on time this afternoon, <u>I'll</u> phone you.
5. <u>I'd</u> apply for that job in Oslo if I <u>knew</u> how to speak Norwegian.
6. If I <u>had</u> a lot of money now, <u>I would</u> give up work.
7. If they <u>don't</u> come soon, <u>we'll</u> never catch that bus.
8. If I <u>were</u> you, <u>I'd</u> definitely accept that new job.

Use the last example in Exercise 3 to highlight the use of *were* with the first person in hypothetical conditionals. We do not think it is necessary to practise this extensively at this stage.

> **Language Point: If I were you …**
>
> In hypothetical conditional clauses containing the verb *to be*, we use *were* for the first and third person singular in formal English.
>
> *If I were in her position, I would leave the company.*
> *If he were a bit stronger, he could lift that.*
>
> In conversational English, *was* is commonly used:
>
> *If I was that rich, I wouldn't be here.*
> *If he was here, he could tell us himself.*
>
> (*Were* is always used in other persons: *If they were quieter, I'd be happy.*)

4

This returns to the theme of new neighbours. Ask the learners to complete all the sentences before discussing them with a partner.

5

The final activity might be more interesting with a mixed nationality group as different cultures may have their own customs with regard to new neighbours. But even within a single culture there are probably differences from personality to personality. You might also ask if there is any difference between a new neighbour in the next house and a new neighbour in the next flat. And with a group who all live in the same town or city, are there certain parts of the town with a greater sense of community than others?

Personal Study Workbook

1: Correct the mistakes
2: Just imagine
8: Conditional sentences
9: Speaking partners

IT'S UP TO YOU

Introduction

There is further practice of the second conditional through an extended speaking activity; groups discuss how they would respond to a series of hypothetical offers and requests. They then listen to native speakers doing the same activity, before examining the exact language that may have been used in the offers and requests. The lesson finishes with the learners acting out some of the situations in order to practise the offers and requests for themselves.

Suggested steps

1

The key to this exercise is that your learners do not realise that different pictures accompany the situations they are going to discuss. For this reason, divide the class into two groups right at the beginning and, if possible, put the groups in different rooms. (If that is not possible, try at least to ensure a physical separation between the groups.) With a large class, you can subdivide each group into smaller groups.

Tell one group to look at the situations on page 123, and direct the other group to the situations on page 172. Tell them to discuss each situation in turn and note down their own answers.

Monitor the discussion and make notes, remembering to write down good language use as well as errors.

2

Mix up the groups and let them compare their answers. After they have given their response to each situation, tell them to look at each other's pictures to see if this would produce a change in their response.

At the end you can give them feedback on their language, but you might also wish to talk about the way in which our reactions to people are governed by what they look like. Is this fair or reasonable? Can the group provide examples of this in their own lives?

3 ▭

Play the recording and let the learners compare their answers in pairs. The tapescript is on page 167.

Answer key

Situation 1: Joumana wouldn't let him in, and neither would Lorelei.

Situation 2: Joumana wouldn't believe her but she would give her something. Lorelei might not believe her but she would give her money.

Situation 3: Joumana wouldn't accept a lift from the man. She would say nothing or scream. Lorelei wouldn't accept a lift with any man she didn't know.

Situation 4: Joumana would like to help but she would phone a locksmith or go to the police to get help for her. Lorelei would probably help her.

Situation 5: Joumana would be suspicious but would take it in the end. Lorelei wouldn't accept it.

4

Put the learners in pairs again. Go through the example in the book and then ask them to write down the exact words used by the speakers in the other situations; just the offer or request, not the whole conversation. Discuss the situations with the class and write up model answers as you proceed.

Answer key

Possible answers:

Situation 2: 'Excuse me. Could you possibly lend me 50 pence? I'm afraid I've left my purse at home and I haven't got any money for my bus fare.'

Situation 3: 'You can't walk in this rain. Would you like a lift?' (Or 'Can I give you a lift?')

Situation 4: 'Excuse me. I'm afraid I've left my key inside. Could you possibly help me to break a window?'

Situation 5: 'Here, would you like this 100 dollars? I'm a rich man, so I don't need it. Please take it.'

5

Ask the pairs to choose one or perhaps two situations and improvise the whole conversation. They can talk about it first and then following the improvisation, they can practise it a second time so that they are more fluent. When you think most pairs are ready, you can select different ones to act it out for the rest of the group. Try to choose conversations which end in different ways, and any that are humorous.

Personal Study Workbook

3: From verb to noun
7: Offers and requests

QUICK NOTES

This went well:

....

....

This didn't quite work:

....

....

Things to think about:

....

....

REVIEW AND DEVELOPMENT

REVIEW OF UNIT 17

1 ▭

Everyone in the class could have different answers to these questions (quite legitimately), but it is surprising how often learners come to similar conclusions. It can be great fun.

Put the learners in groups to discuss the sentences and then conduct a brief feedback

There are two tasks for the recording, but the learners may not need to listen twice. Put them in pairs and ask one to note down the questions asked, while the other notes down the answers. They can check together at the end, and then compare with another pair.

Answer key

See the tapescript on page 168.

Conduct a further feedback on the answers and then put the learners back in groups for the speaking part of the exercise.

2

Check the answers to the first part of the exercise before putting the learners in pairs for the dialogue practice.

Answer key

remember – forget
both – neither
background – foreground
nice – unpleasant
simple – complicated
tense – relaxed
second-hand – new
panic – stay calm
town – countryside
clear – confusing

REVIEW OF UNIT 18

1

When the learners have written their answers, they can discuss them in groups. Follow up with a feedback and discuss any differences.

Answer key

Possible answers

1. I'm afraid I can't come tomorrow because I have to go to the airport to meet a client.
2. I'm sorry I'm late but I missed the bus.
3. That's OK. Never mind.
4. How about 7.30?
5. Could you possibly come and have a look at it?
6. Excuse me, I'm looking for …
   Excuse me, do you know where …?

You could then put the learners in pairs to role play each situation. If necessary role play one of the situations with another learner as an example.

Monitor the pairs while they practise, and at the end choose several pairs to act out their situations for the rest of the group.

2

Follow the instructions in the Class Book.

Answer key

Possible answers

cancel: a flight, a meeting, a football match, a trip, a visit, an appointment

arrange: a meeting, an appointment, flowers, a wedding, a holiday

hire: a car, a bike, a room for a party or reception, a pair of skis

check: doors, windows, electricity

confirm in advance: a flight, a booking for a hotel

solve: a problem

3 ☐☐

Follow the instructions in the Class Book. If you find this type of exercise useful, you could easily construct your own using a different group of words from any of the units.

Answer key

The answers are on the recording. The tapescript is on page 168.

20

THE SENSES

CONTENTS

Language focus: *so do I, neither do I*
will, might and *won't* for predictions
likes and dislikes

Vocabulary: materials, food, nationalities, technology
it smells/tastes/sounds like ...
I like the smell/taste/feel of ...

Skills: Speaking: talking about things you like and dislike
discussing different smells
predicting changes in technology
conducting a survey on the use of perfume
and after-shave

Listening: sounds of the 20th century
information about perfume
people's predictions about future technology

Reading: a text on the smells different nationalities
like and dislike

SENSORY PREFERENCES

Introduction

In the first part of the lesson learners talk about their likes and dislikes of different smells, tastes and things you touch. This introduces a lot of new vocabulary and also creates the need for the constructions *so do I* and *neither do I*. Following practice of this structure, there is a text on smells which different nationalities like and dislike, and the lesson finishes with a freer personalised speaking activity.

Suggested steps

1

Ask your learners if they can name the five senses, and put these on the board. You could ask them which is the most important of the senses and why, as an introduction to the theme.

Put them in small groups, talk them through the examples in the book, and then let them carry out the task. Conduct a brief feedback.

2

You could ask the learners to use the visuals and their dictionaries to find the meaning of new words, or go through the list yourself with the whole class. Whichever approach you use, it is important to check the pronunciation, perhaps by drilling the more difficult items, before the class exchange opinions.

Get them to fill in their ticks and crosses. While they are doing this, you could transfer the table in Exercise 3 to the board (or prepare an overhead transparency in advance if you have a projector).

3

Read the examples and try to elicit the difference. For example, ask the learners if speaker B agrees with speaker A in both sentences. If yes, then what is the difference between them? Why are there different constructions? You should be able to elicit the correct answer here, and you can then follow up with some controlled practice round the class; ask the learners to agree with everything you say.

If you wish, you can also tell the class that the other way of agreeing is to use *me too* in positive sentences, and *me neither* in negative sentences. Explain that disagreement calls for a different response and illustrate with the examples in the book. Drill the class again, only this time tell them to respond truthfully; in other words they may agree or disagree. Make sure that when they disagree they do so with appropriate intonation.

Example: *I don't like the taste of honey.*

Oh, I do – it's wonderful.

Put them in pairs to find out about the examples in Exercise 2. Note that although *touch* is the name of the sense, *feel* is the word we use to talk about it. While the pairs practise, move round and monitor. You may wish to have a brief feedback at the end where pairs do some questions and answers in front of the class and are corrected if necessary.

4

Ask the learners for their *favourite* smells. When you've got two or three examples, introduce the topic of the reading text and get the class to read it and complete the table. Tell them to start filling in the information after the second paragraph.

Answer key

	Likes	Dislikes
English	root beer, anise, lemon (for cleaning products)	oil of wintergreen
Poles	banana, cherry, pickle, pizza	oil of wintergreen
French	anise	garlic, smoke, skunk
Swiss	pizza	oil of wintergreen
Californians	oil of wintergreen	
Germans	lemon	
Norwegians and Swedes	lemon, chocolate, pickle	

(The first two paragraphs also mention more generally that most people like the smell of banana, and dislike the smell of natural gas.)

Option

Write the smells mentioned in the text on the board. Explain words as necessary. Ask the learners to rank them (from best to worst), and then to move round and compare. At the end put a few examples on the board and then get the class to read the text to see how it compares with their own opinions.

5

Finish with the personalised speaking activity.

Personal Study Workbook

1: Agreeing
4: Listen and answer
5: Odd one out
9: Visual dictionary

QUICK NOTES

This went well:

....

....

This didn't quite work:

....

....

Things to think about:

....

....

Introduction

The use of *will*, *might* and *won't* is recycled through an activity in which learners predict changes in technology. The lesson also provides new lexical input as learners try to identify sounds which accompany machines and gadgets, and there are a number of different speaking activities from dialogue building to free discussion.

Suggested steps

1 ▭

Ask the class to give you a few common everyday sounds which are man-made, i.e. not the sound of birds or trees or babies. Then you can tell them that their first task will be to identify a few more. Play the example from the recording and highlight the constructions in the book.

Play the rest of the sounds, pausing each time for the learners to write down their answers. If you have a monolingual class, they could write translations if they recognise a sound but cannot say the word in English. Let them compare answers in pairs and then conduct a short feedback. Explain new words as necessary.

Answer key

2. A washing machine on fast spin
3. a digital wrist watch
4. The hiss of someone else's personal stereo
5. The ping of an oven or microwave when something is ready
6. a video ejecting a cassette
7. a computer keyboard
8. a zoom lens on a camera
9. a doorbell

2

Make sure the class understand the meaning of the adjectives before they begin their discussion. Monitor and provide feedback.

3 ▭

The recording is not intended as a model for the learners, but it does give an example of the type of dialogue they can produce, and the approximate length. Play the recording and ask them if they have experienced (or caused) this particular problem. Put them in pairs for the dialogue building and move round the class to help where necessary. As it is intended to be quite short, encourage the pairs to keep practising until they can produce their conversation clearly and fluently. Choose one or two examples for the rest of the class to listen to at the end.

Option

If you have access to a tape recorder and a quiet area outside the classroom, you could record some or each of the pairs. When one pair has finished, send them outside to record their conversation, then another pair and so on. If you have time, you could then do some very detailed analysis of pronunciation errors at home, and follow it up with more practice in class. For some learners this is the only way they become fully aware of their pronunciation problems.

4

Go through the examples on the board, and ask the class what they think. Make sure they do not say *I think we won't …* . In this case, native speakers prefer to make the first verb negative and say *I don't think we will …* .

Put them in groups to discuss the other gadgets/machines from Exercise 1. Monitor and correct while they work, but try not to interrupt too much unless they clearly need help. Conduct a short feedback when they have exhausted the topic.

5

This is a fairly free activity, although *instead of* is a useful phrase, so explain the example carefully (*in the place of* is a paraphrase that most learners understand), and encourage them to use the phrase in their discussion. They should also, of course, use *will* for their predictions, but otherwise allow them to talk freely without too much correction. The groups can exchange ideas with other groups, or you could finish with an exchange involving the whole class.

Note: Remind the learners to bring some perfume, after-shave, eau de cologne, etc. for the next lesson. Those who do not wish to should bring something that they particularly like the smell of: a drink, something to eat, a bar of soap, etc.

Personal Study Workbook

2: Find the first letter
3: Compound words

```
                 QUICK NOTES

This went well:

...................................................................

...................................................................

This didn't quite work:

...................................................................

...................................................................

Things to think about:

...................................................................

...................................................................
```

CHOOSING PERFUMES AND EAU DE COLOGNE

Introduction

This is primarily a skills lesson, with the theme of perfume and after-shave being exploited for various speaking and listening activities. Learners also have a lot of question practice, and important verbs such as *last* and *affect* are recycled in several activities. Needless to say, the use of *smell* + adjective recurs quite often as well.

Suggested steps

1

You will need to warn your learners in advance about this lesson. Tell them to bring to class an example of perfume, eau de toilette, after-shave, etc. (See the note at the end of the previous lesson's teacher's notes.)

In class, begin by putting some perfume or after-shave on your skin, and then ask the learners for responses, using the verb *smell* plus a suitable adjective or phrase; you could remind them of the use of *like* + noun, that they used in the previous lesson.

Do the same activity in small groups. Ask each group to choose a favourite, then test the favourites with the whole class.

2

Having established an interest in the subject, introduce the quiz. Go through the questions to make sure they understand them, and then let them answer and compare in groups. In their discussion, monitor their use of language and make notes. Conduct a brief feedback on language points and the content of the quiz. Do not confirm or deny any answers at this stage.

3 ▭▭ ▭▭

Play the appropriate recording and ask your class to answer the questions to the quiz. Play it a second time if you think it is necessary. Let them compare answers with a partner before you check with the whole class.

Answer key

1. Perfume is the strongest and longest lasting. Eau de toilette contains about 5–12% perfume, eau de cologne contains only 2–6%. Eau de parfum contains up to 15% pure perfume. After-shave is for men, is similar to eau de toilette, but has more alcohol and less smell.
2. The best time is later in the day.
3. Not more than two at a time.
4. A few hours.
5. Perfumes smell different on different people with different skins. Smoking, medication and certain strong foods can change the smell of a perfume.
6. Six months.

4

Put the learners in small groups. It should not be necessary to give examples here – most learners have a clear idea of the questions they can ask – but the groups may require about ten minutes to complete their questions. If one group finishes before the others, just tell them to add one or two more questions. While they are working, you can monitor to ensure they are forming the questions accurately.

Exchange questionnaires so that each group can answer the questions set by another group. Finish with open discussion if the class has further ideas they want to express.

Option

If you are working in a culture where many people do not wear perfume or after-shave, and where there is obviously less personal experience to draw on, it may be more generative to approach the topic by asking the group to consider one or more of these questions:

Why do people wear perfume/after-shave? Is it:
a. to smell nice?
b. to feel good?
c. to attract the opposite sex?
d. to be fashionable?
e. to appear sophisticated?
f. because they think they should?
g. ....

Does the perfume/after-shave you wear say anything about your personality? If so, what?

How are perfumes and after-shave advertised on TV and in the cinema in your country?

Option

This unit includes a lot of new vocabulary from a variety of sources, so you may wish to finish with Worksheet 20 on page 135, which is a type of mind map drawing together a lot of lexical items from the unit, with an opportunity for further expansion.

Personal Study Workbook

6: Setting the scene
7: Writing a story together
8: Speaking partners

QUICK NOTES

This went well:

....

....

This didn't quite work:

....

....

Things to think about:

....

....

REVIEW OF UNIT 18

1 ⊂⊃

Follow the instructions in the Class Book. When your learners have checked their answers with the tapescript, they can practise the exercise in pairs: one person asks the questions again, and the other answers as quickly as possible. This provides a second concept check on the vocabulary, but can also be used for intensive pronunciation practice of sentence stress and rhythm.

Answer key

See the tapescript on page 169.

2

Go through the situations to ensure that everyone understands. Get the learners, in pairs, to practise each situation, and then reverse roles and do each òne again. The best way to simulate the conditions of a telephone conversation in the classroom is to ask each pair to sit back to back, so that they cannot see each other. With each pair shouting to make themselves heard, this is also an ideal opportunity to teach common telephone phrases such as:

Sorry, I can't hear. Could you speak up a bit?
or
I'm sorry, it's very noisy here. Could you repeat that?

Option

You can make these situations more difficult if you wish. Divide the class in half, and send one group out of the room to prepare the role of the caller in each situation.

When they are outside, give the others this additional information:

In Situation 1, you are busy this evening and tomorrow evening, but free the evening after that.

In Situation 2, you are going away on business tomorrow until the end of next week.

In Situation 3, you only have two single rooms free next weekend, but you are prepared to give the caller these rooms for the price of one double room.

When you have explained this information to the learners, tell them to think about their answers. Meanwhile, go outside and give the others this information:

In Situation 1, you are free tonight and tomorrow, but busy the rest of the week (or for the next five days).

In Situation 2, you really need to see this person before the end of the week.

In Situation 3, you are planning to stay at the hotel next weekend because it is your first wedding anniversary.

When they have understood, you can put the pairs together to role play the situations. When they change roles, tell them to make the situations as easy or as difficult as they wish. At the end, give them feedback on their performance.

3

Follow the instructions in the Class Book.

Answer key

Possible answers

a: bedside table; curtains; chest of drawers; cupboard.
b: police; escape; crime; prison.
c: bank; cheque book; interest; take out money.
d: chairman; vote; cancel; attend.
e: beach; bikini; sunglasses; suntan.

REVIEW OF UNIT 19

1

Follow the instructions in the Class Book. When you check the answers, practise the pronunciation, paying particular attention to these words:

worried /wʌrɪd/
nervous /nɜːvəs/
astonished /əstɒnɪʃt/

Finally, there is the common error of putting the stress on the first syllable of *upset* instead of the second. (The main stress is on the first syllable when *upset* is a noun, but then it has a completely different meaning.)

Answer key

1. terrified
2. nervous
3. upset
4. aggressive
5. astonished
6. delighted

2

As this activity makes use of the adjectives from the previous exercise, it makes sense to do it immediately afterwards. Begin by putting up half sentences on the board, and then complete each one as in the book. Ask for alternative endings to check the learners understand, and then get them to complete the task. Get them to move round comparing their sentences, while you monitor and help or correct where necessary.

QUICK NOTES

This went well:

....

....

This didn't quite work:

....

....

Things to think about:

....

....

21

TIME

CONTENTS

Language focus: *used to* + verb
time clauses: *when, as soon as, until* (+ present simple)
revision of tenses
common errors

Vocabulary: dates and ordinal numbers
time expressions, e.g. *the day before yesterday,*
in 5 days' time, etc.

Skills: Speaking: discussing consequences of a new calendar
talking about changes in your life
board game
Listening: three people's lifestyles
Reading: a text about a new calendar

A NEW WORLD CALENDAR

Introduction

This lesson begins by revising dates, focusing in particular on the pronunciation of ordinal numbers and months, which is often the source of much error even at this level. After a mental arithmetic exercise which leads into the theme of the text, the learners read about a new kind of calendar. There is a focus on comprehension and the rest of the lesson is devoted to speaking: the learners discuss the consequences of the new calendar.

Suggested steps

1 📖

Most learners have no problem recognising dates at this level, but there are many pitfalls of form and pronunciation. (For example, the /θ/ sound on most ordinals is problematic for many learners; also the pronunciation of *5th, 15th, 25th*, the use of *the* and *of* when giving a date, and commonly many learners use cardinals instead of ordinal numbers (e.g. ~~the two December~~). For these reasons, you may need to do this quick revision activity. Get the learners to practise the ones that caused problems. The recording is just there if you want to have a model that your learners can listen to.

2

Highlight the form of dates. If you have a class with more than ten learners, as most teachers do, divide them into subgroups (groups of about 6–8 would be best). Then tell them to learn the birthdates of all the learners in their group. Tell them not to write them down, and this will make them practise the dates a great deal orally. This is best conducted as a mingling activity, in different parts of the room if you have subgroups. At the end, put them in circles in their groups to shout out each person's birthday. Correct any errors of form or pronunciation at the end.

Option

If your learners come from a culture where birthdays are not important, adapt to their own most important day.

3

Do the first question together. Then let them time themselves working in pairs on the exercise. Alternatively, to introduce a game element, set a time limit to see who finishes first. Make sure that the rest do finish the exercise, though.

Answer key

You will need to work out the answers to most of these questions yourself as it depends what the date is today.

2. April: 30; October: 31; February: 28, with 29 in a leap year; March: 31.
3. 29th February

4

Check that the learners understand the word *calendar*, then follow the instructions in the Class Book. They could compare their answers to the true/false questions before you go over them.

Answer key

1. true   2. true   3. false (Monday)
4. false (364 days + New Year's Day = 365)   5. true
6. false (every fourth year)

Leave a few moments for the group to give quick reactions to the text (e.g. interesting, crazy, great, etc.). Then move on.

5

Ask the learners to read through the list and ask about any new vocabulary. Then discuss the first question together. They will need time to think, so don't expect immediate answers. If necessary, do the next question too, then ask them to work in small groups on the remaining questions. (Different groups could begin at different points of the list so that there is variety in the feedback.) You may wish to remind them at this point that they are discussing something imaginary, so they need to use *would*.

During group work, monitor and collect examples of learners' language for feedback at the end.

Answer key

Possible answers:
(Your learners will probably have plenty of other interesting suggestions: note them here for next time.)

1. People's birthdays would be on the same day every year; some people would always have to work on their birthdays. What would happen to people whose birthdays are at present on the 29th, 30th or 31st of the month? Their birthdays would change, perhaps.
2. Businesses would have to change their work timetables.
3. The seasons: Which months would correspond to the seasons? Our ideas might change.
4. Diaries and calendars: We wouldn't need new calendars every year. Some manufacturers might go out of business. You could print one standard diary.
5. Christmas to New Year: Many countries who celebrate this don't work much between Christmas and New Year. This period would be shorter.
6. Astrology: The zodiac would be completely changed.
7. Superstitions: These dates wouldn't exist. Maybe people would invent new ones.
8. Clocks, watches and computers would need to be redesigned, and old ones adapted.
9. National holidays: This would depend on the country.

Give the learners an open forum to feed back on their ideas and discuss names for the 13th month. At the end, write up on the board any of the language examples you collected while monitoring for them to discuss/correct.

Personal Study Workbook

5: Contextual guesswork
9: Speaking partners

```
QUICK NOTES

This went well:
.............................................
.............................................

This didn't quite work:
.............................................
.............................................

Things to think about:
.............................................
.............................................
```

SOME TIME IN MY PAST ...

Introduction

The warm-up at the start of this lesson revises/introduces time expressions for the past and future. The rest of the lesson focuses on *used to do* through a sorting activity, a concept check and a listening. It concludes with a personalised practice activity where learners discuss how their lifestyles have changed.

Suggested steps

1

Ask the learners to look at the expressions and decide which is the furthest away in the past and future. Put these on the board, then ask them to finish the exercise in their books in pairs. Go over the answers together, providing oral practice to check pronunciation.

Follow the instructions in the Class Book for the second part of the activity. Agree together on today's date and put that next to *right now* and *tonight*, then ask them to work out the rest in pairs. This will revise dates and years, too, so in feedback you may need to correct the form and pronunciation of these.

Answer key

in the 19th century; a couple of years ago; a fortnight ago; last week; the day before yesterday; right now; tonight; the day after tomorrow; in five days' time; the week after next; next year.

Option

If you feel your class needs more practice with these expressions, you could do this activity. Ask them in pairs to make up five true statements of which the last words would be the time expressions in Exercise 1.

Examples: *We had a test ... (a fortnight ago.)*
It will be Saturday ... (the day after tomorrow.)
Heinz first met his wife ... (a couple of years ago.)

Monitor and correct as necessary. Then bring the class together and ask a pair to say their sentence beginnings for the rest of the group to complete. Either continue this as a whole class activity, or do it as a mingling exercise.

2

Ask the learners to study the pictures, then read the sentences. Explain any words they do not understand. You will probably need to tell them that *used to do* means something that happened regularly or was true for some time in the past. At this stage, the learners do not need detailed understanding of the concept to do this exercise, though it will be necessary for them to know or deduce that it is used to talk about past time.

Follow the instructions for the first example, discussing together which person probably said it and why. The reasons are important as the listening will show later. When you feel they understand what to do, ask them to continue alone then compare in small groups. There are no correct answers at this stage, so in feedback, accept any reasonable suggestions.

3

Read the explanation together, then check understanding through the sentence extensions. If you and your learners prefer, translation is an option, but bear in mind that few languages have a direct equivalent. Highlight the form *used to* + verb and the negative form used in the exercise: *never used to* + verb.

It is of course possible to say *didn't use to* although our feeling is that *never used to* is a more common form and probably easier at this level in any case. Do some controlled practice on the pronunciation using sentences from either Exercise 2 or 3.

Answer key

Possible answers (there may be other good answers from your learners)

1. I used to play with my computer a lot, but I don't any more / I broke it / I got tired of it.
2. When I was younger, I used to have long hair, but it was too much trouble / I cut it all off one day / I prefer it shorter.
3. I used to love punk music, but I don't like it so much these days / I really hate it now / I don't listen to music these days.

Language Point: used to + verb

1. Grammar books differ on the interrogative and negative forms: some give *didn't use to* and *did you use to?* as the correct forms, others give *didn't used to* and *did you used to?* and some give both.
2. *Used to do* is often interchangeable with other tenses and verb forms, though it always carries an emphasis of discontinued or altered habit. Compare:

   She used to leave for work at five every morning.
   She would leave for work at five every morning.
   She left for work at five every morning.
   She was leaving for work at five every morning.

4 ▭

Follow the instructions in the Class Book. Play the recording more than once if necessary, pausing between each speaker to allow time to write sentence numbers. After feedback on the answers, ask the learners to discuss the reasons why some of their guesses might have been wrong. (This is to focus more intensively on the comprehension of the text.)

Answer key

Jack: 3, 5, 7
Val: 2, 6, 8
Don: 1, 4

5

You could talk through the answers you would write yourself, as a demonstration of what to do. While the learners are working alone completing their sentences, monitor carefully. Sometimes you may need to ask questions to check that they really are expressing what they intend, and that they have not misunderstood the concept.

When they are ready, ask them to discuss their answers in groups and encourage them to go beyond simply saying sentences with *used to do* by asking questions or commenting on/agreeing with each other's sentences. Monitor and collect language points for feedback at the end. At an appropriate point towards the end of the group work, remind them about the last instruction in the lesson. The learners may or may not use *used to do* here: it simply depends what they want to express.

Personal Study Workbook

1: Past versus present
2: Mental gymnastics
7: How do you spend your time?

QUICK NOTES

This went well:

....

....

This didn't quite work:

....

....

Things to think about:

....

....

Answer key

Worksheet 21C

There are many possibilities. Here are some more examples.

to spend money/time

to waste time/money

to waste and to save (opposites)

to fill in your diary

a flight is delayed

you can lose cash

last and next (opposites)

to book an appointment

you put cash in your account

Personal Study Workbook

3: *Saw* or *have seen*?

6: A time for everything

8: Messages

TIME'S UP!

Introduction

This lesson contains a grammar and vocabulary revision game. The sentences in the game are all connected to time in a structural or lexical way. (They are in Worksheet 21A on pages 136 and 137, for you to photocopy and cut up into cards.) There is a copy of all the sentences (without answers) in Worksheet 21B on page 138 to consolidate the activity at the end and to provide a written record.

Suggested steps

Divide the class into groups of four or five. Each group will need a dice, counters and a set of cards (Worksheet 21A) placed face down on the table. Explain the rules of the game to the class.

Player 1 throws the dice and moves the number of spaces shown on the dice. The player on his or her left then turns up the first card and reads the sentence on it. Player 1 has to say whether the sentence is correct or incorrect. If Player 1 is wrong, he or she moves one space back into the past. If Player 1 is right, he or she moves one space forward into the future, two spaces forward if he or she can correct an incorrect sentence. Players must also follow any instructions on the spaces on the board that they land on. However, if correcting an incorrect sentence results in the player moving onto a space that tells them to miss a turn or go back a certain number of spaces, they may ignore this instruction.

The winner is the first player to reach the Finish square.

Option

If you have any time left at the end of this lesson, you could use Worksheet 21C on page 139 which is a vocabulary revision game. Before the learners begin the exercise, let them check the meaning of any items they don't remember.

QUICK NOTES

This went well:

....

....

This didn't quite work:

....

....

Things to think about:

....

....

REVIEW AND DEVELOPMENT

REVIEW OF UNIT 19

1

Ask the learners to read the questionnaire before completing it, and answer any questions they have about unknown words. Then give them time to complete it individually. Remind them they can write their own answers if they wish.

Put them in groups to compare their answers, and monitor to collect examples of language points for feedback at the end. You could open the questionnaire up for whole class discussion before feedback on language.

Give them time to work in pairs on their own questions with three possible answers; monitor, assist and correct as necessary. Then ask them to mingle to ask their questions. At the end, in general feedback, ask them to tell the class any interesting results.

REVIEW OF UNIT 20

1

Follow the instructions in the Class Book. The learners may need to use dictionaries or ask you about a few vocabulary items.

Answer key

Note: Other connections are possible, so accept them if correct, although this will mean that some items are not used.

A doorbell sounds like an alarm.
Sugar tastes like honey.
Yoghurt tastes like sour cream.
Norwegian sounds like Swedish.
Some perfume smells like wild flowers.
Soap powder feels like fine sand.
Chilli tastes like pepper.
Some cheese smells like dirty socks.
A small horse looks like a donkey.
Some plastic looks like wood.
A computer keyboard looks like a typewriter.
Garlic tastes like onion.
Soft fur feels like velvet.

2 ▭

The best way to explain the first task is with an example. Write on the board:

A: *I like the smell of lemons.*
B: *So do I.*

Ask the class if A and B agree. Put a tick beside *So do I.* Then rub out *So do I* and write *Really? I don't.* Ask the class if there is agreement now, and this time put a cross next to the second sentence. From this, the group should get the idea.

Put the learners in pairs and ask one person in the pair to write down Bob's words, while the other writes down Rebecca's replies. Pause the recording as necessary. The pairs can then consult and decide how many times Rebecca agrees with Bob. Check the sentences and the answers with the group.

Answer key

The tapescript is on page 170. Rebecca agrees with Bob six times.

Next ask the learners about Rebecca's tone in replying. Does she sound bored or interested? How do they know? Play her replies again, pause the recording, and get the learners to reproduce the same tone and intonation. When you are happy with their pronunciation, move on to the final part of the exercise.

Go round and monitor the sentences before putting the learners in pairs for practice.

QUICK NOTES
This went well:
....
....
This didn't quite work:
....
....
Things to think about:
....
....

22

A SENSE OF HISTORY

```
┌─────────────────────────────────────────────────────────────────────┐
│                           CONTENTS                                    │
│                                                                       │
│   Language focus:    past simple passive                              │
│                      relative clauses with who and which              │
│                      link words: although and however                 │
│                      remember + -ing                                  │
│                                                                       │
│      Vocabulary:     historical event verbs: resign, assassinate, etc.│
│                        (conflict: enemy, prisoner, army, etc. in       │
│                        Worksheet 22b)                                  │
│                                                                       │
│          Skills:  Speaking:  talking about one's memories of history  │
│                              lessons                                   │
│                              retelling stories learners have read     │
│                              narrating a story from the past          │
│                   Listening: historical facts                         │
│                              anecdotal memories of history lessons     │
│                   Reading:   a text about children's rewriting of     │
│                              history                                   │
│                              texts on historical anecdotes            │
│                   Writing:   sentence transformations and completion  │
│                              a 50–60 word story                       │
└─────────────────────────────────────────────────────────────────────┘
```

HISTORICAL EVENTS

Introduction

The learners begin with a historical quiz which incorporates new vocabulary (historical event verbs). A listening activity enables them to check their answers to the quiz and to find out more about the events. They then focus on the active and passive voice and use the quiz for grammar practice. Towards the end of the lesson, attention is given to the use of passives in terms of information focus; this is followed by a practice activity.

Suggested steps

1 ▭

Let the learners complete the quiz in pairs using dictionaries to check the meaning of new verbs, or pre-teach yourself the items they do not know. If they do not know in which years the events happened, tell them to guess. This is not really a test of history.

Note that two of the verbs are irregular, so ask them to refer to their dictionaries or irregular verb list to check.

Option

We have devised the quiz with an international audience in mind. However, if you wish, you could write your own quiz, using historical facts from the country you are working in. Try to include examples which use the verbs in Exercise 1. This might be time-consuming, but would be a piece of material which you could probably use many times.

Ask pairs to compare their answers with other pairs, then play the recording to enable them to correct their answers. You may need to play it more than once, or pause it occasionally. This would be a good point at which to check that the learners can pronounce the verbs by asking them to say the sentences.

2 ▭

Give the learners time to read the questions. They are not expected to have remembered the answers; the instruction is rather to motivate them to listen again. After playing the recording, let them compare answers, then go over the answers together.

Answer key

1. 36 years.
2. It is one of Queen Elizabeth's official residences; £40 million.
3. Ben Johnson who came first in the race lost his medal because he had been using illegal drugs.
4. Rebel soldiers.
5. Mark Chapman.

3

Encourage the learners to analyse the examples of language and check their answers themselves in the Grammar Reference. We suggest you do this to encourage independence, though you may well feel it necessary to check that their understanding of the difference is accurate. If necessary, show active and passive together, for instance:

John Lennon was murdered in 1980.
Mark Chapman murdered John Lennon in 1980.

(That is, with the passive voice, something is done to someone, and the agent may not be important, or may not be mentioned. You are more interested in the person affected by the action.)

Highlight the form of the past simple passive:

was/were + past participle

and provide controlled oral practice of the two passive examples.

Answer key

Refer to the Grammar Reference on page 169.

4

Follow the instructions in the Class Book, and do one or two examples together as a class before they work individually or in pairs on the exercise. In feedback, focus on pronunciation and provide oral practice of the answers.

Answer key

Examples which can be changed:
3. 45,000 people were killed by an earthquake in Armenia.
4. Part of Windsor Castle was destroyed by fire.
5. The 100 metres gold medal was won by Carl Lewis in Seoul.
6. Lasers were invented by Theodore Maiman in 1960.
7. Boris Yeltsin was elected as President of Russia in 1991. (The agent is not necessary, and you might point this out.)

Example 8 cannot be changed and is a test example.

5

This looks at the issue of focus. Write the first example sentence on the board and ask the learners to tell you who stole the car. Eventually you should be able to elicit that we don't know the answer to that question because we are not told; and we are not told because we are more interested in the fact that the car was stolen (at this stage) than who took it. Write the second example on the board and elicit from the group why the person who stole the car is now mentioned: because the thief is someone connected with the family (this is of interest and clearly the information focus is different).

Do the first two questions together on the board, eliciting possible answers from the group, and then put them in pairs to work on the rest of the exercise in their books. Conduct a feedback at the end.

Answer key

Possible answers
1. A famous doctor gave her antibiotics when she arrived.
2. A masked terrorist assassinated the politician when he began his speech.
3. Rebel soldiers hijacked the plane on the way to Berlin.
4. The furious referee sent the player off for fighting.
5. The famous playwright Dennis Potter wrote the play for television.
6. A part-time postman delivered the money to the wrong address.

Personal Study Workbook

1: He was arrested outside the bank
4: From verb to noun
5: Word stress

QUICK NOTES

This went well:

....

....

This didn't quite work:

....

....

Things to think about:

....

....

REWRITING HISTORY

Introduction

Relative clauses are presented through sentences which refer back to the first lesson in the unit and revise some of the lexis. This is followed by a short practice activity, and then skills work dominates the rest of the lesson: a listening passage about history learnt at school, followed by a speaking activity in which learners talk about history they learnt at school, using *remember* + *-ing*; a short reading text about children's misinterpretation of history; and finally a brief writing correction activity.

Suggested steps

1

Revising work from a previous lesson makes a good warm-up activity, so you can go straight into the memory test. If for any reason you didn't do the previous lesson, this will obviously be a test of knowledge and not a test of memory, but the exercise can still be used.

Check the answers and then introduce the second part. You could ask the learners to underline *who* and *which* in the sentences and discuss their answers in pairs. Elicit their ideas in a class feedback and clarify the rule, perhaps by writing it on the board.

Answer key

Part 1
1. true   2. true   3. false: Watergate
4. false: Boris Yeltsin   5. false: 100 metres

Part 2
Who is used when the subject it refers to is a person, *which* is used for things and abstract nouns, but not people.

> ### Language Point: who and which as the subject of defining relative clauses
>
> When the subject of the main clause and the relative clause is the same, you do not repeat the subject in the relative clause:
>
> *The man who gave me the present was later arrested.*
> and not
> ~~The man who he gave me the present …~~

Ask the learners to complete the gap-fill and, after checking their answers, tell them to complete two sentences, perhaps with a partner. Monitor and correct their sentences. If you can monitor all the learners easily, do so; if not, monitor some of the group and ask the others to read out their sentences in feedback.

Answer key

Part 3
the woman who   the country which
the accident which   the book which
the Prime Minister who   the people who
the murder which

2 ▢▢ ▢▢

Choose the appropriate version of the listening and follow the instructions in the Class Book. Replay the recording as necessary. In feedback, you may wish to encourage the learners to use the phrases in Exercise 3: i.e. *He/she remembers learning …*, although this is not vital.

Answer key

Version 1
Speaker 1 remembers that life began in the sea; the wives of Henry the Eighth; the Wall Street Crash and the Depression in the States. He doesn't remember learning about the American Civil War or George Washington. He remembers studying the history of Ancient Greece and the Romans and about the Romans inventing a kind of central heating system.
Speaker 2 remembers some things about the Roman Empire.
Speaker 3 remembers the Vikings and the boats they used.
Speaker 4 remembers the Russian Revolution and Rasputin.

Version 2
Speaker 1 remembers the Aztecs in Mexico and King Henry the Eighth and his wives. She remembers nothing about modern history.
Speaker 2 remembers acts of parliament and kings and queens, but he remembers very little about the rest of the world, apart from a bit about France and Germany.
Speaker 3 doesn't remember dates or political events. She remembers learning about Ancient Egypt and the gods and also Stone Age Britain. She enjoyed the drawings and what people wore.
Speaker 4 remembers learning about the social and economic history of England, but she doesn't remember much about foreign history, apart from a bit about France.

3

Tell the learners they are going to talk about the history lessons they had at school, as in the recording, and ask them to look at the language suggested. Go over this, providing controlled practice and highlighting in particular the use of the *-ing* form after *remember*. Give a few examples of your own reminiscences using the phrases as a model, or elicit some from the class.

Give the learners time to recollect and think about what they are going to say before they work in groups. Monitor, collect examples of language points for feedback, and encourage the learners to use the phrases. In feedback, you could ask each group to report back on the most amusing points they have discussed, or, especially with a monolingual group, on any common historical facts they remember learning. Indeed, monolingual groups may have the most interesting differences in memories, since in many cases, the curriculum will have been the same. Provide feedback on language.

4

If any misconceptions about history have emerged from the previous activity, use them to introduce this exercise. Follow the instructions in the Class Book. You may wish to teach *inhabitant* from the verb *inhabit*, since both noun and verb occur in the reading and are crucial for an understanding of the text.

5

Ask the learners to read the introductory paragraph of the text, and check that they understand what the text is about. Pre-teach *nonsense* in the instruction. Then look together at the first example, and elicit whether it is true or not (obviously not) and if it is nonsense. (If your learners don't know Karl Marx or the Marx Brothers, tell them, but we assume that most learners will have heard of them.) You could also look at the second example, and elicit any corrections. Ask them to continue the exercise, and compare their ideas in groups. Conduct feedback at the end.

Answer key

Karl Marx was certainly no relation to the Marx Brothers who were American comedians in early Hollywood films.

Mummies are dead bodies which have been preserved, so they cannot *inhabit* anywhere. The *Sahara* Desert is what the child wanted to say, and they probably mean that Egyptians wrote in *hieroglyphics* (a system of writing using pictorial symbols).

William Tell shot an arrow at an apple which was on his son's head.

Magna Carta (a British charter/document from 1215) presumably didn't really think you could hang someone more than once. It stated that a person could not be tried twice for the same crime.

Inhabitants cannot live somewhere else – they live where they live.

Abraham Lincoln didn't build his house when he was a baby.

An *armadillo* is a South American animal. The navy fought against the Spanish *Armada* – a large fleet of warships – in 1588. (The time of Queen Elizabeth the First.)

The American Colonists no longer had to pay *taxes*, we assume.

Option

If your learners enjoyed the American children's mistakes, you could use Worksheet 22A on page 139, which contains some British children's mistakes. These are not just about history.

Answer key

Worksheet 22A
1. Not *artificial* but *evergreen*, although it is true that artificial trees don't lose their leaves.
2. An *autobiography* is a book written by oneself about oneself.
3. This should be an *octagon*.
4. This is nonsense.
5. Isaac *Newton* discovered gravity, and the rest is just silly!
6. Rats don't actually drink the coffee, though they might eat the beans.
7. Mosquitoes are small insects, and people from Moscow are called Muscovites.
8. Joan of Arc was no relation of Noah – and Noah built an ark, it wasn't his surname.

Personal Study Workbook

6: The fate of the Russian royal family – fact or fiction?
7: Dictation
8: Speaking partners

QUICK NOTES

This went well:

....

....

This didn't quite work:

....

....

Things to think about:

....

....

HISTORY YOU DON'T LEARN AT SCHOOL

Introduction

This lesson begins with short historical texts which the learners read and retell to each other. Link words *although* and *however* are then taught from the text and practised in an exercise. At the end of the lesson, the learners write an invented story from history together.

Suggested steps

Option

If you think your learners would find the vocabulary in Worksheet 22B on page 139 useful, use it with your class. Some of the vocabulary it contains occurs in the texts and elsewhere. We realise that in some contexts this focus might be painful and insensitive, so for this reason we have put it in the Teacher's Book, and left you to judge the suitability yourself. There is no doubt, however, that this is a very useful lexical set for many adults.

The learners could work in pairs with dictionaries to check new vocabulary and answer the questions. Alternatively, you could pre-teach a few items you think they might find more difficult before they do the exercise. In feedback provide some controlled oral practice to check that the learners can pronounce the items correctly.

Answer key

Worksheet 22B
1. You fight against the enemy.
2. If a bomb explodes, it might destroy buildings or hurt or kill people.
3. The people of that country are the victims: all members of the population.
4. Armies don't give secrets to the enemy (unless they are giving them false secrets).
5. Military prisoners are usually released after a war (though not always).
6. You can lose a battle and win a war: a battle is a fight and there may be many battles in a war.

1

Divide the learners into groups of three. If you have one or two learners left over, make one or two groups of four. Tell the class that the three people in each group are going to read a different text each, and then tell it to the others in their group. Tell them to read only one story, so that they will have an interest in listening to the other two. Either tell each group who should read each text or let them decide themselves. (If you have a group of four, tell two in the group to read the same text.)

An alternative procedure would be to put them again in groups of three, call each member of a group A, B or C, and allocate texts to be read. Before they begin to relate their stories, they could confer with someone who has read the same text as them (e.g. all As together, etc.).

Since these texts are quite authentic, they contain some vocabulary which will be new to learners. They need to read fairly intensively to be able to recode them, so do let them use dictionaries to check unknown words.

Organise them into groups for the recoding activity, making it clear that they don't have to repeat the text word perfect, but should explain the main information. Closing their books as suggested should help, though you could tell them that they can show the pictures quickly while explaining. Monitor the group activity, and assist any learners who are having particular difficulty in telling their story.

If you have picked up any problems of understanding while monitoring, clarify these in class feedback.

2

Give them a few minutes to decide in groups which they think is false.

Answer key

The second text is largely false. There was no hair illness, and this did not give rise to the introduction of wigs. However, people did wear goats' hair wigs at the time.

3

Ask the learners to follow the instructions. Check that they have underlined four examples of *although* or *however*.

Answer key

Although and *however* show a connection between two *contrasting* ideas, and they have more or less the same meaning as *but*.
Although links two ideas in one sentence and can go at the beginning or in the middle of the sentence.
However links two ideas in two separate sentences.

> ### Language Point: although and however
> The main difference between these connectors is that *although* links two contrasting ideas in one sentence (in a subordinate clause), whereas *however* normally links together ideas in separate sentences, or in main clauses linked by a semi-colon.
>
> Examples:
> *Although she missed the bus, she still got to the office in time.*
> *She still got to the station in time, although she missed the bus.*
> *She missed the bus. However, she still got to the office in time.*
> *She missed the bus. She still got to the office in time, however.*

It will be necessary to practise the pronunciation of *although* and *however* perhaps in isolation, then in sentences. Highlight also the rule in the Language Point above, and note the use of punctuation. You may also wish to contrast these items with the learners' mother tongue, especially for monolingual groups.

4

Elicit sentence completions for one or two examples, then ask pairs to complete them in their own way. Monitor and correct errors. At the end, you could ask the learners to read some of their sentences for the class to decide if they are logical or not.

Answer key

Possible answers
1. Although they lost the race, they were happy with their effort.
2. The illness can last a long time. However, people always get better from it / it is not very serious.
3. Although she wore a wig, nobody noticed.
4. Part of the town was destroyed. However, nobody was killed.
5. The police found the dead body, although they never found the gun.

5

In the final activity, ask the learners to identify the people/things in the pictures, and make sure they know words like *castle* and *princess*. Then go over the instructions in the exercise, and suggest that they spend about five minutes in the group developing a story orally before they start to write. They could work in groups of 3 or 4, and appoint one person to write while the others dictate. You would be wise to give them a time limit of ten minutes for the activity: almost certainly it will take longer, but this will give the learners an indication that they shouldn't spend an hour on it. (Unless of course you wish to develop it into a process writing activity with drafting, peer feedback, redrafting, etc.)

Monitor the groupwork, assisting where necessary. The amount of correction you do is very much up to you and your learners. Some people want to produce a completely accurate piece of writing, some are more concerned with simply creating a narrative.

Stop the activity when they are ready and ask one person from each group to move to another group to read their story to them. Alternatively, ask them to put their stories on the walls, and circulate to read each other's stories. Encourage peer feedback.

Option

Your learners might appreciate a photocopy of their group's story the following day, if you have access to these facilities. You could, if you wish, highlight some errors in their stories before copying them, and use these the following day as a correction exercise.

Personal Study Workbook

2: Lexical sets
3: More horrible history

```
┌─────────────────────────────────────────┐
│              QUICK NOTES                 │
│   This went well:                        │
│   .....................................  │
│   .....................................  │
│   This didn't quite work:                │
│   .....................................  │
│   .....................................  │
│   Things to think about:                 │
│   .....................................  │
│   .....................................  │
└─────────────────────────────────────────┘
```

REVIEW OF UNIT 20

1 ⊞

Follow the instructions in the Class Book for the listening activity. If you like, pre-teach the verb *remind* meaning *it makes me think of/remember*.

Answer key

burning wood: camping as a child.
cigar smoke: an uncle. He was rich, so the speaker associates cigar smoke with pocket money.
leather: a car with leather seats.
snakeskin: a briefcase.
mouthwash: the dentist.
cream: Sundays during childhood.
marble: Spain (the cold marble floors).

Ask the learners to practise the phrase *it reminds me of …* using the examples from the questionnaire as a class activity, before they work with a partner. Monitor the pairwork and provide feedback at the end.

2

Quickly go over the instructions and the examples as a revision of *will* and *might*, if necessary checking that they remember the meaning of *might* in particular. Let them read the words in the box and either explain any they don't understand, or let them check in dictionaries. Most items are revision, but a few are new.

Elicit some example sentences from the class relating to their next 24 hours, then ask them to continue in small groups. If appropriate, conduct a brief feedback on their answers at the end.

3

Demonstrate what to do with a learner in front of the class: explain the aim of the activity, and ask the learner questions till you find something true for the two of you, both negative and positive.

Example:
YOU: *Hiroko, can you swim?*
HIROKO: *Yes.*
YOU: *Oh, I can't. Can you drive?*
HIROKO: *Yes.*
YOU: *Me too. OK, so we can both drive.* (write it on the board) *How about sports. Tell me something you can't do.*
HIROKO: *I can't ski.*
YOU: *Oh, I can't ski either. So …* (elicit and write on board: *Neither of us can ski.*)

You may need to revise the meaning of *neither* briefly. Ask the learners to do the same activity, when appropriate noting a sentence with *both of us* or *neither of us*. They can do this orally or in writing.

When most pairs have found ten similarities, you could either ask them to tell a new partner about them (which would be a natural use of the structures) or ask them to tell the rest of the class in feedback.

REVIEW OF UNIT 21

1

Follow the instructions in the Class Book.

Answer key

For all of these, you will need to work out the answers yourself!

2

Follow the instructions in the Class Book. If you like, you could ask the learners to make up their own similar statements at the end to test each other.

Answer key

1, 3, 6, 7 and 9 used to be true.
2, 4, 5, 8 and 10 are still true. However, these facts may change in the future.

QUICK NOTES

This went well:

....

....

This didn't quite work:

....

....

Things to think about:

....

....

23

WHOSE LIFE IS IT ANYWAY?

CONTENTS

Language focus: adverbs of manner and adjectives
adverb word order
expressing preferences: *I'd rather do/I'd prefer to do*

Vocabulary: wordbuilding: nouns, verbs, adjectives, adverbs
social issues: politics, education, etc.
names and naming: family name, nickname, etc.

Skills: Speaking: easy and difficult choices
who influences your choices?
talking about your name
naming animals, houses, etc.
discussing factors in choosing a partner for life
discussing social issues

Listening: advice about choosing names for babies
people talking about factors in choosing a
partner for life

Reading: a text about daily routine

WHO CHOOSES?

Introduction

This lesson begins by asking the learners to discuss what they find easy and difficult to choose, then moves on to develop the theme of choice in our daily lives through a reading activity. The text is further exploited for focus and practice of adjectives and adverbs. Finally, the learners come back to the theme of choice and free will, and discuss who, if anyone, influences them in their daily choices.

Suggested steps

1

Pre-teach and check that the learners can pronounce the verb *to choose* (*chose/chosen*) and know the collocation *to have a choice* since they are likely to need these items throughout the unit. Then ask them to read the prompts for discussion, and check that they understand what to do. If necessary, talk briefly about those choices which you have problems with, saying why or giving examples. Then ask the learners to do the same with a partner. Monitor and conduct feedback on the content of the activity afterwards.

Option

You could ask the learners to add to the list in Exercise 1, saying any choices they find particularly difficult. Put these on the board, and ask them to include the topics when they are discussing the prompts in the book. Or if they prefer, discuss these instead.

2

As an introduction to the reading passage, ask the learners to look at the picture and discuss what is happening, how the person feels and why that might be. This will set the tone of the passage for them. Ask them to read the instructions and then to read the text, and compare in groups. There is likely to be some disagreement here over what constitutes choice, and this is to be encouraged. Conduct feedback at the end.

Answer key

Possible answers (but be prepared to accept others that can be justified)

1. Things the person chooses: to have a shower; to use the shower gel (but not which one); to drive to work (rather than take public transport); to go to the staff canteen; not to eat the vegetable soup; to drive home fast; to go to bed at 11 o'clock.
2. Things the person doesn't choose: the radio station; the clothes they're wearing; the kind of car they drive; the colleagues at work; the menu in the canteen; the TV programmes at home; the time to wake up the next morning.
3. Things in between: to work hard; to work late.

3

Ask the learners to work together. If necessary, put further examples on the board.

Answer key

Adjectives tell you more about a person or thing or state, for example, age, colour, character. They refer to nouns.

Adverbs of manner tell you how something happens or how it is done. They refer to verbs.

4

Follow the instructions in the Class Book.

Answer key

adjectives	adverbs
slow	slowly
quick	quickly
careful	carefully
clever	cleverly
lucky	luckily
hard	hard
fast	fast
stupid	stupidly
interesting	interestingly

Many adverbs of manner are formed by adding *ly* to the adjective.

Example: *slow – slowly*

Adjectives ending in *-y* change to *-ily*.

Examples: *lucky – luckily*
happy – happily

Adjectives ending in *-ful* change to *-fully*.

Example: *beautiful – beautifully*

Hard and *fast* are irregular, being the same form for adjective and adverb.

(*Hardly* has another meaning: = *almost not*.)

5

Follow the instructions, then divide the learners into pairs A and B. Tell the As to write an adjective in each sentence (1–6), and the Bs to write adverbs. Ask them to work alone or with someone doing the same thing (i.e. two As could work together). Monitor and correct any errors.

When they have finished, you could have a quick feedback to check by asking them to read out some of their sentences.

Now put the learners in A and B pairs, this time to compare sentences and to try to combine them as suggested. Demonstrate this first by eliciting an A and a B's first sentences and asking them to combine them. Sometimes their sentences will not make sense, so ask them to make them more realistic. Monitor and assist the pair activity.

When they have finished combining, either ask the learners to read out some combined sentences to the class, or put them with a new partner to exchange sentences.

6

Ask the learners to read the discussion points 1–10 and think for a few moments about who chooses these things in their life. Highlight the example expressions, clarifying the meaning if necessary, then elicit a few personal opinions from the class about the first topic. When you are sure the learners understand the activity, ask them to continue in groups. Monitor and collect examples of language (correct or incorrect) for feedback at the end.

Option

You could ask the learners to add more topics to the list in Exercise 6, to discuss with the others in their group.

If you run out of time, do the discussion in Exercise 6 as a warm-up next time you meet the class. You might want to ask them to think about it for homework, or write down a few thoughts on it.

Personal Study Workbook

2: *Careful(ly)*
7: Good morning

```
┌─────────────────────────────────────────────┐
│              QUICK NOTES                      │
│  This went well:                              │
│  ...........................................  │
│  ...........................................  │
│                                               │
│  This didn't quite work:                      │
│  ...........................................  │
│  ...........................................  │
│                                               │
│  Things to think about:                       │
│  ...........................................  │
│  ...........................................  │
└─────────────────────────────────────────────┘
```

CHOOSING A NAME

Introduction

This lesson centres on naming, beginning with our own names, nicknames and titles. After practice in stating preferences about names, the learners listen to a text which discusses suitable names for children. Finally, they invent their own names for pets, people and objects.

Suggested steps

1

The first two activities include items of vocabulary to do with names and naming. You may wish to pre-teach the following items, using your own name(s) and/or those of members of the class:

first name/Christian name
family name/surname
title (e.g. doctor, professor, Mr, Mrs, Miss, Ms)
nickname
to call someone by their first name / surname, etc.

Option

If you think it would be particularly useful for your class to explore this further, do Exercise 1 in the Personal Study Workbook. It includes speaking and listening on forms of address for different people, and the listening activity contains information which may be interesting cross-culturally.

> ### Language Point: Christian name
>
> We recognise that *Christian name* is a term which may surprise some nationalities, or in some cases offend. However, the term is a common lexical item in English, and learners may come across it on forms or in their reading. We suggest that if the subject arises, you can explain that nowadays most English speakers do not think of the religious origins of the word and that it is synonymous with first name. Nevertheless, do not ask learners who might be offended to practise it.
>
> If appropriate, tell the class to ask you the questions and answer them. Tell them they do not have to divulge anything they do not wish to. Then ask them to discuss the same questions in groups. Monitor and do feedback at the end.

Option

In different cultures around the world there may well be a wide range of questions one might ask learners to discuss on the subject of naming, e.g. *Are you named after anyone?* Adapt these questions to suit a monolingual group if necessary.

2

Pre-teach the structures *would rather do* and *would prefer to do* for expressing preferences. You could do this using your own examples (e.g. tell the class about two options you have for the weekend, having dinner with friends or going to the theatre, and say which you would rather do/prefer to do). Or use the first example: *I'd rather have / I'd prefer to have one first name.* Check that the learners understand the expressions through translation or by a check question: *Do I like one more than the other?* You could also give them a number of choices for controlled practice, using flashcards of two places, two types of food, two different drinks, etc., then elicit sentence responses.

Highlight the forms, especially noting the contraction 'd' for *would*, the presence of *to* with *prefer*, and the pronunciation of *rather*.

Use the prompts for some initial controlled practice of the structures. Ask the learners to ask questions to others across the class, encouraging them to follow up with the question *Why?*

Example: A: *Would you rather have one surname or two?*
B: *I'd rather have one.*
A: *Why?*
B: *Because it's easier.*

When you feel they are ready for it, ask them to do the exercise with a partner. Monitor and correct any errors, and if appropriate, have a quick feedback on their ideas at the end.

> ### Language Point: would prefer to do / would rather do
>
> In Exercise 2, we have kept the practice activity quite simple in terms of the language we expect the learners to produce. This is because expressing preferences can be quite complex syntactically.
>
> Once you introduce two elements of choice into a sentence, you need to use *than*:
>
> *I'd rather stay here than go out.*
> *I'd prefer to stay here than (to) go out.*
>
> *Prefer* in the simple tense is often followed by the *-ing* form, and two choices are linked by *to*:
>
> *I prefer gardening to cooking.*
>
> *Would rather* requires a past tense (as in the second conditional) if two different subjects are involved:
>
> *I'd rather he told me the truth than lied to me.*
>
> For these reasons, we suggest you limit the practice to sentences such as:
>
> *Would you rather have one first name or two?*
> *I'd rather have one.*

3

Refer the learners to the headline to see if they can explain it. Then ask them to read the paragraph and give their reactions as suggested in the Class Book.

4 ▭

Check that the learners understand what they have to write. They will probably need to listen two or three times if they are to make notes at the same time. You may wish them to listen the first time without taking notes, to encourage them to get a general understanding of the text. Don't worry about the spelling of names; an approximation will do, and don't expect them to get all the names.

Ask them to compare answers and do feedback.

Answer key

Jo-Ann's advice	*Examples*
1. Don't name a child after his father.	George Foreman
2. Don't give a child a joke name.	Lloyd Boyd
3. Don't choose strange names.	Seagull; America; Free; Chastity; Elijah Blue; Sage Moonblood
4. If your name is common, don't give children a common first name. Give them more distinctive names.	Jane Smith, John Jones Sigourney Weaver
5. Don't choose funny little (silly) names or animals' names.	Bitsy; Buffy; Fifi

After the listening activity ask the learners to comment on the advice in pairs and groups.

Option

Learners could be asked to add to the advice, particularly if there are factors in their own culture which are most relevant to naming. They could also swap examples of names of people they know which they find amusing or which are other examples of the strange names in the recording.

5

Learners will probably need to use their dictionaries to help them use suitable names. This is intended as an amusing end to the lesson, so encourage any humour. Follow the instructions in the Class Book and conduct feedback on the ideas at the end.

Option

As an activity to revise professions and link with the theme of the lesson, you could use Worksheet 23 on page 140. Follow the instructions on the worksheet.

Personal Study Workbook

1: What do you call them?
5: The origins of first names
6: Expressing preferences
8: Speaking partners

CHOOSING A PARTNER

Introduction

This lesson begins by introducing vocabulary to do with issues in society (politics, finance, religion, etc.) and focuses initially on wordbuilding. The vocabulary is then incorporated into a speaking activity on the importance of such issues when choosing a partner for life. Learners then listen to a recording of reactions on the same set of issues. Finally, some general issues on choice are discussed as a way of providing free speaking practice and rounding off the theme of the unit.

Suggested steps

1

Either pre-teach the meaning of items which are new for your learners, or ask them to check the meaning in dictionaries. Divide the class into As and Bs and ask the As to do the left-hand table and the Bs to do the right-hand table. (Learners doing a similar task can work together.) Before they begin their separate tasks, do one example from each table together.

After A and B pairs have compared answers, go over them together. You will almost certainly need to highlight and practise the pronunciation (particularly word stress which you could mark on the board over the stressed syllables for the learners to copy). Oral drilling is the obvious answer and you could then ask them to test each other in pairs:

Example: A: *What's the adjective from finance?*
       B: *Financial.*

Answer key

Stressed syllables are underlined.

Noun	Adjective	Noun	Verb
finance	financial	choice	to choose
religion	religious	advice	to advise
education	educational	marriage	to get married
politics	political	belief	to believe
culture	cultural	comparison	to compare
society	social	divorce	to get divorced

2

Ask the learners to read the table and explain anything they do not understand. Then ask them to complete the table alone. Explain that in groups they should discuss their ideas and give their reasons.

Note: Respect the views of any learner who for whatever reason does not wish to speak or give their opinion on one of the topics.

While the learners are comparing in groups, monitor and collect any interesting examples of language for feedback at the end. This is a challenging task for the level, and be ready to praise communication as long as it takes place!

Option

If a group finishes early, ask them to think of more factors which might affect your choice of partner.

3 ⬚⬚⬚

After feedback on the activity (content and language) play the appropriate recording(s): version 1 and/or 2, and follow the instructions in the Class Book. You know your class best, so how much detail you can expect them to understand is up to you. However, they should all be able to say which subjects are mentioned and whether they are important or not. Do feedback at the end of the activity.

Answer key

Version 1
The speaker talks about interests, finance, education and coming from different countries.
Similar interests and hobbies: very important; if you only have a little free time, it's better to spend the time together doing things you both like.
Similar financial situation: not very important; can help each other.
Similar education: very important to be able to speak to each other on the same level.
Same country: quite important; coming from different countries can be exciting but can cause problems culturally.

Version 2
The speaker talks about interests, food, politics and education.
Similar interests: very important; he likes going to the theatre and cinema and he wants a partner to share the same interest.
Similar food: important to him as he is vegetarian, but maybe not for the partner.
Similar political views: quite important to have similar views.
Similar education: not very important; education comes after leaving school; being the same sort of people is the most important thing.

4

Give the learners time to read and ask if they do not understand any of the questions. Tell them to choose questions which interest them most, then discuss them, again in small groups. Monitor and collect language points for feedback. Give them an opportunity for an open forum of discussion at the end, but beware of letting a few learners dominate. Either encourage others to speak, or bring the forum to an end, since everyone should by this stage have had plenty of opportunity to express themselves.

Option

You could make a worksheet of the language examples you collect (say 8–10) and give the learners a photocopy the following day to study and correct where necessary. Be sure to include examples of good use of language, and tell the learners that not all the sentences have errors in them. In our experience, learners are highly motivated by this kind of activity.

Personal Study Workbook

3: Politics and religion
4: Sounds and spelling

```
┌─────────────────────────────────────┐
│            QUICK NOTES              │
│                                     │
│  This went well:                    │
│  ...............................    │
│  ...............................    │
│                                     │
│  This didn't quite work:            │
│  ...............................    │
│  ...............................    │
│                                     │
│  Things to think about:             │
│  ...............................    │
│  ...............................    │
│  ...............................    │
└─────────────────────────────────────┘
```

REVIEW AND DEVELOPMENT

REVIEW OF UNIT 21

1 ⬚⬚

Pause the recording after each sentence so that pairs can consult on the number of words. You can then elicit answers, and when you have a correct answer, play the recording again for the group to write down the sentence. Check the answers at the end of the exercise.

Answer key

See the tapescript on page 172.

2

Before the learners complete the task, you could point out that a few of the questions are factual and have a clear concrete answer, but most of them are a matter of personal opinion. When the learners have finished the first task, they could work in pairs on the second part in which they add one more question to each section.

Follow the instructions in the Class Book for the final part of the exercise.

REVIEW OF UNIT 22

1

Follow the instructions in the Class Book. At the end, you could ask the class to explain the significance of the exercise title. And you may wish to point out that it has become a kind of fixed expression in British English, and is normally used with reference to someone's resignation. The implication is clearly that the person resigned because the alternative was getting the sack.

Answer key

1. was invented
2. was won
3. died
4. were released
5. became
6. were destroyed
7. was arrested
8. threw

2

Follow the instructions in the Class Book.

Answer key

Part 1
1. which
2. who
3. which
4. who
5. who
6. which
7. who
8. which

Part 2
Possible answers
1. wig
2. John Kennedy; Robert Kennedy; Martin Luther King
3. a bat
4. a postman; a milkman; a newspaper delivery boy; a florist
5. It is impossible to provide a fixed answer to this, but the learners should be able to provide examples from their friends or public life (perhaps themselves).
6. See 5.
7. See 5.
8. *Oliver Twist; War and Peace*

QUICK NOTES

This went well:

....
....

This didn't quite work:

....
....

Things to think about:

....
....

24

CINEMA AND THE ARTS

CONTENTS

Language focus: present simple active and passive
past simple active and passive
present perfect simple
be able to + verb; *good at* + *-ing*

Vocabulary: cinema, theatre, music, artistic jobs
adjectives describing people

Skills: Speaking: talking about jobs you like and hate
discussing best films/actors of all time
comparing cinema-going in different places
Listening: people describing jobs they could or couldn't do
a quiz about the Oscars
Reading: a text about the Oscars
a questionnaire about cinema going
Writing: preparing a quiz

CREATIVE PEOPLE

Introduction

The first part of the lesson practises a lexical set of professions associated with the arts, before the learners go on to discuss the qualities needed for these professions using the target structures for the lesson (*be able to* and *good at* + *-ing*). This is consolidated through a listening passage, and the lesson finishes with a personalised speaking activity in which the learners talk about the jobs they would personally like or hate.

Suggested steps

1

You could begin by asking the class if they can identify the people in the pictures and name their jobs. From this, move into the table and get the learners in pairs to complete as much as possible. Conduct a feedback at the end, and ask them to go back and mark the main stress on each of the professions. Check and practise around the class.

Answer key

Possible answers

Person	What they do	Example
novelist	writes novels	John le Carré
opera singer	sings in operas	Maria Callas
painter	paints pictures	Rembrandt
film director	directs films	Akira Kurosawa

Person	What they do	Example
poet	writes poems	John Keats
composer	writes/composes music	Mozart
photographer	takes photographs	Henri Cartier-Bresson
musician	plays music	anyone in an orchestra
actor	acts	Meryl Streep
conductor	conducts an orchestra	Georg Solti
fashion designer	designs clothes	Coco Chanel
sculptor	makes sculptures	Eduardo Chillida
architect	designs buildings	Antoni Gaudi

For the practice activity, demonstrate with several learners first and mix up both question types – this not only provides practice of nouns and verbs, but also ensures that the listener has to pay attention. Put the class in pairs for further practice and monitor.

Option

You could also use this activity to revise relative clauses by adding a further question for the pair to practise, for example:

Give me the name of someone who writes novels.

2

Direct the learners to the three sentences and ask each person to write down the name of the job being described. Discuss their answers, then choose another job and elicit ways of finishing the sentences using the target structures. If there are problems, you can then explain the structures more carefully. You will need to highlight the use of the *-ing* form after a preposition.

Answer key

a novelist

When you are happy that your learners are clear about the form and meaning of the target structures, let them write similar descriptions for another pair to guess. If you like, they could write descriptions of several jobs. At the end some of the pairs could read out their sentences for the whole class to guess.

3 ▭

Ask the learners to look at the photos, and see if anyone knows what a holographer does. If they don't, which is quite possible, give them a quick explanation, i.e. a holographer makes holograms, which are three-dimensional photographic images created by laser beams. Clarify the meaning of *costume designer*, then explain the task, i.e. that they will hear the speakers talking about other jobs and whether they would be good at them or not. They may need to listen to the recording two or three times.

Answer key

Nickie
1. fashion designer: yes
2. photographer: no
3. architect: yes, possibly
4. painter: yes – but not a good one

Martin
1. architect: no
2. photographer: yes
3. fashion designer: no
4. painter: yes – but not a good one

4

In the final activity, you could demonstrate what you want the learners to do by giving your own examples using *I'd like to be … / I'd love to be … because … .* Highlight the *'d*. Elicit a couple of examples from the class, then ask them to discuss in groups. Monitor and collect language points for feedback at the end.

Option

Tell the learners to think about their own lives, their jobs and hobbies. Which of the jobs in Exercise 1 relate to them?

Personal Study Workbook

2: Theatre and cinema
4: First names in English
5: The artistic process

```
QUICK NOTES

This went well:
...................................................
...................................................

This didn't quite work:
...................................................
...................................................

Things to think about:
...................................................
...................................................
```

THE OSCARS

Introduction

The opening reading text on the Oscars is also the basis for a listening activity and language revision on a range of tenses. At the end of the lesson, the learners have an opportunity for free speaking, again linked to the subject of Oscars.

Suggested steps

1

Follow the instructions in the Class Book.

Answer key

The statue is an *Oscar* which is an award given to people in the film industry (the best film, the best director, the best actor, etc.). The award ceremony takes place every year in Los Angeles.

This would be a good point to teach the words *award* (noun and verb), *prize* and *ceremony*. A *prize* is given for an achievement such as coming first, second or third in a race/competition; an *award* is given also in competition, but can be something a person receives as a result of an official decision, e.g. *She was awarded $10,000 as compensation for the accident.*

2

Introduce the text and emphasise that they should read carefully and remember as much as possible. The learners should have access to dictionaries to look up new words; if they are not available, you may decide to pre-teach/check the meanings of *nomination*, *category*, *postpone* and *cancel*, although these words will not interfere with the learners' ability to answer later questions on the text.

---

3 ▭

After reading the text, move straight into the listening. Make sure all books are closed, and pause the recording after each question to give the learners time to consider and choose their answer. At the end, let them compare with a partner before they open their books to check their answers. The tapescript is on page 172.

4

This is also based on the text, so ask your learners to cover the text while they answer the questions. You could begin by asking them to give you examples of the four tenses they should choose from in order that you can find out if they are familiar with all the forms.

Once again, let them check with a partner before they refer back to the text. Move round and find out what each learner has written, and this will tell you which concepts may require further consolidation. If there are particular problems you could go straight to one of the tense exercises in the Personal Study Workbook and/or the Review and development section.

Answer key

1. was formed; were chosen; are chosen
2. are selected
3. has won; collected
4. was postponed; postponed
5. has won
6. won

5

We have only suggested that the learners choose one example from music, special effects and costume design, because we are not sure how knowledgeable they will be about the cinema. You will obviously know much more about your class and you could increase the categories or leave them out altogether. Follow the instructions in the Class Book.

Option

If the class are quite interested in cinema, you could follow up with Worksheet 24 on page 140, which tests knowledge of films alongside teaching the names of a number of different animals.

Answer key

Worksheet 24
1. *Dog Day Afternoon*
2. *Crocodile Dundee*
3. *The Silence of the Lambs*
4. *Duck Soup*
5. *Lord of the Flies*
6. *A Fish Called Wanda*
7. *Planet of the Apes*
8. *The Deer Hunter*
9. *Batman*
10. *The Elephant Man*

Option

Here is another idea for a follow-up to the lesson on Oscars. This is an activity called Classroom Oscars. Each member of the group has ten minutes to do one of the following:
– write down a joke
– draw something
– make something
– make up a story
– prepare a song (that they are going to sing)

They can do these things individually or in pairs. In some cases, learners may want to be on their own; others may want the extra security of a partner. Move round and assist with the stories, jokes and songs; and look at the drawings or objects that people have made (origami is very popular among Japanese learners). Then bring the class together and elicit what categories there are, e.g. best joke, best picture, best song, etc. Ask each person or pair to perform/show their work and then let the group decide on the best of each category.

Personal Study Workbook

1: Test your knowledge
3: Crossword
6: Playing in a band

```
┌─────────────────────────────────────┐
│            QUICK NOTES               │
│  This went well:                     │
│  ..................................  │
│  ..................................  │
│  This didn't quite work:             │
│  ..................................  │
│  ..................................  │
│  Things to think about:              │
│  ..................................  │
│  ..................................  │
└─────────────────────────────────────┘
```

CINEMAS AND THEATRES

Introduction

The lesson begins with a group of lexical items connected to cinema and theatre, in preparation for an extended speaking activity in which the learners compare cinema-going in different towns and/or countries. The lesson finishes with the learners writing their own quiz on cinema, theatre or music.

Suggested steps

1

This is a warm-up activity, although it could go on for quite a long time. Move round, monitor the conversations and make notes. You may find a number of lexical items the learners clearly want but don't know, and you could teach them at the end of the activity.

2

Put the learners in pairs or groups so they can share their knowledge. Most new items can be retrieved from a dictionary, but if the learners are unable to guess/work out the meaning of *continuous performance* and *numbered seats*, you may have to explain. Check the answers with the class, and practise the pronunciation of *aisle* /aɪl/, *curtain* /kɜːtn/ and *audience* /ɔːdiəns/.

Answer key

These answers are true for the UK but may be different in other countries.

Cinema only	Theatre only	Cinema/Theatre
continuous performance	stage	to book seats
subtitles	numbered seats★	curtain
adverts	interval★	box office
screen	to clap	aisle
trailers		audience
dubbing/dubbed		

★It is possible to have an interval and numbered seats in cinemas in the UK but not that common.

3

Ask the class to read through the questionnaire to check that they understand the questions. You should check their pronunciation of *advertisement* /ədvɜːtəsmənt/, and it is also worth highlighting the use of *common* in several questions. A very common utterance from learners of English is *It's very usual in my country (to book seats in advance)*. This does not sound natural in English, and most native speakers would almost certainly prefer to use *common* in this context.

Put the learners in groups to discuss their answers. This might lead to some very interesting cross-cultural differences in a multilingual group, but in a monolingual situation with learners from one country the topic may not generate as much discussion. If that is the case, you could introduce additional questions or even a different questionnaire for the group to consider. For example: What differences are there between cinemas in their town? Which do they prefer and why? Have they been to cinemas elsewhere that were very different? What makes a good cinema? Are there more cinemas in the town compared with ten years ago, or fewer? Obviously the type of questions you ask will depend on your own environment, but there should be some questions of interest wherever you work.

4

Allow the learners to decide whether they want to write questions about cinema, theatre or music, and then organise the three groups accordingly. Move round and monitor while the groups prepare their questions and help where necessary.

You could stage the quiz with the whole class. One group asks their questions and the other two groups write down answers. The next group asks their questions, and so on. After all three groups have asked their questions, you can go through the answers and see who has the most right. Award points if you feel the class would enjoy this kind of competitive element.

Personal Study Workbook

7: Film diary
8: Speaking partners
9: Visual dictionary

```
QUICK NOTES

This went well:
.............................................
.............................................

This didn't quite work:
.............................................
.............................................

Things to think about:
.............................................
.............................................
```

REVIEW AND DEVELOPMENT

REVIEW OF UNIT 22

1

Follow the instructions in the Class Book.

Answer key

1. crashed; killed *or* hurt *or* injured
2. hijacked; release
3. recognise; got up *or* stood up
4. battle; wounded *or* injured *or* hurt
5. assassinated *or* killed *or* injured; exploded *or* went off
6. died; illness

2

You could try to elicit from the class four sentences from *live* and *parents* using the four different constructions. If any pose problems, highlight the examples given in the book. Get the learners to complete the rest of the activity, and emphasise that they should be true sentences. At the end they can compare their answers with a partner, or they could mingle in groups and exchange answers. At the end, collect examples from the class to check grammatical accuracy.

Answer key

Possible answers

1. I usually write at least two letters every week.
   I'm writing a letter to my accountant at the moment.
   I wrote a letter to my sister last week.
   I haven't written a letter this week.
2. I spend a lot of money every week on food.
   Are you spending much money at the moment?
   I spent a lot of money yesterday.
   I've spent a lot of money this month.
3. I always work hard.
   I'm working very hard at the moment.
   I didn't work hard last week.
   I've worked very hard this week.
4. I have lunch at 1 o'clock.
   I'm having lunch with my mother.
   I had pasta for lunch yesterday.
   I've had pasta for lunch every day this week.
5. I usually drive to work.
   I'm not driving to work at the moment.
   I drove to work last week.
   I've driven to work twice this week.

REVIEW OF UNIT 23

1

You will need to go through the sentences to check that the learners understand. Do that before you explain the purpose of the exercise, otherwise the immediacy of the choice they have to make will be lost.

When the vocabulary is clear, explain what they have to do and put them in pairs to complete the activity. At the end you could go round the class with a few more examples.

2

Follow the instructions in the Class Book. Check the eight mistakes with the group before they complete the second part of the activity. At the end, let the pairs read their stories to another pair.

Answer key

1. It should be *he cuts hair beautifully*.
2. It should be *He's always very polite*.
3. It should be *he works hard*.
4. It should be *Ray just listens patiently*.
5. It should be *makes suggestions gently*.
6. It should be *He always behaves extremely professionally*.
7. It should be *he's quick*.
8. It should be *and he's never late*.

QUICK NOTES

This went well:

....

....

This didn't quite work:

....

....

Things to think about:

....

....

WORKSHEETS

WORKSHEET 2

Ask the right question

1. Here are some questions you could hear in a railway station. Some of them are correct, but others have mistakes in them. Can you find the mistakes and correct them? Compare your ideas with a partner.

1. How long does it takes from London? ....

2. How often the trains run in the morning? ....

3. How far is it to Dover? ....

4. What train is quicker – the 9.00 or the 11.00? ....

5. How much is the supplement for first class? ....

6. Do you know where is platform 5? ....

7. How many trains are there in the morning? ....

8. Is the 9.00 train stop at Amiens? ....

9. What kind of reduction is there for students? ....

10. How much costs a return? ....

2. Now write your own answers to the questions above on another piece of paper. Invent any answer you like.

3. Memorise the questions, then turn the paper over.

4. Work in groups. Give your answers to others in the group. See if they can remember the questions.

WORKSHEET 3

How good is your sense of direction?

Do you ever confuse left and right? Do you know where north is? Read through the statements on the left and put your score in the column on the right.

	(I can't do it.)				*(It's very easy.)*
	1	2	3	4	5

1. I can draw a clear map to show someone the way to my house from here.

2. I can follow street maps easily.

3. I can find my way around in a new place easily.

4. I can use my watch to find out which direction north is.

5. I can use a compass.

6. If I get lost in the countryside, I can find where I am on a map.

7. I can use the stars to work out my direction.

8. I can find my way around the building we are in now in the dark.

Tell your partner your score. Find out who has the best sense of direction in the group.

Total

WORKSHEET 5

Are you in good condition?

Answer the questions and use the time expressions on page 31 of the Class Book.

1. Do you ever do the following things? If so, how often?
   – do breathing exercises
   – do aerobics
   – go for a run
   – do yoga

2. How often do you
   – run upstairs?
   – run for a bus?
   – leave the car at home and walk to your destination?
   – use stairs instead of a lift?

3. When did you last
   – play an energetic physical game?
   – walk more than 4 km in a day?
   – go on a bicycle ride?
   – do some serious swimming?

4. How long do you spend
   – sitting at a desk?
   – sitting in front of the television?
   – outside in the fresh air every day?
   – in smoke-filled rooms?

TRUE TO LIFE PRE-INTERMEDIATE   © Cambridge University Press 1995

WORKSHEET 6

useful	useless	progressive	traditional	interesting
boring	old	modern	wide	limited
nice	unpleasant	easygoing	strict	hardworking
lazy	good	poor	large	small

TRUE TO LIFE PRE-INTERMEDIATE   © Cambridge University Press 1995

WORKSHEET 7

Discussion about handwriting

Discuss these questions in any order in small groups.

1. Do you like your handwriting? If not, what do you want to be different about it?

2. How do you sign your name? Is it easy to read?

3. What can you remember about first learning to write?

4. Are there any professions in your country which are famous for good or bad handwriting?

5. Do you think examiners should give lower marks in exams for bad handwriting or spelling or punctuation mistakes?

6. Should you complete a job application form using a typewriter or by hand? Why?

WORKSHEET 8

Where can you buy these things? There is more than one possibility. Work with a partner, and use a dictionary if necessary.

Example: *You can buy chewing gum in a sweet shop, a newsagent's, a supermarket, at a kiosk, sometimes in a chemist's.*

Which is the best place to buy each of these? Why? (Don't think only of the cheapest place!)

Work with another pair and compare your answers.

WORKSHEET 9

What do you know about wine?

1. Read the statements below. Write *True*, *False* or *Don't know* for each one.

1. White wine is made from white/green grapes and red wine is made from red/black grapes. ....

2. You should store wine on its side like this. ....

3. You shouldn't fill a wine glass more than half full. ....
4. Most red wine gets better if you keep it for at least a couple of years. ....
5. You should generally serve red wine at room temperature. ....
6. You should always open a bottle of red wine at least an hour before you drink it. ....

7. You should serve champagne in a glass like this.

....

8. You should never serve red wine with fish. ....
9. If you open a bottle of red wine and drink just a little, you can put the cork back in and it will keep for a few days. ....
10. If you eat a meal in a restaurant, you have to order a bottle of wine. ....

Compare your answers in small groups.

2. Read the questions and add two more questions of your own for discussion.

1. At what age can you buy/drink alcoholic drinks in your country? Do you think this is the right age? Or is alcohol not permitted at all?
2. What are the laws about drinking and driving in your country? Do you agree with them?
3. How do you feel if you see people drunk around you?
4. Do you think it is acceptable for people to drink during working hours?
5. ....?
6. ....?

Work in small groups and discuss all six questions.

When you have finished, tell the rest of the class your group's opinions.

TRUE TO LIFE PRE-INTERMEDIATE   © Cambridge University Press 1995

WORKSHEET 10

Think about the activities in the box and divide them into four groups: those you love, those you like, those you don't mind and those you hate.

> getting letters from very old friends
> people arriving to stay with you unexpectedly
> children you don't know talking to you in public places
> sending and receiving greetings cards
> phoning companies (airlines, stations, etc.) to get information
> walking into a roomful of strangers at a party
> meeting your old school teachers
> receiving phone calls late at night
> having a party with all your family and relations
> making appointments with the doctor, dentist, etc.
> complaining about a meal in a restaurant
> standing next to strangers in a crowded train or lift

Now write one more sentence of your own for each category.

Work with two or three other people. Compare your answers and tell them why you like, hate or don't mind these things.

TRUE TO LIFE PRE-INTERMEDIATE   © Cambridge University Press 1995

WORKSHEET 11

Work in small groups. Think of as many advantages and disadvantages as possible for these weather conditions.

Example: *Windy weather is good for* **drying wet clothes, sailing, windsurfing, windmills**
is not good for **cycling, your hairstyle, playing golf**

Hot sunny weather is   good for ....
                        not good for ....

Heavy rain is   good for ....
                        not good for ....

Fog is   good for ....
                        not good for ....

Thunderstorms are   good for ....
                        not good for ....

Cold weather is   good for ....
                        not good for ....

TRUE TO LIFE PRE-INTERMEDIATE   © Cambridge University Press 1995

WORKSHEET 12

1. Valentine cards are not the only cards we send. There are also:

Christmas cards
Birthday cards
Good luck cards
Anniversary cards
Congratulations cards
Get well cards
Bereavement cards
Mothers' Day cards

Check that you understand these. Can you think of any other cards you send?

2. What type of card would you send to the people in these situations? Compare your answers with a partner.

1. Kate and Simon who got married exactly two years ago.
2. Linda who is 26 tomorrow.
3. A colleague of yours who has just broken her leg.
4. Your mother. Next week is December 25th.
5. Tony who is taking his driving test next week.
6. Christine and Jim who have just had a baby girl.
7. A friend whose wife has just died.
8. A friend who has just got his degree in law.

3. Write some messages to other people in the group on different pieces of paper. Then give them your messages.

Examples: *To a classmate who is taking an exam next week:*

> *To Enzo,*
> *Good luck with your exam! I hope you pass.*
> *Best wishes, Carla*

To another classmate who has a birthday tomorrow:

> *To Yumi, wishing you a very happy birthday,*
> *love from Hitomi and Erica.*
> *See you at the party.*

TRUE TO LIFE PRE-INTERMEDIATE © Cambridge University Press 1995

Match the verbs with the pictures, and make a sentence describing each one.

to get on something
to get off something
to get in(to) something
to get out of something
to pick something up
to put something down
to put something in (something)
to take something out (of something)
to turn something on
to turn something off

Work with a partner. Think about a journey from the beginning to the end. Continue this story using all these verbs.

When I was packing my suitcase, I took my clothes out of the wardrobe and put them …

TRUE TO LIFE PRE-INTERMEDIATE © Cambridge University Press 1995

WORKSHEET 14A

General Knowledge Quiz

Fill the gaps in the sentences using information in the box. Be careful: there are more suggestions in the box than you need. Work with a partner.

1967	Rio de Janeiro	Steffi Graf	1990	USA	1960	Argentina	17th	Arabic
6	1920	Brasilia	1978	Chinese	Finland	9	Japan	the 1920s
Belgian Congo	Italians	Martina Navratilova	Ecuador	1981	São Paolo	13th
The Gold Coast	the 1820s

1. Zaire has been independent since .... Before that, it was called ....

2. The woman tennis player who has won the highest number of Wimbledon finals titles since the Second World War is .... She has won the championship .... times, winning it for the first time in ....

3. .... has been the capital of Brazil since 1960. Before that it was ....

4. Spectacles have been in existence since the .... century, when they were invented by the ....

5. Turkey has used Roman script since .... Before that, the script that was used was ....

6. Sweden has driven on the right since .... Before that, it drove on the left, like Britain and ....

7. Greece has been a member of the EU (then called the EEC) since ....

8. Women have been able to vote in the USA since .... In Latin America, the first country to give women the vote was .... in 1929.

Ask your teacher for the answers. Score one point for each gap correctly filled. Which pair has the highest score?

TRUE TO LIFE PRE-INTERMEDIATE © Cambridge University Press 1995

WORKSHEET 14B

Look at the list in the box. When people replace these items, is it usually because they *need* to replace them, or just because they *want* to replace them? Is there any reason to possess more than one of each? Discuss in groups.

video camera	washing machine	car	tyre	computer	toothbrush	watch
watch strap	umbrella	wallet	iron	telephone	television	suitcase	handbag
pens and pencils

TRUE TO LIFE PRE-INTERMEDIATE © Cambridge University Press 1995

Read the text and answer the question.

A DANISH HEARING AID MANUFACTURER DECIDED THE WAY AHEAD WAS TO GET RID OF ALL PAPER. SO THEY DID!

A few years ago the Danish hearing aid manufacturer Oticon made some radical decisions about the way it ran the company and organised its offices. First, the company tried to get rid of all paper. The Accounts Office kept folders and ring binders, and employees could have a few personal files, but everything else went into the shredder and most information is now stored on computer. And out with the paper went most of the desks and filing cabinets.

Next, the company got rid of individual job responsibilities. When employees arrive at work, they collect their own personal trolley with essential files, and then they decide what job they want to do. There are some limits here: if you don't have the technical qualifications there are some jobs you can't do. Generally though, the aim is a team of all-rounders and not a number of individual specialists. 'There is nothing more expensive and time-consuming than trying to co-ordinate a group of specialists,' says managing director, Lars Kolind. In this way an engineer might do some market research, and an economist may teach people how to fit a new hearing aid. And if there are no special job responsibilities, then employees don't have their own special desks. People decide where they want to sit when they arrive in the morning.

The company also decided to get rid of the traditional management hierarchy. At Oticon decisions are taken by the team on a consensus basis.

Make notes on the important changes with your opinion of each one.

Major changes   *Good or bad?*

1. ....

2. ....

3. ....

4. ....

Compare your answers in groups.

TRUE TO LIFE PRE-INTERMEDIATE © Cambridge University Press 1995

WORKSHEET 17

1. What kind of pictures do people usually take? Put the following categories in order (1–8) from the most common to the least common. Remember, it is people in general, not yourself.

Family ☐   Familiar places, e.g. your flat, a hotel you stayed at, etc. ☐

Friends ☐   Landscapes, e.g. the sea, the countryside ☐

Animals ☐   Famous buildings and monuments ☐

Plants and flowers ☐   Unusual or interesting people, places or objects ☐

2. Interview other members of the class who have cameras and find out if your order is the same as theirs.

TRUE TO LIFE PRE-INTERMEDIATE © Cambridge University Press 1995

WORKSHEET 18

Here are two rather unusual lists. Read them using a dictionary if necessary. Then complete the two lists with a partner.

TEN BEST PIECES OF ADVICE

Never give your telephone number to an insurance salesman.
Never agree to 'try something a bit different' at the hairdresser's.
Never buy clothes that are a bit small hoping that you will lose weight.
Never buy a hamburger at a funfair.
Never put the snacks and peanuts on the table before your guests arrive for dinner.
Never go on holiday with friends for longer than a week.
Never buy a white car.

....
....
....

THE TEN MOST USELESS THINGS TO DO IN THE WORLD

Saying 'Come on! Hurry up!' to a red traffic light.
Shouting at your horse while watching a horse race on television.
Writing in a letter, 'I hope I've got your address right'.
Looking at the hi-fi while listening to a cassette, record or CD.
Saying 'and this is the bathroom' when you are showing people round your house.
Changing to a different queue in the post office.
Making gestures when you are talking on the telephone.

....
....
....

Tell another pair your ideas.

TRUE TO LIFE PRE-INTERMEDIATE © Cambridge University Press 1995

WORKSHEET 19

1. Try to guess the meaning of the underlined words and phrases. Sometimes you can guess the exact meaning, and sometimes only the general meaning. If you cannot explain the meaning in English, write a translation.

1. It was a very funny joke and we all started <u>giggling</u>.
2. It's a very interesting book. I was <u>fascinated</u> by it.
3. When we got back after the storm the flat was <u>flooded</u>; there was about 20 centimetres of water in the kitchen and the dining room.
4. I love <u>cabbage</u>, but it's not my sister's favourite vegetable.
5. He was trying to open the bottle with this knife, and I'm afraid he <u>bent</u> it.
6. He arrived late for work every day, so his boss <u>gave him the sack</u>.
7. Most people were here on time, but Carlos didn't <u>turn up</u> until after ten o'clock.
8. I think the <u>cardigan</u> goes very well with that shirt and tie.
9. She <u>spilled</u> her coffee all over me, so I had to wash my shirt and jeans immediately.
10. I thought the film was <u>appalling</u>, but I believe it has been very successful.
11. Our flight was <u>held up</u> for three hours because of bad weather.
12. She told me the ring cost fifty pounds, but I think it's probably <u>worth</u> more than that.
13. He has been very ill but he's <u>getting over it</u> now.
14. When the bus arrived, everyone started to push and <u>shove</u>.
15. The economic situation is still very bad. Over five hundred companies <u>went bankrupt</u> last year.

Compare your answers in groups.
Now check your answers in a dictionary or with your teacher.

TRUE TO LIFE PRE-INTERMEDIATE   © Cambridge University Press 1995

WORKSHEET 20

Write an example next to each of the adjectives on the mind map. Compare your answers with others.

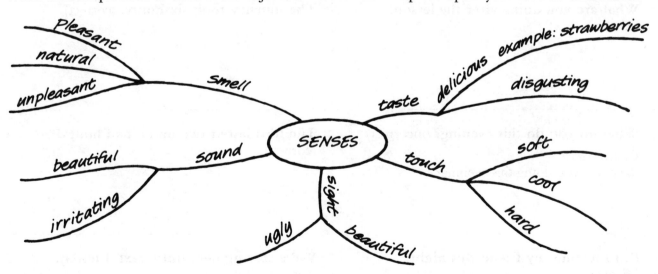

Work with a partner. Create another mind map around a different topic, and then show it to others in the group.

TRUE TO LIFE PRE-INTERMEDIATE   © Cambridge University Press 1995

I'll be at this hotel for another week.
(correct)

How long time have you been a doctor?
(incorrect)

Correct sentence:
How long have you been a doctor?

I arrived here two days before. (incorrect)

Correct sentence:
I arrived here two days ago.

What does she do after work? (correct)

I've been here during six months.
(incorrect)

Correct sentence:
I've been here for six months.

I go often to the cinema at the weekend.
(incorrect)

Correct sentence:
I often go to the cinema at the weekend.

I am here since yesterday. (incorrect)

Correct sentence:
I have been here since yesterday.

She's getting married the day before yesterday. (incorrect)

Correct sentence:
She got married the day before yesterday.

What are you doing after the lesson?
(correct)

The journey took six hours. (correct)

What do you do this evening? (incorrect)

Correct sentence:
What are you doing this evening?

The film lasted two and a half hours.
(correct)

I'm meeting my friend this night.
(incorrect)

Correct sentence:
I'm meeting my friend tonight.
or: I'm meeting my friend this evening.

We're staying here until next Tuesday.
(correct)

He's here from 7 till 10 every day. (correct)

I haven't seen her this morning. (correct)

I spent an hour to wash the car. (incorrect)

Correct sentence:
I spent an hour washing the car.

My little sister is two years. (incorrect)

Correct sentence:
My little sister is two.
or: My little sister is two years old.

I went there for my holidays the last year. (incorrect)

Correct sentence:
I went there for my holidays last year.

I always clean my teeth before to go to bed. (incorrect)

Correct sentence:
I always clean my teeth before going to bed.

I answered the phone as soon as it rang. (correct)

I'll tell him when I will see him. (incorrect)

Correct sentence:
I'll tell him when I see him.

I've seen him yesterday. (incorrect)

Correct sentence:
I saw him yesterday.

My car was stolen while I was at the travel agent's. (correct)

I'm going to work hard; I don't want to lose my time. (incorrect)

Correct sentence:
I don't want to waste my time.

We can leave whenever you like. (correct)

I saw all my family in Christmas. (incorrect)

Correct sentence:
I saw all my family at Christmas.

Some machines save a lot of time. (correct)

TRUE TO LIFE PRE-INTERMEDIATE © Cambridge University Press 1995

These are the sentences from the game you played. Were they correct or not? If not, correct them.

I'll be at this hotel for another week.

I arrived here two days before.

I've been here during six months.

I am here since yesterday.

What are you doing after the lesson?

What do you do this evening?

I'm meeting my friend this night.

How long time have you been a doctor?

What does she do after work?

I go often to the cinema at the weekend.

She's getting married the day before yesterday.

The journey took six hours.

The film lasted two and a half hours.

We're staying here until next Tuesday.

He's here from 7 till 10 every day.

I spent an hour to wash the car.

I went there for my holidays the last year.

I answered the phone as soon as it rang.

I've seen him yesterday.

I'm going to work hard; I don't want to lose my time.

I saw all my family in Christmas.

I haven't seen her this morning.

My little sister is two years.

I always clean my teeth before to go to bed.

I'll tell him when I will see him.

My car was stolen while I was at the travel agent's.

We can leave whenever you like.

Some machines save a lot of time.

TRUE TO LIFE PRE-INTERMEDIATE   © Cambridge University Press 1995

WORKSHEET 21C

Word Game

Do this exercise in small groups. Each person in turn must choose two words which are connected in some way.

Examples: *waste and time. You can waste time if you don't spend it well.*
calendar and diary. They both tell you the date.

The group must decide if each answer is acceptable. Continue until you cannot think of any more connections and all the words have been used at least once.

spend	delay	flight	late	diary	cash	lose
book	account	cancel	early	next	last	waste
time	save	money	fill in	appointment	calendar	course

WORKSHEET 22A

Are these British children's mistakes nonsense or can they be corrected?

1. Trees that stay green all year round are called artificial.
2. An autobiography is a book about cars.
3. Oxygen has eight sides.
4. To germinate is to become a German.
5. Gravity was discovered by Isaac Walton. You can see it best in the autumn when the apples are falling off the trees.
6. In India, rats eat 20% of the rice crop. In Brazil, they drink 20% of the coffee.
7. The inhabitants of Moscow are called Mosquitoes.
8. Joan of Arc was Noah's sister.

WORKSHEET 22B

Vocabulary of conflict

Answer these questions with a partner. Use a dictionary to help you.

1. Do you fight against the enemy or your friends?
2. What happens if a bomb explodes?
3. Who are the main victims in a civil war?
4. Does an army usually give secrets to the enemy?
5. In a war, when are military prisoners released?
6. Can you lose a battle and still win a war?

WORKSHEET 23

Look at the list of jobs below and make sure you know the meaning and the correct pronunciation.

| farmer | lawyer | plumber | novelist | pilot | florist | butcher | banker | carpenter |

From the following list, choose the best name for each of the jobs above.

| James Wing | Ken Wood | Jill Court | Pat Cash | |
| W C Leak | Rose Thorn | Larry Lamb | Frank Field | Arthur Page |

Example: *Frank Field the farmer.*

Work with a partner. Try to think of funny names for people in different professions, then tell the class.

Suggestions for jobs:

| doctor | decorator | army officer | teacher | shoe repairer | chef |

WORKSHEET 24

Animals and films

1. Complete these film titles with the names of the animals in the pictures.

1. .... Day Afternoon

2. .... Dundee

3. Silence of the ....

4. .... Soup

5. Lord of the ....

6. A .... called Wanda

7. Planet of the ....

8. The .... Hunter

9. ....man

10. The .... Man

2. Choose a category for each of the films from the following:

| war film | comedy | drama | science fiction | horror film |

3. Can you think of any more films with names of animals in the title? Translate them into English and tell your partner.

ROLE CARDS

WAITER/WAITRESS

You are a polite and professional waiter/waitress but you are very busy tonight and you may get a little bit impatient with customers who cannot decide quickly.

Unfortunately the lobster is no longer available this evening but in its place you have crab.

There is a vegetarian dish of the day, which is aubergine and tomato gratin (that's aubergine and tomato with grilled cheese on top). It may take a little longer to prepare than the other dishes.

The restaurant has a good wine list, but no half-bottles. However, you serve wine by the glass, if requested.

Be prepared to answer questions from your customers.

CUSTOMER 2

You always find it very difficult to choose things in a restaurant and you often want extra information about the dishes, e.g. Does the dish have a sauce? Is there very much garlic in the dish with snails? Is the duck well-cooked or quite rare? Are there other sorbets in addition to mango? etc.

CUSTOMER 1

You are a vegetarian and you are surprised and disappointed that the restaurant does not have a vegetarian main dish. You are also on a diet.

CUSTOMER 3

You are not very hungry and don't want a starter, but you love lobster. You are also very keen on wine, and you would like to have half-bottles of white and red to go with the different dishes.

TESTS

1 Questions   10 marks

Complete these questions with the correct word.

1. How .... money have you got?
2. How .... books do you need?
3. .... you have a good journey?
4. What .... of car has she got?
5. .... you like a cup of coffee?
6. How .... is the station from here?
7. .... is their flat like?
8. .... you like your job?
9. .... you seen Carlos?
10. How .... are you planning to stay?

2 Tense review   10 marks

Underline the correct answer in brackets.

1. She (*comes / is coming*) from Australia, but she (*works / is working*) in New Zealand at the moment.
2. I can't go out very much because I (*revise / am revising*) for an exam.
3. I usually (*spend / am spending*) about £5 a month on books.
4. The company (*makes / is making*) electrical appliances.
5. Go away. I (*read / am reading*) a newspaper.
6. (*Did you do / Have you done*) your homework last night?
7. I (*arrived / have arrived*) ten days ago.
8. (*Did you ever write / Have you ever written*) a short story?
9. I (*had / have had*) three meetings this week.
10. Last month I (*saw / have seen*) five films.

3 Adjectives   10 marks

Write opposites for these words.

1. tidy – ....
2. hardworking – ....
3. efficient – ....
4. positive – ....
5. rude – ....
6. organised – ....
7. pleasant – ....
8. useful – ....
9. interesting – ....
10. do well – do ....

4 Parts of the body   8 marks

Label the pictures.

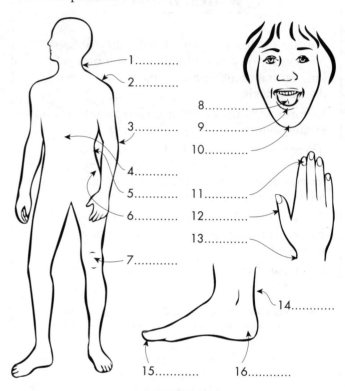

1 ....
2 ....
3 ....
4 ....
5 ....
6 ....
7 ....
8 ....
9 ....
10 ....
11 ....
12 ....
13 ....
14 ....
15 ....
16 ....

5 Word order   5 marks

Make sentences from these words.

1. ever/go/the/I/hardly/cinema/to

....

2. home/of/the/weather/stayed/because/we/at/bad

....

3. know/the/do/station/where/is/you?

....

4. you/when/could/train/tell/arrives/us/the?

....

5. tired/so/I/to/went/was/bed/I

....

6 Verb + noun collocation   10 marks

Complete the sentences with the correct verb.

1. I often .... mistakes.
2. I didn't .... my homework.
3. Do you ever .... your nails when you're nervous?
4. Have you ever .... in a play?
5. Did you .... in the last election?

TRUE TO LIFE PRE-INTERMEDIATE   © Cambridge University Press 1995

6. I .... the children when their mother is at work.

7. I'm .... a course at the moment.

8. I'm afraid she .... the exam, so she will have to take it again.

9. I .... a lot of time at school because I didn't do any work.

10. We .... cards every week.

7 Directions   10 marks

Complete the text.

.... along this road and .... left into Brooklands Avenue. Then .... going, ... the cinema, until you .... to a .... Go .... across, take the second .... on your right, and the hospital is .... the end of the road on the left- .... side.

8 Prepositions   10 marks

Complete the sentences with the correct preposition.

1. The books are .... the desk.

2. I usually sit .... a desk when I'm working.

3. She's not very good .... English.

4. Is he interested .... classical music?

5. I can't stop; I'm .... a hurry.

6. I prefer to work .... silence.

7. We stayed .... home because .... the bad weather.

8. Do you often sit .... the floor?

9. I always lock the door .... night.

9 Grammar   8 marks

Correct the mistakes in these sentences. (There is one in each sentence.)

1. The film was quiet good.

....

2. I must take some pictures before to leave.

....

3. How much people were there?

....

4. She went there for buy some shoes.

....

5. I introduced me to the guests.

....

6. We might to see a film.

....

7. How is the film like?

....

8. I go often to the park.

....

10 Common phrases   6 marks

Complete these dialogues. Each space is one word.

1. A: .... going to a restaurant, this evening?

   B: Yes, good idea. Perhaps we .... try that new French restaurant.

2. A: .... you like to go out tonight?

   B: Yes, I'd .... , but I'm afraid I'm busy.

3. A: Sorry to .... you waiting.

   B: That's OK.

4. A: How old are you?

   B: I .... not say.

11 Street vocabulary and pronunciation   8 marks

Add a word to each of these words to form nouns. Then underline the compound word where the stress is on both parts of the compound.

high-rise ....

parking ....

pedestrian ....

traffic ....

litter ....

car ....

bus ....

department ....

12 Pronunciation and listening   5 marks

Circle the underlined sound which is different from the others in each group.

1. f<u>ou</u>nd   backgr<u>ou</u>nd   s<u>ou</u>venir   l<u>ou</u>nge

2. st<u>o</u>mach   c<u>o</u>st   l<u>o</u>ve   rec<u>o</u>ver

3. b<u>oo</u>k   cart<u>oo</u>n   l<u>oo</u>k   f<u>oo</u>t

4. fount<u>ai</u>n   p<u>ai</u>nt   str<u>aigh</u>t   portr<u>ai</u>t

5. w<u>ea</u>pon   br<u>ea</u>d   br<u>ea</u>st   br<u>ea</u>k

Total = 100 marks

1 Professions 10 marks

Here are some definitions. What are the jobs?

1. They design buildings.
2. They fly planes.
3. They write books.
4. They wear and demonstrate designer clothes.
5. They treat sick animals.
6. They operate on people in hospital.
7. They repair pipes and problems with water.
8. They tell funny jokes.
9. They run shops which sell medicine.
10. They represent the views of people, especially in parliament.

2 Wordbuilding and pronunciation 10 marks

Complete the table. Then mark the main stress on each of the nouns.

Adjective	Noun
reliable	....
honest	....
imaginative	....
popular	....
sensitive	....
self-confident	....
intelligent	....
political	....
responsible	....
humid	....

3 Tense review 15 marks

Underline the correct answer in the brackets.

1. A: What (*do you do / are you doing*) this weekend?
   B: I (*'m going to / 'll*) visit some friends.
2. A: It's very dark in here.
   B: OK. I (*'m going to / 'll*) turn on the light.
3. A: Peter (*is staying / will stay*) with us next week.
   B: Oh, great. How long (*will he / is he going to*) stay?
   A: I don't know. I(*'ll ring / 'm ringing*) him now and ask him.
4. The books (*publish / are published*) in Germany.
5. We (*grow / are grown*) the vegetables in our garden.
6. I (*cooked / was cooking*) breakfast when he (*rang / was ringing*).
7. I (*went / was going*) to bed quite early, but I couldn't get to sleep because someone (*played / was playing*) very loud music next door.
8. When I (*left / was leaving*) home it (*rained / was raining*), so I (*took / was taking*) an umbrella.

4 Spelling 6 marks

Correct the spelling mistakes in this text.

Dear Grandma,

I'm writting to thank you for the wonderfull bycicle you gave me for my birthday. It's what I've allways wanted and I'm going to ride it evry day during my holyday. Mum bought me a helmet to wear – it isn't really necesary, but she says it's importante.

Last week we went to Wales and climbbed a mountain wich was great. Stephen is biger than me but I got to the top first. Next week we're going to a forrest. It should be fantastic.

Love,

5 Food vocabulary 10 marks

Identify the things in the picture.

6 Comparatives and superlatives 10 marks

Complete the table.

Adjective	Comparative	Superlative
big	....	....
beautiful	....	....
careful	....	....
clean	....	....
good	....	....
bad	....	....
happy	....	....
modern	....	....
more		....
less		....

TRUE TO LIFE PRE-INTERMEDIATE © Cambridge University Press 1995

TESTS

7 Modal verbs: have to, don't have to, mustn't, should(n't) 10 marks

Complete the sentences with one of the above verbs.

1. The doctor said he .... smoke or drink.
2. We .... work on Saturdays, but some people do.
3. In my country you .... do military service for one year.
4. If you don't feel well, you .... have a rest.
5. You .... leave milk in the sun for very long.
6. I wore a uniform five years ago, but we .... wear one now.
7. You .... drink if you are going to drive.
8. You .... keep fruit in a cool place.
9. You .... eat too much sugar or salt.
10. If you drive a car, you .... have insurance in most countries.

8 Infinitive or –ing form? 6 marks

Are these verbs followed by -ing or by an infinitive?

enjoy   want   refuse   decide   don't mind
promise   can't stand   imagine   avoid   hope
expect   regret

9 Shopping 6 marks

Complete this dialogue. You need one word for each space.

A: Could I .... on this suit please?

B: Yes, the .... room is just down there.

A: Right. Thanks.

B: How's the suit?

A: Well, the trousers .... quite well round the waist but I'm afraid they're not long

....

B: And the jacket?

A: I'm afraid it's .... small. Do you have it in a bigger ....?

B: No, I'm afraid not.

10 Compound nouns 5 marks

Match words from the left with words from the right to form ten compound nouns.

writing	conditioning
art	lotion
light	heating
thunder	paper
washing	shirt
air	gallery
short–sleeved	bulb
suntan	storm
central	assistant
sales	powder

11 Prepositions and adverbs 6 marks

Complete the sentences with the correct word.

1. It was hot so I took .... my jacket.
2. When we left the cinema it was pouring .... rain.
3. We may get there .... time; it depends .... the traffic.
4. I decided to give .... sweet things and go .... a diet.
5. We listened .... her story .... silence.
6. I could see the church .... the distance.
7. She's very keen .... tennis.
8. He fell .... love while he was .... holiday.

12 Pronunciation 6 marks

Circle the odd one out in each group.

1. pro<u>m</u>ise   de<u>c</u>ide   qu<u>i</u>te   m<u>i</u>nd
2. ar<u>ch</u>itect   <u>ch</u>emist   s<u>ch</u>ool   wat<u>ch</u>
3. c<u>ou</u>ntry   c<u>ou</u>ple   r<u>ou</u>te   en<u>ou</u>gh
4. <u>u</u>mbrella   h<u>u</u>mid   <u>th</u>under   s<u>u</u>ntan
5. plu<u>mb</u>er   re<u>m</u>e<u>mb</u>er   la<u>mb</u>   thu<u>mb</u>
6. kn<u>ow</u>   gr<u>ow</u>   t<u>ow</u>el   bl<u>ow</u>

Total = 100 marks

1 Tense review   10 marks

Underline the correct words in the brackets.

1. I (*live* / *'ve lived*) here (*for*/*since*) fifteen years.
2. She (*worked* / *has worked*) in the bank for five years and then she (*went* / *has gone*) into the police force. She (*is* / *has been*) there (*for*/*since*) 1992.
3. I (*had* / *'ve had*) this watch since I (*was* / *'ve been*) ten years old.
4. If I (*see* / *'ll see*) Tom, I (*give* / *'ll give*) him your message.
5. We (*get* / *'ll get*) there in time if we (*hurry* / *'ll hurry*).

2 Vocabulary   16 marks

Identify the objects in the picture and organise them into four groups below. Give each group a heading using a general word. For example, *fruit* would be a general word for *apple, orange, banana*.

....
1. ....   4. ....
2. ....   5. ....
3. ....   6. ....

....
7. ....   10. ....
8. ....   11. ....
9. ....   12. ....

3 Use of articles   10 marks

Complete the sentences with *the*, *a*, *an*, or no article.

1. We saw .... Mount Everest as we passed over .... Himalayas.
2. I met .... interesting woman on the way to .... station.
3. We drove across Canada from .... Lake Michigan to .... Pacific Ocean.
4. My sister bought me .... CD for my birthday because she knows that I love .... music.
5. It was at .... Odeon Cinema but I can't remember what .... film was called.

4 Opposites   10 marks

Write opposites for these words.

polite   ....
knowledgeable   ....
badly dressed   ....
friendly   ....
full   ....
confusing   ....
legal   ....
delighted   ....
comfortable   ....
reliable   ....

5 Plural and uncountable nouns   8 marks

Underline the correct words in the brackets.

1. We need (*an*/*some*) information.
2. My (*trouser is* / *trousers are*) in the bedroom.
3. Her (*luggage is* / *luggages are*) very heavy.
4. Could you give me some (*advice*/*advices*).
5. Your pyjamas (*is*/*are*) in the cupboard.
6. The equipment (*was*/*were*) excellent.
7. Some people (*is*/*are*) here already.
8. I must get some travel (*insurance*/*insurances*).

6 Verb + noun   10 marks

Match the verbs on the left with the nouns on the right.

shake   the gas
wear   insurance
wait   hands
do   someone a tip
take out   your turn
lock   a flight
book   your nose
turn off   a uniform
give   the door
blow   your packing

TRUE TO LIFE PRE-INTERMEDIATE   © Cambridge University Press 1995

7 Pronunciation   10 marks

1. Underline the silent letter in each of these words (excluding the final 'e'):

   island   castle   receipt   aisle   fasten

2. Mark the stress on these words:

   Japan   electricity   insurance   accommodation   museum

8 Phrases and phrasal verbs   8 marks

Each space in these sentences represents one word. Complete the sentences with suitable phrases.

1. A: I'm sorry I'm late.

   B: .... That's OK.

2. A: How old was he?

   B: I'd say he was at .... 20, but not more than 25.

3. A: How many passed the exam?

   B: Everyone, ... Marcel.

4. A: Did they catch the thief?

   B: No, he ....

5. A: What time do you want to meet?

   B: Uh, ... 7.30?

   A: Yes, that's fine.

6. A: Did she go with friends?

   B: No, I think she went ....
   ....

7. A: The plane .... ten minutes early, but it still landed ten minutes late.

8. A: Can I help you with that suitcase?

   B: Oh, that's ....
   .... Thank you.

9 On the phone   5 marks

Correct the mistakes in this dialogue.

A: Hello.
B: Oh, is it Olga?
A: No, my name is Denise.
B: Oh, could I speak with Olga, please?
A: Yes. One moment.
C: Hello.
B: Hello, Olga. Here is Dieter. How are you?
C: Thank you. And you?
B: I'm fine. Listen Olga, what do you do tonight?

10 Link words   5 marks

Complete these sentences with a suitable link word.

1. We'll stay at home .... the weather is bad tomorrow.

2. We must go now .... we'll be late.

3. I bought a portable computer .... I could work on the train.

4. I'll phone him .... I get home.

5. Could you look after my dog .... I'm away?

11 Verbs   8 marks

Complete these sentences with a suitable verb.

1. A: Does this suitcase .... to you?

   B: No, it's not mine.

2. This lesson .... one hour.

3. The journey to work .... me half an hour.

4. A: How often do the buses ....?

   B: Every ten minutes.

5. I always .... my money in a money belt.

6. We want a quiet holiday, so we will try to .... crowded places.

7. I always .... lots of picture when I go on holiday.

8. Bill came into the room but I didn't ....
   him without his beard.

Total = 100 marks

1 Tense review and verb forms   15 marks

Put the verbs in brackets into the correct tense.

1. The man (take) to the police station last night and detectives (interview) him this morning. Two hours later he (release).
2. They (grow) a lot of coffee but most of it (export).
3. The letters (send) to the wrong address and nobody (realise).
4. I'll tell him when I (see) him.
5. Do you think it (rain) this afternoon?
6. I (see) that woman before.
7. She (arrive) ten days ago.
8. The children (go) to stay with their grandmother.
9. I (listen) to rock music all the time when I (be) younger, but now I much prefer jazz.
10. I remember (go) to the seaside when I was a little girl.

2 Adjectives ending –ed and –ing   6 marks

Choose the correct adjective in the brackets.

1. I was (bored/boring) for most of the film.
2. I think she found the situation very (embarrassed/embarrassing).
3. It's a (fascinated/fascinating) book.
4. The children were very (disappointed/disappointing) with their results.
5. We were (shocked/shocking) when we heard the news.
6. The weather is very (depressed/depressing) at the moment.

3 Conditional sentences   6 marks

Complete these sentences with a suitable verb in the correct form.

1. If I .... my wallet, I would go to the police.
2. If I .... the match tomorrow, I'll be delighted.
3. If he .... from the job, it will be very difficult to find someone else with his knowledge and experience.
4. I'd earn more money if I .... longer hours.
5. He would tell me if he .... the answer.
6. If it .... my car, I'd sell it.

4 Sense verbs   8 marks

Complete the sentences with a verb in the box or a verb in the box + like.

sound   smell   taste   feel   look

1. This perfume .... sweet.
2. That noise .... a flute.
3. Cats' fur .... velvet.
4. Marble .... cold.
5. Lemons .... limes.
6. My brother .... one of my cousins.
7. This soup .... salty.
8. That piano .... awful.

5 Wordbuilding   10 marks

Complete the table.

Verb	Noun
compare	....
complain	....
believe	....
advise	....
choose	....
educate	....
invent	....
die	....
imagine	....
explain	....

6 Agreeing   8 marks

Agree with these statements using so or neither.

1. I like lemon.
2. I don't like chocolate.
3. I'm a bit disappointed.
4. I can't speak Norwegian.
5. I love hot weather.
6. I'm not angry.
7. I didn't want to go.
8. I can swim.

7 Pronunciation   9 marks

Mark the stress on these words.

vegetable   supermarket   develop   fascinating escape   accident   photographer   musician colleague

8 Time expressions 6 marks

Correct these sentences.

1. I'm going to Australia the next year.
2. We met yesterday night.
3. We are meeting again this night.
4. My birthday is the sixteen of July.
5. I spent two hours to do my homework.
6. I've been here during six months.

9 Arts vocabulary 10 marks

Organise these words into three groups and give each one a title. (Two or three words can go in more than one group.)

> subtitles   director   audience   composer   actor
> dubbed   conductor   play   film   orchestra   clap
> stage   musical instrument   trailer   screen

10 Adjectives and adverbs 8 marks

Underline the correct words in the brackets.

1. It's a (beautiful/beautifully) evening.
2. I've worked very (hard/hardly) this month.
3. He closed the door (quiet/quietly).
4. She's always (polite/politely).
5. I had a (quick/quickly) shower.
6. She drove very (fast/fastly).
7. It was a (slow/slowly) race.
8. He (careful/carefully) opened the door.

11 Link words 8 marks

Complete the sentences with a suitable link word or relative pronoun.

1. .... there was a lot of traffic, we still arrived early.
2. Take an umbrella .... you might get wet.
3. The first part of the book was a bit slow. ...., I enjoyed the rest of it.
4. Nurses work very hard .... they don't earn a lot.
5. She gave up her job .... she could spend more time with her children.
6. That's the man .... gave us the money.
7. Have you read the book .... won the prize?
8. There are some people .... never stop talking.

12 Expressions 6 marks

Add one word to each sentence to complete a common expression.

1. I'm sorry to .... you, but do you know where I can buy a newspaper near here?
2. A: Are you waiting for a bus to the centre?
   B: Yes.
   A: Well, I'm going to the centre. Can I give you a ....?
3. He's in a bad .... today because he left some books on the bus, and then he had an argument with the driver.
4. I had to get up early so I .... the alarm for 6 o'clock.
5. I liked the book to some ...., but there were certain parts I didn't like.
6. A: Would you like to see a film?
   B: Actually, I'd .... stay at home.

Total = 100 marks

TEST ANSWER KEYS

1 Questions

1. much   2. many   3. Did   4. kind/sort/type   5. Would
6. far   7. What   8. Do   9. Have   10. long

2 Tense review

1. comes/is working   2. am revising   3. spend   4. makes
5. am reading   6. Did you do   7. arrived
8. Have you ever written   9. have had   10. saw

3 Adjectives

1. untidy   2. lazy   3. inefficient   4. negative   5. polite
6. disorganised   7. unpleasant   8. useless   9. boring
10. badly

4 Parts of the body

1. neck   2. shoulder   3. elbow   4. stomach   5. waist
6. hip   7. knee   8. tongue   9. lip   10. chin   11. nail
12. thumb   13. wrist   14. ankle   15. toe   16. heel

5 Word order

1. I hardly ever go to the cinema.
2. We stayed at home because of the bad weather.
3. Do you know where the station is?
4. Could you tell us when the train arrives?
5. I was tired so I went to bed. *or* I was so tired I went to bed.

6 Verb + noun collocation

1. make   2. do   3. bite   4. acted   5. vote   6. look after
7. doing   8. failed   9. wasted   10. play

7 Directions

Go; turn; keep; past; get *or* come; roundabout; straight;
turning *or* road; at; hand

8 Prepositions

1. on   2. at   3. at   4. in   5. in   6. in   7. at; of   8. on
9. at

9 Grammar

1. The film was *quite* good.
2. I must take some pictures before *leaving*.
3. How *many* people were there?
4. She went there (in order) *to buy* some shoes.
5. I introduced *myself* to the guests.
6. We might *see* a film.
7. *What* is the film like?
8. I *often go* to the park.

10 Common phrases

1. How about; could   2. Would; love to   3. keep
4. 'd (would) rather

11 Street vocabulary and pronunciation

1. high-rise building   2. parking meter
3. <u>pedestrian crossing</u>   4. traffic light (or traffic jam)
5. litter bin   6. car park   7. bus stop (or bus station)
8. department store

12 Pronunciation

1. souvenir   2. cost   3. cartoon   4. fountain   5. break

1 Professions

1. architects   2. pilots   3. authors/writers   4. models
5. vets   6. surgeons   7. plumbers   8. comedians
9. chemists *or* pharmacists   10 politicians

2 Wordbuilding

relia<u>bi</u>lity	self-<u>con</u>fidence
<u>ho</u>nesty	in<u>te</u>lligence
imagi<u>na</u>tion	<u>po</u>litics
popu<u>la</u>rity	respons<u>i</u>bility
sensi<u>ti</u>vity	hu<u>mi</u>dity

3 Tense review

1. are you doing; 'm going to
2. 'll (will)
3. is staying; is he going to; 'll ring
4. are published
5. grow
6. was cooking; rang
7. went; was playing
8. left; was raining; took

4 Spelling

wri<u>t</u>ing	nece<u>ss</u>ary
wonder<u>ful</u>	important
<u>bicycle</u>	clim<u>b</u>ed
a<u>l</u>ways	w<u>h</u>ich
ev<u>e</u>ry	bi<u>gg</u>er
holi<u>d</u>ay	fo<u>r</u>est

5 Food vocabulary

1. garlic   2. carrots   3. onion   4. strawberry
5. pineapple   6. peach   7. pepper   8. mushrooms
9. lemon   10. aubergine   11. cabbage   12. lettuce
13. prawns   14. knife   15. fork   16. melon   17. potato
18. avocado

6 Comparatives and superlatives

bigger	the biggest
more beautiful	the most beautiful
more careful	the most careful
cleaner	the cleanest
better	the best
worse	the worst
happier	the happiest
more modern	the most modern
	the most
	the least

7 Modal verbs

1. mustn't (or shouldn't)   2. don't have to   3. have to
4. should   5. shouldn't   6. don't have to   7. mustn't
8. should   9. shouldn't (or mustn't)   10. have to

8 Infinitive or –ing form?

enjoy + *-ing*   want + infinitive   refuse + infinitive
decide + infinitive   don't mind + *-ing*
promise + infinitive   can't stand + *-ing*   imagine + *-ing*
avoid + *-ing*   hope + infinitive   expect + infinitive
regret + *-ing*

9 Shopping

try; changing (fitting); fit; enough; too; size

10 Compound nouns

writing paper	air conditioning
art gallery	short-sleeved shirt
light bulb	suntan lotion
thunderstorm	central heating
wa<u>sh</u>ing powder	sales assistant

11 Prepositions and adverbs

1. off   2. with   3. in; on   4. up; on   5. to; in   6. in
7. on   8. in; on

12 Pronunciation

1. promise   2. watch   3. route   4. humid   5. remember
6. towel

1 Tense review

1. 've lived; for
2. worked; went; has been; since
3. 've had; was
4. see; 'll give
5. 'll get; hurry

2 Vocabulary

Jewellery	Animals (or Pets)	Musical instruments	Furniture
1. earrings	4. parrot	7. flute	10. sofa
2. necklace	5. horse	8. guitar	11. wardrobe
3. ring	6. rabbit	9. saxophone	12. bookcase

3 Use of articles

1. (–); the   2. an; the   3. (–); the   4. a; (–)   5. the; the

4 Opposites

impolite/rude	ignorant
well dressed/smart	unfriendly
empty	clear
illegal	miserable/unhappy/sad
uncomfortable	unreliable

5 Plural and uncountable nouns

1. some   2. trousers are   3. luggage is   4. advice   5. are
6. was   7. are   8. insurance

6 Verb + noun

shake hands	lock the door
wear a uniform	book a flight
wait your turn	turn off the gas
do your packing	give someone a tip
take out insurance	blow your nose

7 Pronunciation

1. i<u>s</u>land   ca<u>st</u>le   recei<u>p</u>t   ai<u>s</u>le   fas<u>t</u>en
2. Ja<u>pan</u>   electri<u>c</u>ity   in<u>s</u>urance   accommo<u>da</u>tion   mu<u>se</u>um

8 Phrases and phrasal verbs

1. never mind   2. least   3. apart from   4. got away
5. how about   6. on her own   7. took off
8. very kind of you

9 On the phone

– is <u>that</u> Olga?
– Could I speak <u>to</u> Olga?
– <u>It's</u> Dieter
– <u>Fine</u>, thank you
– What <u>are you doing</u> tonight?

10 Link words

1. if   2. otherwise   3. so that   4. when   5. while/when

11 Verbs

1. belong   2. lasts   3. takes   4. run   5. keep (or put)
6. avoid   7. take   8. recognise

TEST 4

1 Tense review and verb forms

 1. was taken; interviewed; was released
 2. grow; is exported
 3. were sent; realised
 4. see
 5. will rain
 6. 've seen
 7. arrived
 8. have gone
 9. listened *or* used to listen; was
10. going

2 Adjectives ending -ed and -ing

1. bored   2. embarrassing   3. fascinating   4. disappointed
5. shocked   6. depressing

3 Conditional sentences

1. lost   2. win   3. resigns   4. worked   5. knew
6. were (or was)

4 Sense verbs

1. smells   2. sounds like   3. feels like   4. feels
5. taste like   6. looks like   7. tastes   8. sounds

5 Wordbuilding

comparison	complaint
belief	advice
choice	education
invention	death
imagination	explanation

6 Agreeing

1. So do I.
2. Neither do I.
3. So am I.
4. Neither can I.
5. So do I.
6. Neither am I.
7. Neither did I.
8. So can I.

7 Pronunciation

<u>ve</u>getable   <u>su</u>permarket   de<u>ve</u>lop   <u>fa</u>scinating   es<u>ca</u>pe
<u>a</u>ccident   pho<u>tog</u>rapher   mu<u>si</u>cian   <u>co</u>lleague

8 Time expressions

1. I'm going to Australia next year.
2. We met yesterday evening (*or* last night).
3. We are meeting again this evening (*or* tonight).
4. My birthday is the sixteenth of July.
5. I've spent two hours doing my homework.
6. I've been here for six months.

9 Arts vocabulary

Cinema	Theatre	Music
subtitles	director	composer
actor	actor	audience
audience	audience	conductor
director	play	orchestra
film	clap	clap
dubbed	stage	musical instrument
trailer		
screen		

10 Adjectives and adverbs

1. beautiful   2. hard   3. quietly   4. polite   5. quick
6. fast   7. slow   8. carefully

11 Link words

1. Although   2. otherwise   3. However
4. although (*or* but)   5. so that   6. who   7. which
8. who

12 Expressions

1. bother   2. lift   3. mood   4. set   5. extent   6. rather

TAPESCRIPTS

UNIT 1 GETTING STARTED

Exercise 4

Version 1

JOAN: When I work at home, I work in my study, usually sitting at a desk. Erm, I like to work alone, and, er, in silence and I usually use a pencil. I find that working early in the morning is best for me. Erm, I don't have a fixed routine; I work when I feel like it, in blocks of about an hour, and, er, and then I have a break. I drink a lot of coffee, and, um, usually my place of work is quite untidy, but I do know where everything is. I, um, also bite my nails.

Version 2

RICHARD: When I work at home, I usually work in the kitchen, because there's a nice, big table in there, and a window for me to stare out of. Erm, I study and work when I feel like it, but I try to make it in the morning if possible. I find I'm more energetic in the morning. I study for quite long periods without realising it, really, erm, and then I have a cup of tea; I drink quite a lot of tea while I work. Erm, I usually use a ballpoint pen, and I usually work alone and in silence if possible. I make a bit of a mess, but I usually know where everything is, and I tend to scratch my head quite a lot when I work.

AT THE MOMENT I'M ...

Exercise 2

TONY: So, you working hard at the moment?

JULIET: Yeah, yeah. I'm revising for my for my A levels; they're next month. I'm really, really nervous about it, though.

CHRIS: How many are you doing?

JULIET: I'm doing three. I'm doing music, art and, um, English.

CHRIS: You nearly forgot that, didn't you? Spending so much time studying the music!

JULIET: I I'm spending ... you know, every night I'm sitting there over books and it's just, it's just driving me mad, it really is. What about you?

CHRIS: Well, I don't want to depress you, but I'm revising for an exam as well.

JULIET: Oh, no.

CHRIS: I thought when I left school it was all over, but no, I'm doing an Open University degree, and, uh ...

TONY: What subject?

CHRIS: Sociology. It's good fun, but it takes so long, because you, you know you work during the day and then you come home and you ... and they want you to do two hours a week, but tend not to I'm afraid. I tend to, er, tend to lose it. Not doing any exams at the moment?

JENNY: I'm doing a test.

CHRIS: Are you?

JENNY: I've got my driving test coming up.

JULIET: Oh, good luck!

JENNY: I'm dreading it. I hate it, I go and hide when my driving teacher knocks on the door. I don't want to do it, but I know I've got ...

CHRIS: How many lessons have you had?

JENNY: I've had about thirty.

CHRIS/TONY: Thirty?

JULIET: That's not that many ...

SPEAKING PARTNERS

Exercise 2

Q: So what did you talk about, Jackie?

J: Well, at first it was really, really difficult to think of anything to talk about. But well, now we talk about what we are doing, or, you know, what we're going to do at the weekends. or, I mean, anything. It does help if, if the teacher can give you sort of topics to talk about. I mean, sometimes we just talk about the lesson, or, or we simply do our homework together.

Q: How did you feel, when you were doing it?

J: Ooh, sort of oh, really stupid at first, I mean you feel silly. But well, you get used to it – well, after a few times, I mean it just seems silly. And we, you know, sometimes we did things in a sort of half English, half Spanish way. Half a sentence would be English and then we would finish it in Spanish. And then we'd just translate some things.

Q: And do you do it sort of on a regular basis, or ...?

J: Erm, well, first of all we didn't, you know, just before we went to class we would meet and have a coffee and just chat then, erm, but the first person that I used to, you know, have these sort of speaking sessions with wasn't any good, I mean, ... and I felt really silly, and we didn't meet often enough. But my friend now that I do it with is really, really good. And we've actually set up a routine, so that we meet regularly, and if we can't meet, well, we just speak to each other on the phone, just a little but, you know, very often.

Q: And do you get bored with it ever, lose interest?

J: Erm ... yes, after a few months, we did – you know, just the two of us talking all the time. So we thought: what could we do? And we just invited some other friends to join us, and now we go to a pub every single week and we all talk in Spanish, and we even try to find some real Spanish people. And in fact we've made two really good friends who are genuine Spanish speakers.

UNIT 2 ASKING QUESTIONS

ASKING ABOUT PERSONAL HISTORIES

Exercise 4

Version 1

Well, um, I was born in Africa; that's where I grew up. And I went to a local school, where my parents made my brother and me work very hard, so that's probably why I did so well at school in my exams. I passed them all, actually.

Anyway, I left school at 18 and went to university in England. I got a place at Bristol University to study agriculture. It was a bit strange living in England after Africa, but, um, I had quite a good time at university.

After that, I went back to Africa where I met my husband. And we got married after a couple of years and came back to live in the village he'd lived in. And afterwards, um, we went back to my university town with our three-year-old son, and I've lived there ever since.

Version 2
INTERVIEWER: Right, so, er, could you tell me something about yourself? Er, where are you from?
WOMAN: Well, um, I was born in Africa: just outside Nairobi.
INTERVIEWER: Oh, right, and that's where you grew up?
WOMAN: Um, I, I was there until I was 18, yes.
INTERVIEWER: Fine. So you, you were educated over there. Did you have a, a tutor at home or …?
WOMAN: Er, no. I was educated there, though. I, I, um, went to a local school.
INTERVIEWER: Ah.
WOMAN: Hmm.
INTERVIEWER: And how did you find that, the, er, the local schooling, was it good?
WOMAN: It was, it was. I worked very hard. Um, my parents were very strict, which is probably why I, I passed all my exams and got to university.
INTERVIEWER: Oh, and that was in Africa?
WOMAN: No, no, I came back to England, um, for university.
INTERVIEWER: Fine. Which university?
WOMAN: Bristol.
INTERVIEWER: Ah, nice. And, er, what did you study?
WOMAN: I studied agriculture.
INTERVIEWER: And how did you find that? Coming over to England after living in Africa?
WOMAN: Oh, it was very strange. Er, it couldn't be more different. Living in Africa and living in Bristol.
INTERVIEWER: Much colder, eh?
WOMAN: That's right.
INTERVIEWER: And, er, so have you been in England ever since university?
WOMAN: Oh, no. I went back to Africa for a short while. And I met my husband there.
INTERVIEWER: And you got married out there?
WOMAN: Yes, we got married in Africa, and, um, after a few years, we came back, um, to live in the village he was from in England.
INTERVIEWER: Ah, right, and, er, that's where you still live now?
WOMAN: Um, no, we, we went back to my university town with our three-year-old son, and I've lived there ever since.

REVIEW AND DEVELOPMENT

REVIEW OF UNIT 1

Exercise 1B
1.
A: So, what do you think of this picture?
B: Er, what, number one?
A: Mm.
B: Right, well, she's holding a cup – is it a coffee advert or something?
A: No …
B: So, nothing to do with drinks of any kind, then?

A: Not drinks, no.
B: She's smiling. That's a pretty strange smile …
A: Yes, exactly!
B: Toothpaste?
A: Yes; actually it's smokers' toothpaste!

2.
A: OK, er, what do you make of this one?
B: Well, it's actually quite a funny picture, because there's a girl, and she's standing in front of a house, and then there's a piano, right, which is falling from one of the windows. Is it for an insurance company?
A: No, I'm afraid not. It's more to do with her clothes.
B: Oh, her trainers? They're very white!
A: Yes, you're nearly there. It's a special kind of sole which absorbs the shock!
B: She's going to need that when the piano falls on her!

3.
A: So, what can you see here?
B: Well, we've got a man and a woman – thirtysomething – and they're walking down a street, lovely golden leaves, and they've got a bicycle each.
A: Right.
B: So I suppose they are either advertising the bicycles, or the clothes they're wearing.
A: A very good guess. Yes, it is *one* of those.
B: The clothes?
A: No.
B: It's the bicycles, then.
A: Yep.

4.
A: Right – it's a middle-aged woman, and she's holding a bunch of flowers.
B: Yes.
A: And she's crying – well, probably with happiness, oh, well, she's not really crying of course … Is this an advertisement for flowers?
B: Not exactly.
A: A service for sending flowers to people?
B: Yes, that's it, you've got it.

5.
A: How about this chap?
B: It's a typical British scene. There's dad, and, er, he's sitting out in the garden, having a sleep under the Sunday paper. Then, there's a rather nice coffee set on the table. Is it a coffee advertisement?
A: No.
B: Anything to do with the grass? You know, 'you can, um, cut your grass in ten minutes with our machine …'
A: No, no. Let me give you some help. The white thing on the table in front of the coffee pot.
B: An alarm?
A: Sort of. It's a doorbell extension, actually.
B: Oh, so if someone comes to see this man, he can hear it from the end of the garden?
A: Absolutely.

Exercise 3
1. Is a ruler bigger than a rubber?
2. Can you put papers in a file?
3. If a room is in a mess, is it tidy?
4. Can you read anything on a blank sheet of paper?
5. Can you write something on a word processor?
6. Is efficient the opposite of organised?
7. Can you drink from a lighter?
8. If you throw something away, do you want it?

9. Can you sharpen something with a dictionary?
10. If you have a break, do you stop working?
11. Do people usually listen to background music?
12. Can you scratch your head?
13. If you are doing a course, do you usually need a notepad?
14. Do people usually revise after an exam?
15. Does your teacher give you housework?

UNIT 3 STREETLIFE

FINDING YOUR WAY

Exercise 4

Version 1

WOMAN: So, did you find the hospital OK?

MAN: Er, not exactly. I came up Holywell Hill as you said, and when I got to the High Street, I went straight across, and I saw the town hall, and turned left, just like you said.

WOMAN: No, I didn't say turn left *immediately* after the town hall …

MAN: Yes, well, that's what I thought you meant. Anyway, I walked along this road – er, Mount Pleasant, I think it was – and I took the second road on the right, but it wasn't Normandy Road. So I stopped and asked an old lady the way, and she told me to go straight ahead, until I got to, er, Folly Lane, then turn right and take the first turning on my left. And this time it *was* Normandy Road.

WOMAN: Oh, well, you weren't very late, and I expect the exercise did you good …

Version 2

MAN: When I got to the station, I remembered you'd said turn right.

WOMAN: Mm.

MAN: So I came out of the station and I looked … right didn't seem to be right, but I did turn right and walked up Holywell Hill.

WOMAN: Yeah, yeah.

MAN: Came up Holywell Hill past the information centre which you mentioned. And I got up to the town hall … and the road in front of me didn't sort of look right so I turned left.

WOMAN: What at the town hall?

MAN: That's right. Yeah, didn't you say turn left?

WOMAN: No, you're supposed to go straight on.

MAN: Oh, no. Well, anyway, I turned left which I suppose was my mistake, and I walked up Mount Pleasant Road and got to the end of that and it sort of took a turning down a branch road, then I carried on again and by that time I knew I was on the wrong road because it started to turn into countryside and things.

WOMAN: Are you kidding?

MAN: No. And I thought, oh, no. And I walked on and it … up this other road called, I think it was Hatchwood Drive, I think or something. And there was a golf course there, anyway. So I got to the golf course.

WOMAN: That's miles away!

MAN: Yeah, I found that out. And I got to the golf course and I went in and I phoned for a taxi.

WOMAN: Yeah.

MAN: Because I wasn't going to walk any further around St Albans. A taxi came and got me and I told him where I wanted to go and on the way back we discussed the route and he said you've taken the wrong turning …

Exercise 4

1.

MAN: Excuse me, do you know where the nearest paper shop is?

WOMAN: No, I'm sorry, I've no idea.

MAN: OK, never mind, thanks anyway.

2.

WOMAN: Excuse me, can you tell me where the post office is?

MAN: Yes, it's just along here. I'm going that way – I'll show you.

3.

MAN: Excuse me, how do I get to the cathedral from here?

WOMAN: It's a bit complicated. Go along here and ask again when you get to the traffic lights.

MAN: Oh, thank you.

4.

WOMAN 1: Do you know what time this shop opens?

WOMAN 2: It usually opens around now – they must be late.

5.

MAN 1: Excuse me, have you got the time, please?

MAN 2: Sure, it's ten past four.

MAN 1: Thanks.

6.

MAN 1: Is this your car, sir?

MAN 2: Er, no, nothing to do with me.

REVIEW AND DEVELOPMENT

REVIEW OF UNIT 2

Exercise 2A

Where do you live?
What's the time?
Haven't you got any money?

What are you doing?
When does he work?
What have you got in your bag?
Where do they live?

1. What's your name?
2. Where are you from?
3. Where do you live?
4. What do you do?
5. Do you enjoy it?
6. Why are you studying English?
7. How do you get to school?
8. What have you got in your pocket?

UNIT 4 CREATIVITY

CREATIVITY TESTS

Exercise 3

Version 1

1. Joe was 84 and couldn't walk any more. His wife Moira looked after him. One day two men came to the house and said they were from the electricity company. They wanted to check the electrical wiring. Moira let them in and then went back to look after Joe. Later she went into the kitchen

and found one of the men holding her handbag. When he saw her he dropped the bag, pushed past her and ran out of the house … the other man quickly followed. Moira picked up her handbag and sure enough, the money was gone. Earlier that day she had been to the bank, taken out £75, and put it in her bag. Now there was nothing left. What was she going to do …

2. Joe was 84 and couldn't walk any more. His wife Moira looked after him. One day two men came to the house and said they were from the electricity company. They wanted to check the electrical wiring. Moira let them in and then went back to look after Joe. Later she went into the kitchen and found one of the men holding her handbag. 'What are you doing with that?' she said. 'Oh, I'm sorry, Mrs Jones, but I'm afraid your wiring is so dangerous that we're gonna have to ask you to leave the building while we check the place.'

'Oh, dear,' she said. 'Will we able to come back?'

'Oh, yes,' he said. 'It won't take long.' So the two men took both Moira and Joe next door and told them to wait outside for a moment. Then the door opened and a group of people all shouted, 'Happy Birthday, Joe!' It was a surprise birthday party.

Version 2

1. Joe was 84 and couldn't walk any more. His wife Moira looked after him. One day two men came to the house and said they were from the Electricity Board. They wanted to check the electrical wiring. Moira let them in and then went back to look after Joe. Later she went into the kitchen and found one of the men holding her handbag. He said he recognised it. It had belonged to his mother whom he hadn't seen since he was a baby. He insisted that Moira was his mother, but Moira and Joe hadn't had any children, they were childless. The man threw his arms around her and called her mother.

2. Joe and Moira, a really nice old couple, they've been married for years. Joe was injured at work and so he took retirement and Moira looks after him. One day a couple of men came to the house and said that they wanted to check the electrical wiring, so Moira let them in and she went back to look after Joe. When she came into the kitchen, she saw one of the men had her handbag in his hand. But when he saw her, he put the handbag down, said that the wiring was OK, and the two men left very quickly. Of course, Moira thought that they had stolen something from her bag. So she went to open it, but instead of finding her purse gone, she found a bundle of five-pound notes and a letter from the two men saying that they were old workmates of Joe and they just wanted to help him out.

YOUR CREATIVE EXPERIENCES

Exercise 2

A: Sally, have you ever written a poem?
B: Yes, I have.

A: Have you ever acted in a play?
C: No, never.

A: Andy, have you ever written a poem?
D: Yes, I wrote one last year.

A: Have you ever drawn a cartoon?
E: Oh, yeah; I drew lots of cartoons when I was at school.

CREATIVE IMPROVISATION

Exercise 2

Dialogue 1
LUCY: Mark!
MARK: Hi, Lucy.
LUCY: Well, come on in.
MARK: Thanks. Hope I'm not late.
LUCY: Late?
MARK: Well, we did say tonight for dinner, didn't we?
LUCY: Did we?
MARK: What? Yes, on the phone, last week.
LUCY: I thought we said Tuesday.
MARK: But it is Tuesday, isn't it?
LUCY: No, it's Monday.
MARK: Oh, my goodness. I'm terribly sorry. Well, how embarrassing … perhaps we could have dinner anyway.
LUCY: Erm … yes, yes, let's.
MARK: Great.

Dialogue 2
LUCY: Mark!
MARK: Hi, Lucy.
LUCY: Well, come on in.
MARK: Thanks. Hope I'm not late.
LUCY: Late?
MARK: Well, we did say tonight for dinner, didn't we?
LUCY: Did we? Oh, look, just hold onto that cloth and come into the kitchen.
MARK: What?
LUCY: Quick, just do as I tell you – the cat's having kittens. Quick, I need help.
MARK: Oh, I can't face that. Look, I'll come back tomorrow.
LUCY: Oh, Mark!

Exercise 6

A: Hello Jenny.
B: Hi.
A: Guess what I've got.
B: What?
A: Tickets for the opera.
B: Brilliant! When?
A: Well, tonight of course.
B: Tonight?
A: Of course, tonight. You know what tonight is?
B: No.
A: It's our anniversary. You can't have forgotten our anniversary.
B: Well, I …
A: Oh, I don't believe it!
B: It's just that … my mother's here.
A: Oh, no!
B: Happy anniversary, darling.
A: Happy anniversary.

REVIEW AND DEVELOPMENT

REVIEW OF UNIT 3

Exercise 1

1. Can you see the street from where you are sitting?
2. Does the room you are in have a carpet?
3. If you open the door of your room, is there another door opposite?
4. If you open the door of your room, can you see any stairs?

5. Can you walk out of your room, turn left and go straight on?
6. Can you walk out of your room, turn right and go straight on?
7. Can you go down a floor?
8. Do you have to go to the next floor to go to the toilet?
9. Can you take a lift to the next floor up?
10. Can you jump out of the window safely?
11. Can you get anything to drink on your floor?
12. Can you phone from your classroom?
13. Can you walk out of your room, along a corridor and out of the building?
14. If you leave the building, do you go past a coffee machine?
15. Do you have to go down some steps to leave the building?

UNIT 5 YOU AND YOUR BODY

KNOW YOUR OWN BODY

Exercise 2

1. How many knees have three people got?
2. Add the number of toes to the number of ankles one person has got.
3. Multiply the number of thumbs you've got by the number of fingers.
4. How many wrists and elbows have ten people got?
5. Add together the number of chins, lips and tongues in two human heads.
6. Take the maximum number of teeth an adult has got and divide it by eight.
7. How many waists, hips, and knees have three people got?
8. Multiply your fingers and thumbs by your shoulders. What number do you get?

LOOKING AFTER YOURSELF

Exercise 5

Version 1

I once was roller skating outside my house and I just fell over … I don't know what happened … and unfortunately I broke my ankle and I had to go to hospital, and I remember it was very, very painful and it was in a plaster for six weeks, but thankfully when they took the plaster off, although I couldn't move it very well, after about six weeks it was fine.

Well, I hurt my wrist when I was a little girl. Um, and I was playing the flute in the school band and, er, my chair was on the end of the row and somebody moved their chair and I fell off the stage, which was very embarrassing. Anyway, I hurt my wrist quite badly and it meant that I couldn't play the flute for a long time, which was probably quite a good thing, actually.

Version 2

I have a scar on my chin which came about because when I was five years old, living in America I was playing in a sandbox and there was a tin can there, and I decided to bite into it. And I cut my, my chin open and I had to go to the hospital and they patched me up, but I still have that scar today.

When I was eleven, I was junior champion of a horse show, and I was so excited that I went to get back onto my horse. It was really old, thirty years old. And he bolted on me, and I fell off, and I broke my arm. And now I can't straighten it, and when I show people, and I hold both my arms out, they think I'm joking, and I'm doing some sort of gag, but it's really true – I've got one bent arm.

REVIEW AND DEVELOPMENT

REVIEW OF UNIT 3

Exercise 2A

town hall; parking meter; traffic lights; railway station; litter bin; post office; bus stop; ring road; office block; pedestrian crossing; shopping centre; car park; department store; golf course

Town hall and *pedestrian crossing* are the only two with equal stress on both words.

UNIT 6 LEARNING – PAST AND PRESENT

AN ADULT LANGUAGE CLASS

Exercise 2

A: You're studying a foreign language at evening school, aren't you?
B: Yeah, that's right, I'm doing a German course two evenings a week.
A: What's it like?
B: Well, it's really different from when I was at school. I mean, the way people behave is quite different.
A: How?
B: Well, for a start, the teachers were really strict at school – I suppose they had to be; there were 30 of us in the class, and most of us were very lazy. But um in this German class, we call the teacher by her first name, and we we talk to her more like she's our equal. And she doesn't force us to do homework if we don't want to.

Oh, and the classroom itself is very different – like at school, we had to sit at desks, and they were nailed to the floor, so you couldn't really move about at all. And here we sometimes sit in a circle and sometimes in a semi-circle, and er quite often we just work in groups, so it's, it's much much more flexible. Oh, and the other thing is we get up and walk about a lot too.
A: It sounds a bit of a madhouse!
B: Yes, oh, it can be. Oh, it's not like school; you don't have to sit in silence or put your hand up – here, everyone just shouts out if they know the answer. And, er, if there's anything you don't understand, you just ask the person sitting next to you, or, or the teacher.
A: But you still use set texts, course books, that sort of thing?
B: Yeah – we still have a course book, but we can ask the teacher to teach us something in particular if we want to. Um, like in my class, there's this banker who always wants to know lots of economic vocabulary.
A: But, suppose the other learners in the class aren't interested in that?
B: Well, we're adults – so if we don't want to do something, we don't have to. Or we can at least, um, tell the teacher we don't want to do it. But most of the time there's a pretty good atmosphere in the class, apart from a couple of people who often just come in ten or fifteen minutes late and don't even apologise. And that's really annoying because then of course the teacher wastes a lot of time explaining things that that the rest of us already know.

REVIEW OF UNIT 5

Exercise 1A

1. Is your skin on the inside of your body?
2. Can people walk on their heels?
3. Is your elbow between your hand and your shoulder?
4. Can you put your thumb in your mouth?
5. Can you bend your chin?
6. Are your fingernails at the end of your hands?
7. Is your neck near your toes?
8. Are your knees above your throat?
9. Is your bottom near your ankle?
10. Is your wrist next to your arm?
11. Can you touch your lips with your tongue?
12. Can you hurt yourself with your waist?

UNIT 7 LETTERS THAT TELL A STORY

HANDWRITING STYLES

Exercise 1

Julia rang and said, could you meet her outside the art gallery at nine thirty and not nine forty-five. She told me to tell you not to worry about Sandra. She will ring her herself later this evening. That's it.

OTHER PEOPLE'S LETTERS

Exercise 3

Version 1

Ella was delighted with the handkerchiefs that her friend Bertie gave her, and very angry that she couldn't write to thank him. Letters, I'm afraid, were impossible because Bertie's mother always opened his mail.

When Bertie told his friend Clovis about this, it gave Clovis an idea. The next morning, a letter arrived for Bertie, marked 'Private'. Naturally, Bertie's mother, Mrs Heasant, picked it up and opened it. It read as follows:

My dearest Bertie,

Do you think you will be brave enough to do it? It will take some courage. Don't forget the jewels. They are a detail, but details interest me.

Yours as ever,
Clothilde

Your mother must not know of my existence. If she asks you about me, tell her you have never heard of me.

Mrs Heasant never trusted Bertie, and now it seemed she was right. 'Bertie is in the power of a terrible girl!' she cried, and when Bertie arrived, she demanded to know who Clothilde was.

Bertie said he didn't know anyone called Clothilde. This made his mother very angry, but he just disappeared and shut himself in his room.

A little while later, another letter, marked 'Private', appeared in the letter box.

So, you have really done it. Poor girl! Poor Dagmar! Now she is finished, I almost feel sorry for her. You did it very well, you wicked boy; the servants all think she killed herself, and there will be no trouble. But it will be best not to touch the jewels just yet.

Clothilde

Mrs Heasant read it, ran upstairs and shouted, 'Miserable boy! What have you done to Dagmar?'

'Oh, it's Dagmar now, is it?' he answered.

Mrs Heasant's eyes filled with tears. 'Don't lie to me. Clothilde's letter tells me everything.'

'Oh, really, mother. If you go on like this, I shall fetch a doctor.'

A bit later, the last post arrived, with another letter for Bertie. As Mrs Heasant read it, the terrible truth became clear to her.

Dear Bertie,

I hope you aren't upset about the stupid letters that I have been sending in the name of an imaginary Clothilde. You told me the other day that the servants, or somebody at your home, opened your letters, so I thought I would give anyone that opened them something exciting to read. The shock may do them good.

Yours,
Clovis Sangrail

Mrs Heasant knocked once more on Bertie's door. 'It's a letter from Mr Sangrail. It's all been a stupid trick.'

Bertie opened the door. He was wearing his hat and overcoat.

'Where are you going?' she said.

'I'm going for a doctor to come and see you. Of course it was a trick, but no normal person would have believed all that nonsense about murder and jewels.'

'All right,' she said. 'I promise I'll never open your letters again.'

Version 2

Ella was delighted with the handkerchiefs that her friend Bertie had given her, and very angry that she couldn't write to thank him. But letters, I'm afraid, were impossible because Bertie's mother was a nosy old woman, and always opened his mail. Bertie had often had arguments with his mother about this habit of hers, but it made no difference.

When Bertie mentioned this to his friend, Clovis, a few days later, it gave Clovis an idea. The next morning, a letter arrived for Bertie, marked 'Private'. Naturally, Bertie's mother, Mrs Heasant, picked it up and opened it. It read as follows:

My dearest Bertie,

Do you think you will be brave enough to do it? It will take some courage. Don't forget the jewels. They are a detail, but details interest me.

Yours as ever,
Clothilde

Your mother must not know of my existence. If she asks you about me, tell her you have never heard of me.

Mrs Heasant always thought that Bertie could easily get into trouble, especially with girls around, and now it seemed she was right. 'Bertie is in the power of a terrible girl!' she cried, while Bertie's sisters were forced to sit on the sofa and listen. And when Bertie himself arrived an hour later, she demanded to know who Clothilde was. Bertie said, quite innocently, he didn't know anyone called Clothilde. This just made his mother very angry, but Bertie disappeared and shut himself in his room. His mother made several more visits to the locked door and repeated her question, but got no further reply from Bertie.

A little while later, another letter marked 'Private' appeared in the letter box.

So, you have really done it. Poor girl! Poor Dagmar! Now she is finished, I almost feel sorry for her. You did it very well, you wicked boy; the servants all think she killed herself, and there will be no

trouble. But it will be best not to touch the jewels just yet.
Clothilde

Mrs Heasant ran downstairs, opened it, let out a brief cry, and then ran upstairs and beat madly at her son's door. 'Miserable boy! What have you done to Dagmar?'

'Oh, it's Dagmar now, is it?' he shouted. 'It will be Geraldine next!'

Mrs Heasant's eyes filled with tears. 'Don't try to hide things from me. Clothilde's letter tells me everything.'

'Oh, really, mother. If you go on like this, I shall fetch a doctor. I know you blame me for most things, but you've never introduced imaginary girls into our conversation before.' And with that, Bertie would say nothing more.

A bit later, the last post arrived, with another letter for Bertie. Mrs Heasant, almost out of control by now, tore it open and began to read – and as she did, the terrible truth began to emerge.

Dear Bertie,
I hope you aren't upset about the stupid letters that I have been sending in the name of an imaginary Clothilde. You told me the other day that the servants, or somebody at your home, opened your letters, so I thought I would give anyone that opened them something exciting to read. The shock may do them good.
Yours,
Clovis Sangrail

Mrs Heasant knocked once more on Bertie's door. 'It's a letter from Mr Sangrail. It's all been a stupid trick.'

Bertie opened the door. He was wearing his hat and overcoat.

'Where are you going?' she said.

'I'm going for a doctor to come and see if anything's the matter with you. Of course it was a trick, but nobody in their right mind would have believed all that nonsense about murder and jewels.'

Bertie realised it was his great opportunity. If the story became known Mrs Heasant would look very stupid.

'All right,' she said. 'I promise I'll never open your letters again.'

REVIEW AND DEVELOPMENT

REVIEW OF UNIT 5
Exercise 2

Examples: this, then, mother.
            think, fourth, mouth.
Column 1: bath, breath, teeth, thumb, throat.
Column 2: there, breathe, another, themselves, without.

REVIEW OF UNIT 6
Exercise 1

1. Have you had an English lesson this week?
2. Have you learnt a new sport this year?
3. Did you see your parents last night?
4. Have you shouted at anyone today?
5. Did you have a dream last night that you can remember?
6. Have you cleaned your shoes this month?
7. Have you refused to do anything this month?
8. Have you moved house this year?
9. Have you wasted any time today?
10. Did you buy a new car last year?
11. Have you learnt a new spelling rule this month?
12. When did you start this exercise?

UNIT 8 TAKE IT OR LEAVE IT

BUYING SOMETHING TO WEAR

Exercise 5

1. It's very hot in this room.
2. The music is too loud.
3. This alarm clock isn't working.
4. It'll be very expensive to take a taxi.
5. We need some more bread.
6. The baby is crying.

PAYING FOR THINGS

Exercise 2

A: In America I pay for my supermarket shopping in cash.
B: In England I pay for my supermarket shopping with a debit card.
A: Mmm. But I pay for petrol for my car, well the gas for my car, I pay for by credit card.
B: Yeah, I use a credit card as well so I can keep track of it.
A: I pay for new clothes by credit card and far too often, I'm afraid.
B: I pay for new clothes with a cheque.
A: I pay for my daily transport in cash though because that's easiest.
B: Yes, me too, I pay in cash.
A: Um, if I'm buying an airline ticket, I like to pay by credit card.
B: I pay by credit card too because you get travel insurance on it.
A: Hmm. I pay for my car insurance by direct debit once a month.
B: I pay my car insurance by cheque at the beginning of the year.
A: I pay for stamps in cash, of course.
B: I pay for stamps in cash too.
A: I pay for a restaurant meal in cash if it isn't too much. If it's expensive I pay by credit card.
B: I pay by credit card always.
A: I pay my phone bill by direct debit.
B: I pay my phone bill by cheque.

REVIEW AND DEVELOPMENT

REVIEW OF UNIT 7
Exercise 1

1. I'm writing to their boss.
2. I mustn't lose the address.
3. We planned the meeting last Tuesday.
4. I always forget how to spell *quite*.
5. Whose handwriting is the easiest to read?
6. It's wetter and warmer than yesterday.
7. He's bigger than me.
8. Which suitcase is heavier?
9. She's sitting down over there.
10. I'm putting on weight, but she's much thinner.

UNIT 9 FOOD AND DRINK

EATING OUT

Exercise 2

When you get to a restaurant, you normally ask for a table – you don't ask for seats – but you wouldn't normally say 'I want a table' – it sounds a bit rude.

Um, when you want to call the waiter or waitress, um, in, in Britain you normally try to attract their attention with your hand or your eyes – you don't actually say anything most of the time. But if you want to say something, it's usually 'Excuse me'. 'Waiter' or 'Waitress' is just about possible but I don't know many people who would say that. And 'Hey' is very rude.

Um, for question 3, b is the only answer – a is rude and c is wrong – it's a menu not a card.

In the next question you could say a or b, but c is grammatically wrong. And you could also say either a or c in question 5 – but b sounds a bit rude.

For number 6, there is a difference here between Britain and America. In Britain we normally ask for the toilet, whereas in the United States, you ask for the washroom. We never use that expression in Britain. And the first answer is wrong – it's basically a translation mistake.

In number 7, there is another difference here between Britain and the United States – they ask for 'the check' whereas in Britain we ask for 'the bill' … but I think it's probably true to say that most waiters in Britain would understand if you asked for 'the check'. I don't know if Americans would understand the word 'bill' …

REVIEW AND DEVELOPMENT

REVIEW OF UNIT 7

Exercise 1B

1st syllable	2nd syllable	3rd syllable
politics	intelligent	sensitivity
architect	reliable	politician
character	imaginative	personnel
necessary	advertisement	popularity
advertising	analysis	application
sensitive	computer	

UNIT 10 FEELINGS: THE GOOD, THE BAD AND THE UGLY

WHAT MAKES YOU HAPPY?

Exercise 1

Asked what makes her happy, nursing sister Georgina Salmon listed:

Log fires and Christmas tree lights
Being alone; walking the dog in the country, surrounded by fields
Jacket potatoes oozing with butter
Receiving long letters from friends not often seen
Newborn babies and the expressions they make
A mother's expression when she sees her baby for the first time
Books and music
The car starting first time in winter
The look on children's faces as you tell them a story
Knowing a patient will recover when at times it's seemed impossible
Bubble baths and the feeling after a sauna
Looking at my old photographs
Watching a good suspense film
Church bells
Taking communion and knowing that God is real
Liqueur coffee after a delicious meal
Robins watching you as you dig over the garden
Waking up to the knowledge that it's a day off from work.

HOW TO BEAT A BAD MOOD

Exercise 3

Version 1

Doctors may sometimes give patients tranquillisers for depression, but there are many other ways to beat a bad mood.

The first of these is *exercise*; running, cycling and swimming are all good for you and aerobics is especially good. Natural changes are better than drugs, and exercise makes better use of the oxygen you take in. Basically, you need to do these things for about 20 minutes, three to five times a week.

Colour can also have an influence. Don't wear dark colours like black and blue if you are depressed: go for bright colours. But if you are angry, red is not a good colour to wear, and if you are worried or anxious, try and choose soft, neutral colours.

If you want to use *music* to change your mood, start with music which is similar to your bad mood, and then change it gradually until you finish with happier music.

Scientists have also found a connection between *food* and mood. Carbohydrates, for example, make you feel calm and relaxed, but too much tea and coffee will make you depressed and anxious.

Finally, there is *positive thinking*. If you think positive thoughts and try to take an interest in other people, you will begin to feel happier.

Version 2

Moods are emotions that can become fixed and influence you for hours, days or even weeks. If your mood is sad or depressed or angry, that can be a real problem. Too often, doctors recommend tranquillisers and anti-depressants. But there are other ways which are not toxic or addictive.

Exercise, especially aerobics, seems to be a very good way to get out of a bad mood. Researchers have found that biochemical changes produced by exercise are better than drugs at beating a bad mood. Running, cycling and swimming make the heart beat faster and improve the use of oxygen. You need about 20 minutes of this, three to five times a week.

Colour psychologist Patricia Szczerba suggests that you should avoid red if you are angry or annoyed. And don't wear dark colours like black or dark blue if you're depressed – go for bright colours. If you are anxious, it's best to choose neutral, soft colours.

Music therapists say the best way to change your mood is to play music which is similar to your bad mood, then little by little, over about four pieces of music, change the music to the mood you want to be in.

Scientists have found a link between *food* and mood. Carbohydrates eaten alone make you feel calm and relaxed.

There are plenty of low calorie foods like popcorn which work, as well as crisps and doughnuts. And too much tea or coffee makes you depressed and anxious.

And finally *positive thinking* is a very good way to change your mood. An experiment on a group of students who were depressed and anxious found that if they looked for something funny, it helped them more than if they cried. If you think positive thoughts, and try to take an interest in someone else, you'll probably begin to feel happier.

REVIEW OF UNIT 8

Exercise 2B

Questions the customer could ask:
Can I try this on, please?
Have you got a bigger one?
Have you got this in another colour?
Can I pay by credit card?
Where's the changing room?
Could I have my money back?
Do you take American Express?
Could I speak to the manager?
Can I wash it?
Is this in the sale?
Can I have a discount?
How does it look?

Questions the assistant could ask:
Could I have your cheque card, please?
Would you like to try it on?
Can I help you?
Do you need any help?
How would you like to pay?
Does it fit OK?
Is it the right size?
Do you want a tie to go with that shirt?
Do you want a handbag to go with those shoes?

UNIT 11 WEATHER

Exercise 1

On a cold winter's morning I just want to stay in bed all day.

I love the feeling on a warm summer's evening, um with a gentle sea breeze, you just feel very relaxed and happy, and especially if you're in good company.

On a hot summer's day I love to be in the countryside, but if I'm in a town or city, I feel hot and sticky and miserable.

On a wet and windy day I like to stay in bed, put the covers over my head and not get up.

Towards the end of a long spell of very hot humid weather, I normally feel as though I've got no energy at all, and I just want to drink a lot.

Well, just before a violent thunderstorm I usually feel, um, in a bad mood and anxious because I hate thunderstorms.

Exercise 2

Because the weather in Britain is so changeable – cold and wet one day, then hot and sunny the next – the weather forecast is especially important to supermarkets and shops that sell food, and changing weather conditions can have quite a dramatic effect on sales of different things ... and sometimes they can be quite surprising.

For example, did you know that in Britain we drink more coffee in wet weather, and during sunny weather, we buy more tea? And the situation with soft drinks, such as orange juice and Coca-Cola, is very interesting, because the sales of these drinks rise dramatically as soon as the temperature goes above 15°.

With things like salad (lettuce, tomatoes, cucumber, etc.), the important factor seems to be the first weekend of good weather that we get in the spring. After that sales go up very quickly and, um, people buy lots of food and drink we associate with summer. When autumn comes, we don't stop buying these foods quite so quickly.

The sale of bread is also directly related to the weather. Basically people buy more bread as the weather gets colder.

Supermarkets also sell lots of prepared sandwiches and every day they order these from the factory. One rather surprising statistic here is that sales of beef sandwiches go up in the winter, but in summer it is chicken sandwiches that are more popular.

REVIEW OF UNIT 9

Exercise 1

1. salad   bacon   cabbage   carrot
   (So *bacon* is the odd one out.)
2. cook   food   spoon   room
   (So *cook* is the odd one out.)
3. peach   meal   beans   healthy
   (So *healthy* is the odd one out.)
4. menu   lettuce   refuse   cucumber
   (So *lettuce* is the odd one out.)
5. diet   recipe   fried   pineapple
   (So *recipe* is the odd one out.)
6. pork   cork   fork   work
   (So *work* is the odd one out.)

UNIT 12 ROMANCE

Exercise 2

As most people in the English-speaking world know, Valentine's Day is celebrated every year on February 14th, and on this day people send Valentine cards to their husbands, wives, boyfriends, girlfriends or just someone they are fond of – even if they don't actually know them.

Sometimes people sign their cards, but it's quite common among teenagers to leave them blank. Then, if you receive an anonymous card, you have to try and guess who it came from.

And it's an enormous industry too. On average, people in Britain send over l5 million cards every year. But it's not just cards: people also send chocolates or flowers to their loved ones

– roses are the most popular – and they even put messages in daily newspapers.

No one is quite sure about the origin of St Valentine's Day, and there are several popular theories. One theory is that it comes from the tragic figure of Saint Valentine. This poor man fell in love with a blind girl, performed a miracle by giving her back her sight, but was then killed by the girl's father. A very sad story.

We normally associate Valentine's Day with young people, but that's not strictly true. It is more common among younger people, but usually 25% of all Valentine cards are bought by the over 45s.

SHORT BUT SWEET

Exercise 2

Version 1
When I was 13, I went on holiday with my parents and, uh, we went to, er, Florence in Italy and, and we stayed in a villa, uh, just outside Florence; and it was most beautiful, it was set in the middle of a vineyard, and, er, it was very lovely. Anyway, we once went to the swimming pool, the local pool, and, uh, while we were there, um, I met this boy whose name was Fabrizio, and, er, he was probably about 18, and, uh, very beautiful – he was blond with blue eyes. And, er, I fell completely madly in love with him. And, uh, he didn't speak very much English at all, and of course I didn't speak any Italian, and so communication was a problem, but in a way it wasn't because, um, you know there was this sort of connection between us. And anyway, er, I was constantly asking my parents, you know, 'Can we go to the swimming pool, please?' And I wasn't remotely interested in exploring the beauties and art of, er, of Florence, and all I really wanted to do was go to the swimming pool and see Fabrizio.

So after my parents had taken me grudgingly around the Uffizi gallery and, you know, to look at David and what have you, I finally persuaded them, you know, that we had to go back to the swimming pool, because I, you know, I really wanted to swim. And, er, and we, we I got into the pool and, and I looked everywhere for Fabrizio, and, and then finally I saw him, and he was sitting on the edge of the pool, holding hands with another girl. And, uh … well, that was, that was the end of my love affair.

Version 2
When I was about 19, I took a bus from Regina, Saskatchewan to New York City. And it's about three and a half days on a bus. And I got on the bus I remember, I got on in Regina and I got down in and I was excited about going to New York for the first time. And I took my seat and I looked across the aisle and there was a girl sitting there, who had blond hair, bright teeth, blue eyes and I just fell in love (badoomph) right there. And I had three and a half days on the bus with this girl and I thought, this is going to be magic, this is going to be wonderful. And I started talking to her and she was really nice, and she had a tape recorder with her, which I didn't have and she had recordings of music and she had, I remember, a tape by the Eagles with *Hotel California* on it, and she used to play it over and over again, which at the beginning was really good and I thought, boy she likes music, and we talked and we stopped; when the bus stopped, we got off and had coffee and we were getting to know each other really well and it was actually becoming pretty romantic, but after about a day and a half of *Hotel California* being played over and over again, I started to fall out of love with her, and by the time we got to

Toronto, the batteries were running down on her tape recorder and she was still playing it even though it was playing even slower and slower, and people on the bus were getting really aggravated, and I actually got off the bus in Toronto because she was going on, on the same journey I was; I actually got off the bus to avoid this girl and fell deeply out of love with her by Toronto. So I changed my ticket and got off the bus.

REVIEW AND DEVELOPMENT

REVIEW OF UNIT 10

Exercise 1

1. Can you wear a jacket potato?
2. If a patient recovers, do they get well?
3. Can you use a bubble bath in a sauna?
4. Do you have communion in church?
5. Is a day off a nice thing?
6. Is gardening an outdoor hobby?
7. If something is delicious, do you like it?
8. Is a stranger someone you know well?
9. Can you put logs on a fire?
10. Is spare time the same as work time?
11. Can you repair a pet?
12. Can you start a car?
13. If something is unexpected, does it surprise you?
14. If you regret something, are you happy about it?
15. If you make a promise, should you keep it?

UNIT 13 IT'S BETTER TO TRAVEL THAN TO ARRIVE

LET'S GET ORGANISED!

Exercise 3

Version 1
Well, I'm a very organised person, so I made a list of everything I had to do in advance, and weeks before I went to Tunisia, I booked my flight and got travel insurance at the same time. In fact, it was a package holiday so the accommodation was all arranged there and then. Um, I always make a point of checking my passport to make sure I don't need to renew it.

The day before I left, I did my packing, and then I realised I didn't have a guidebook, so I rushed out and bought one. I like to know a bit about the place I'm going to. I, er, ordered a taxi to take me to the airport, because the taxi company I use can get rather busy on the day and I want to be sure that I've got one.

Just before I left the house, I checked everything as usual – the, er, doors and windows, the gas, um, turned the electricity off, and also, as usual, spent the next half hour in the taxi worrying that I had forgotten something …

Version 2
Last year when I went to, er, Malaysia on business I was really organised which I'm not normally, and, uh, quite a few weeks before I decided I'd better go out and get a big suitcase because I knew that I was going to be staying for quite a long time. So I bought the suitcase and at the same time I saw a wonderful guidebook on Malaysia which I bought and used a lot. Um, also about four weeks before I went, um, I booked my flight and at the same time with the travel company I took out some, some insurance … and, er, in fact with the same travel

company I was able to order all my, er, Malaysian money and my traveller's cheques which was great because it made it much easier ... uh, and they told me that I had to get some injections and that had to be done, um, so many weeks before, so I went to the doctor and had my injections, and then I realised that I ought to arrange for someone to come and look after the cat. Um, so I phoned up a local cattery and booked the cat in, and that was about, I think, three weeks before I left. And then the day before I left, er, I finished my packing, I did all the packing, and, er, I went and collected the, the foreign currency that I'd ordered. And then the day that I left, just about an hour before I actually left the house, um, I gave my next-door neighbour a box with all my jewellery and all that sort of thing in, um, and I checked that I'd locked all the doors and the windows, and made sure that all the plugs were switched off and the fridge was switched off, and took my suitcase, double-locked the front door and then got a bus to the airport.

REVIEW AND DEVELOPMENT

REVIEW OF UNIT 11

Exercise 2

1. There's often fog in the winter.
2. We don't have icy roads in winter.
3. Do you get a lot of sun in spring?
4. We had showers in March.
5. I love the mist in the mornings in spring.
6. We get a lot of wind in the autumn.
7. Did you say it was cloudy outside?
8. We had horrible thunder and lightning in the mountains.

UNIT 14 POSSESSIONS

MY FAVOURITE THINGS

Exercise 1

A

Well, I guess the thing which is most important to me is my father's watch. My mother gave it to me on my eighteenth birthday, so I've had it now for thirteen years. What's more, I think I've worn it almost every day. It has great sentimental value and would be difficult to replace because it's been in the family since before the Second World War.

B

Well, I'm a great jazz fan, and I have a really large collection of records – well over four hundred – which is very important to me. I started buying records when I was at school, but I've only been a serious collector since about 1980 – that's when I left university and started earning money. And I guess that most of the records I've had for sixteen years, I think it is, are impossible to replace, so I'd hate to lose them.

THROUGH THE KEYHOLE

Exercise 2

1. Well, I'm standing in the lounge ... and looking around me, I get the impression that this person certainly likes having all the latest hi-tech equipment – TV, video recorder, hi-fi with compact disc player – they're all here ... and behind me a small white desk with a fairly expensive-looking word processor.

There's nothing out of place here. In fact, the whole room is very neat and tidy. But what's this over here? A black leather case and inside ... my word, a very fine-looking saxophone. Have we got a musician here, perhaps?

I'm in the hall now, and, glancing at the bookcases here, I think this is a person with fairly general interests – reference books, novels, one or two travel books – and perhaps significantly, lots of maps.

Moving through to the bedroom ... still very neat, very functional ... there's only a bed, bedside table and wardrobe for furniture, and the walls are just plain white. So, let's have a look inside the wardrobe ... aha ... tracksuits, a pair of skis and a tennis racket. And I suspect the racing bike outside the house belongs to our owner too!

2. As I came into the house, I noticed a very smart-looking sports car in the drive, but inside the impression I get is more traditional, more conservative ... large portrait paintings on the walls, elegant silver candlesticks on the dining table; moving through to the conservatory, a beautiful bronze statue sitting proudly in front of the french windows.

Moving through to the bedroom, there is a huge wardrobe occupying the whole of one wall, and inside ... wow, evening dresses, fur coats, and at least a dozen pairs of high-heeled shoes – I don't imagine this person does a lot of walking in their spare time. But with that sports car outside, who would want to?

REVIEW AND DEVELOPMENT

REVIEW OF UNIT 13

Exercise 2

1. Is the flight to New York boarding now?
2. Is the Mexico City flight delayed?
3. What is the gate number for the flight to Tokyo?
4. Is the Cairo flight taking off soon?
5. Why is the Bangkok flight delayed?
6. Is it the final call for the Chicago flight?
7. Is the Los Angeles flight boarding?
8. Is it gate 30 for New York?
9. How long is the delay on the Mexico City flight?
10. How many flights are taking off in the next half hour?

UNIT 15 RULES

RULES OF BEHAVIOUR

Exercise 4

Version 1

WOMAN: Well, I've lived in Japan for a few years now, and, er, if you go to the theatre, you wear smart clothes usually.

MAN: Well, in Britain you can wear what you like really. I mean, some people do wear smart clothes, but you don't have to.

WOMAN: Public phones: yes, you, you do have to wait your turn.

MAN: That's true in Britain too. But if it's a real emergency, you can tap them on the shoulder and ask them to let you make your call.

WOMAN: Hmm. In a coffee bar, if you, yes, if you ask very *politely*, and if there are no other seats free, you, you can usually sit at someone else's table.

MAN: Yes, you can do that in Britain too. And you can also say 'Bless you' if someone sneezes, but you don't really need to say anything.

WOMAN: Well, in Japan, sneezing in public is very rude …

MAN: Really?

WOMAN: … and people certainly don't say anything like 'Bless you'. It's considered embarrassing. And of course it is *terribly* rude to blow your nose in public.

MAN: Well, in Britain you should blow your nose. In fact, it's rude not to.

WOMAN: Talking to strangers – well, there isn't an exact, um, equivalent of 'sir' and 'madam', but well, yes, I suppose in Japan they, they show respect to an older person through different levels of politeness in the language they use.

MAN: Hmm. In Britain that's not so true nowadays. You certainly don't call someone 'sir' or 'madam' just because they are older. Er, how about this question on tipping taxi drivers?

WOMAN: Oh, no, they don't usually tip them.

MAN: In Britain you do, usually – well, not everyone does, but …

WOMAN: Oh, yes, and if you are meeting someone, you must never arrive ten minutes late – that's incredibly rude. You arrive on time or, or even ten minutes early.

MAN: Oh. Well, in Britain it's quite normal to be ten minutes late if you're meeting a friend. Nobody worries about that. And the other thing is that if you go into a bar, you go and pay for your drinks, *then* you sit down.

WOMAN: Ah, well, in Japan you sit and then wait to be served.

MAN: Hmm. How about this last one?

WOMAN: In Japan people bow of course. Though I think with Westerners, for instance, Japanese people do tend to shake hands.

MAN: Hmm. Yeah, I've seen that. In Britain, shaking hands is common at a formal first meeting, but, well, if you were just meeting a friend, you wouldn't even bother, wouldn't even think about it.

Version 2

WOMAN: Um. Number 1, going to the theatre. What do you think about that?

MAN: I think in Britain nowadays people more or less wear what they like. Whatever they're comfortable in.

WOMAN: Mmm. I think in, in Japan it really is necessary to wear smart clothes. Absolutely.

MAN: If you're waiting to use a, a phone box, a public phone box, I think probably if you need to make a call urgently in an emergency, then it is OK to tell the person on the phone to hurry up.

WOMAN: Yes, I don't think you would in, in Japan. I think you wait your turn. That's very important.

Um, on number 3 um, sitting down at a table in a coffee bar with someone, it's OK in Japan, but you must ask them very, very politely.

MAN: In Britain I think it's, it's OK in a crowded coffee bar.

WOMAN: Yeah.

MAN: That's fine. If somebody sneezes, er, next to you, um, traditionally in Britain you'd say 'Bless you'.

WOMAN: Yes, I think that's OK, but you wouldn't do that in Japan. It's, it's actually considered very rude to sneeze, and it's better just not to say anything.

MAN: Is it the same as in five, with blowing your nose. Is that considered rude?

WOMAN: Uh, well, yes – you, you leave the room. You never blow your nose in public.

MAN: Really?

WOMAN: Mmm.

MAN: I think it's OK here, assuming you've got a clean handkerchief, and preferably you're not doing it when people are eating.

WOMAN: Um, on 6, er talking to a stranger, there, um, there are different levels of politeness in Japan to show your, your respect. It's not, it's not exactly 'sir' or, or 'madam'. It's a little bit different.

MAN: I think probably in Britain people don't differentiate necessarily between, er, people, talking to young people or older people. There doesn't seem to be much difference in the respect you'd show to a stranger.

In, in a taxi, er, question 7, um, traditionally you do tip. Er, I think normally you tip ten to fifteen per cent.

WOMAN: Yes. You don't normally tip at all in Japan. Certainly not in a taxi, anyway.

Um, this number 8, meeting someone for a drink. It would be really, really rude to arrive late. Um, you should really arrive early, ten minutes early, or most definitely on time.

MAN: Really?

WOMAN: Mmm.

MAN: Mostly I think people are more flexible about time in Britain.

WOMAN: I think that's right.

MAN: You can afford to be a little bit late without causing too much offence.

In a bar of course, er, in, if you go into a bar for a drink in Britain, um, usually you have to go up and ask the, the bartender for the drink and pay after he's served you.

WOMAN: That's right, you pay for it straightaway. Er, in, in Japan it's more normal to go, sit at a table, wait to be served, er, more as, as a restaurant, really.

MAN: And, uh, meeting people?

WOMAN: Mmm.

MAN: What, what, what happens in Japan?

WOMAN: Well, of course Japanese people bow to each other, but I think when they're meeting Westerners it's more usual to, to take the custom of shaking hands rather than bowing.

MAN: Yes, and of course in Britain that's, that's the usual way.

WOMAN: Yes.

MAN: … is to shake hands.

GRAMMAR RULES

Exercise 4

1. Which continent is Rwanda in?
2. Which islands in the Mediterranean lie off the coast of Spain?
3. Which sea is surrounded by Egypt, Saudi Arabia, Yemen, Sudan and Ethiopia?
4. Which group of states includes Abu Dhabi and Dubai?
5. Which famous street in the USA is the American financial centre?
6. In which museum will you find the *Mona Lisa*?
7. What is the name of the famous park in New York?
8. What is the highest mountain in Japan?
9. What is Venezuela's main export?
10. Chicago is on a lake. Which one?

SCHOOL RULES

Exercise 3

1.
I went to, erm, a girls' grammar school, in just to the east of London, and it was a really nice school. It was very relaxed and very happy. Erm, we had to wear a uniform, erm, and we couldn't wear make-up, or high heels or anything like that. Erm, but we liked our teachers and we had a good time. And I stayed on until the Sixth Form when we didn't have to wear uniform, and we didn't have to play sport, which was great if you were lazy like me. And I really enjoyed school, I had a lovely time and made lots of friends and was very happy there.

2.
I remember we had some rather strange rules. One thing that we always had to do, erm, we had to cover all our textbooks with brown paper, and then write the title of the book on the front of the brown paper again, so we couldn't just use the books as they were. And er, another thing that we had to do was, we had to measure our skirts, because you weren't allowed to wear a skirt that was either too short or too long. You had to make sure that it was exactly five inches from the floor when you were kneeling down. And we definitely had to wear hats, and we couldn't hold hands with each other in the playground.

3.
I went to a grammar school in South Wales. It was an all boys' school and there were about a thousand pupils. And we had a headmaster who was rather old-fashioned. And he insisted on all sorts of rules. We had to wear our school caps between home and school. We had to take our caps off when we met a teacher or an older person. And we couldn't get on buses before the public. We had to wait for them to get on buses first to show that we had good manners ...

REVIEW AND DEVELOPMENT

REVIEW OF UNIT 13

Exercise 1A

listen	know	thumb
knee	lamb	wrist
bomb	foreign	wrong
castle	island	whistle
fasten	sign	aisle

UNIT 16 KEEPING THE CUSTOMER SATISFIED

CUSTOMER SERVICE

Exercise 5

Version 1
I've just been on holiday to Lanzarote and I was really impressed at the people who worked, er, in one of the little restaurants near where we stayed. They were so helpful and efficient and they were so friendly towards the children. It was lovely.

I was in a queue at the post office the other day and there was a huge queue, everybody was waiting for ages, and the staff were so rude and unfriendly, and just didn't seem at all interested in any of us.

I lost a contact lens once at a pool in London and, um, the lifeguard was really friendly and polite, and she said leave my phone number and she'd look for it. And a day later the phone rang and she'd spent two hours going over the floor and found my contact lens and gave it back to me, and I think that's really nice.

Version 2
I went to change money in a bank in India a couple of years back, and I was struck at how friendly and efficient everybody was. They invited us to sit down and have tea with them, and, er, I've never really quite experienced anything like that since.

Uh, one of our local clothes shops, the people that serve there are so ignorant of anything that they're trying to sell. They're badly-dressed, unfriendly and cold. Really, I'd rather go without any clothes than shop there.

There's a hotel near Bath in the west country which is a special hotel that welcomes children. It's one of the nicest hotels I've ever been to. All the staff are so helpful and polite and friendly. They're all smartly-dressed, but they look friendly and the children just love going there.

A CHANGE OF IMAGE

Exercise 5

Situation 2
1.
Well, I think the bar certainly will be cleaner if people aren't smoking. But I do think that it might be bad for business because most people who go into pubs, it seems to me, um, like to smoke – well, a lot of people I should say like to smoke, that's why they go; you know, one of the reasons they go there, they can have a smoke and a drink and meet all their friends and ... I think it, yeah, I think it might be bad for business.

2.
The bar will be a more pleasant place to spend time in, um, because usually with all that smoke it's an extremely unpleasant place to be in. And I think that ... while the barman might, you know, he might lose business, I'm sure that even more people will actually come to the bar because it's a, a smoke-free zone on those days. I certainly would, anyway.

Situation 3
1.
I don't think this is going to be very easy for the company to adjust to. But I do think that people doing different jobs in different departments will totally change the character of the company and everybody will end up doing a better job.

2.
I don't think this will have a very good effect on the company, um, I know it's already happened, but I think that people will get very angry, actually, that somebody else is now doing the job that they've spent their life training for.

3.
Well, I think this will have a very positive effect on the company because I think people will feel that they are working much more as a team together, and I think if people have open minds, they will be able to learn a lot about their own jobs and other people's.

4.
It seems to me a good idea because it will bring variety into the workplace and keep people's interest alive. And I think it will make people feel more equal with fellow workers if they've been doing similar or the same jobs.

UNIT 17 PICTURE THIS!

TAKE MY ADVICE!

Exercise 4

Version 1

WOMAN: You know, I bought this food mixer yesterday and I got it home and I plugged it in and it doesn't work.

MAN: Oh, well, you must definitely take it back. And don't forget to take the receipt or some evidence of where you bought it from, you know the shop.

WOMAN: Mmm, I think I'll demand to see the manager as well.

MAN: Certainly, and be aggressive, be as aggressive as you like.

Woman: Mmm. D'you think I should take someone, someone else with me?

MAN: Yes. I'll come with you if you like.

WOMAN: Oh, that would be great.

MAN: I think it would be sensible though, if we do try and avoid a busy time in the shop.

WOMAN: Yes, and I'd better check the guarantee before I go as well.

MAN: Absolutely, yes. That's very important. But don't forget, try and make a lot of noise and a lot of fuss. I find that always works.

WOMAN: And what, well what if they don't give me my money back?

MAN: Oh, well, make sure that you tell them you'll call the police if you don't get your money back. That is important.

WOMAN: Right. I'll do that. Well shall we go tomorrow then?

Version 2

WOMAN: I've bought these shoes, and, uh, and the sole of one of them has just completely fallen off. What do you think I should do?

MAN: Well … you bought them recently?

WOMAN: Yes, I bought them last week. I've worn them once.

MAN: Oh, well, just take them straight back, take them straight back, and, uh, you know, and then you'll get, you'll get a new pair if you want them, or your money back.

WOMAN: Well, what should I say to them? Do you think?

MAN: Well, well, for a start, right, take the receipt with you …

WOMAN: Yeah …

MAN: … right, just as proof, cos I mean, you know what shoes are like, they can say you've worn them for ages or whatever. So if you've got the receipt …

WOMAN: Yes, I've kept the receipt, so that's all right. Now do you think … I was wondering … shall I get really angry or …

MAN: Yeah, I know what you mean. I, I wouldn't make a lot of noise about it, cos they can just make a lot of noise back at you, and you know, it'll end up getting all nasty and rude. I mean, I think you should possibly be aggressive …

WOMAN: D'you think?

MAN: Yeah, but don't shout at them, don't make a lot of noise, but just, you know, be …

WOMAN: Right, well I was thinking of taking my friend Jane with me, you know, because I thought, you know, she'd back me up a bit.

MAN: Yeah, that's, I mean that's true, but I've done that before, and I don't I don't think you should take someone else with you because it confuses the issue a bit.

WOMAN: Yes.

MAN: You know, and the people in the shop feel they're being ganged up on.

WOMAN: Yeah, I see what you're saying.

MAN: If you go in on your own, take your receipt with you, and just, just be … pushy.

WOMAN: But I tell you what, I'm really frightened that you know … how far can I take it? What about, you know … Could I threaten to, to get the police involved?

MAN: Oh, abso… Well, first of all, I think you should, uh, you know, demand to see the manager because you'll probably be just talking to one of the little sales assistants, you know, and say well I'm sorry, I don't believe what you say, I want to see the manager. Demand to see the manager, and then … yeah, if they're going to be rude to you, then tell them that if you don't get your money back, you're going to call the police.

WOMAN: All right.

MAN: All right.

WOMAN: OK. That sounds good.

MAN: Right, when are you going to do it, then?

WOMAN: Well, I'll not … I won't go when it's really busy. I'll go maybe, you know, sort of first thing in the morning, maybe.

MAN: Yeah, that's a good idea. Obviously try to avoid the busy times cos, you know, there's too many people and they're busy running off everywhere.

WOMAN: Yeah.

MAN: Well, I want to hear how you get on.

WOMAN: OK.

DESCRIBING PICTURES

Exercise 3

It's difficult to see from this picture, but in fact, this is the living room of a houseboat. The boat used to carry rubbish down the River Thames in London, but it was bought by a millionaire businessman from Sweden who wanted a natural, simple but luxurious interior. The room is, of course, very light because of the windows along the side and in the ceiling, and because the light comes off the river.

The white object on the left is a kind of box which covers the staircase down to the bedrooms. The woman in the photo is, in fact, the present owner with her son.

REVIEW AND DEVELOPMENT

REVIEW OF UNIT 16

Exercise 2

1. If he makes a noise, I'll tell him to shut up.
2. If she does it again, he'll ask her to stop it.
3. If they sit down, I'll tell them to stand up.
4. If he comes, she'll ask him to go away.
5. If she smokes, I'll tell her to put it out.
6. If they get on, he'll tell them to get off.
7. If he puts it on, she'll ask him to take it off.
8. If they turn it on, we'll ask them to turn it off.

UNIT 18 LISTS

WHO MAKES LISTS?

Exercise 1

Take out a piece of paper. Now, on this piece of paper you are going to write a list. First of all, think what your list is going to be. For example, it could be a list of people you want to invite to a party, or a list of things you have to do this week.

Now write the first thing on your list and then pass it to the person on your left.

You now have a piece of paper in front of you with one thing written on it. What do you think this list is? Write the second thing on this list and pass it on.

You now have a piece of paper with a list containing two things. Write the third thing on the list and then pass it back to the person who started the list.

Look at your list. Did the other people continue it in the way you intended? Talk to them about it.

LISTS IN LANGUAGE LEARNING

Exercise 3

Well, this particular student has used translations for all the words. Now, that's a good idea for lots of words, but sometimes there isn't a very exact translation, and then perhaps you need an explanation in your first language, or in English if possible.

Another good idea is to write an example sentence for some words. This helps you to remember the word, but it can also be important if a word has any special features that you need to know. For example, in this list, *escape* can be a verb or a noun, so you could write two different sentences to show that. And in fact, it's always a good idea, I think, to write down the part of speech. It's easy, after each word you just write *v* for verb, *n* for noun, *adj* for adjective, and so on.

Then, you need something to help you with words that are difficult to pronounce. The best thing here is phonetics, but if you can't write phonetics, your own system will do. For example, with the word *average*, you need to remember that the last three letters are pronounced *idge* and not *age*, so after the word you could write *bridge* in brackets, to remind you of the correct pronunciation.

Finally, I think it's always a good thing to organise words in groups that are connected in some way. This helps you to remember them, and in this list, there are several words that go together – for example, *get away* and *escape* are synonyms, they mean the same thing. And with the phrase *on foot* you could add the other ways of travelling, that's to say, *by car, by bus, by train*, etc. And so that you can add more words later, leave lots of space on the page.

ORGANISATION

Exercise 4

1.
MARY: Hello.
BOB: Hi, is that Mary?
MARY: Yeah.
BOB: Hello, Mary, it's me.
MARY: Oh, hi, Bob, how are you?
BOB: I'm fine, thanks. And you?
MARY: Yeah, OK.

BOB: Listen, Mary, as you know I'm off to Lisbon next week, and I can't leave Felix with my mother because she's ill. Would it be possible for you to feed him while I'm away?
MARY: Yeah, sure. How long are you going for?
BOB: Ten days.
MARY: Yeah, that's no trouble at all.
BOB: Oh, that's very kind of you, thanks.
MARY: No problem. So where are you staying in Lisbon then …

2.
A: Bardens.
B: Oh, good morning. I wonder if you could help me? I'd like to hire some champagne glasses for the weekend. Is that possible?
A: How many d'you want?
B: About 50.
A: Yeah, that's fine.
B: Great. And how much will that be?
A: There's no charge.
B: Really. That's amazing. But … do I have to leave a deposit?
A: Yes. Twenty pounds.
B: OK. And when could I pick them up?
A: Ah, well …

3.
A: Good morning.
B: Oh, hello. Could I speak to Mrs Howard, please?
A: Yes, speaking.
B: Oh, hello, Mrs Howard, it's John Cudmore from BF here.
A: Oh, hello. How are you?
B: Fine, thanks. I'm just ringing to arrange our meeting.
A: Oh, yes. How about sometime next week?
B: Well, I'm afraid I have to go to Paris tomorrow, and I'll be away till the weekend. But how about Thursday the 24th? Is that convenient for you?
A: Um, let me just look in my diary …

UNIT 19 PUT YOUR TRUST IN OTHERS

IT'S UP TO YOU

Exercise 3

1.
JOUMANA: I'd really like to believe this man. He looks wonderful. He looks like a nice, old man, like you expect a grandfather to look, but I don't think I'd let anyone in my house if I didn't know them.
LORELEI: It breaks my heart to say this but I wouldn't let this man in my house. He looks very sad. I might want to give him some money, but I certainly wouldn't want to let him in my house.

2.
JOUMANA: I most definitely would not believe this woman. I wouldn't believe that she lost her purse or she left it at home, but I would believe that she didn't have any money. And I wouldn't believe that she would want to use the money for a bus fare, either. Erm, but I think I'd give her something anyway.
LORELEI: This woman – I, I might not believe it, only because I'm suspicious by nature. But I certainly would give her the money. She looks very sweet, and a bit like a grandma, and er, yes, I'd, I'd be inclined to want to take care of her, so I would give her money, yes.

3.

JOUMANA: I definitely would not accept a ride from this man, whatever happened. And I think I wouldn't say a thing, hoping he'd go away, but if he doesn't go away, I'd threaten to scream very loudly.

LORELEI: I certainly wouldn't take a ride with this man although he looks pleasant enough. And it's not because I hate his shirt, it's just because I don't think it is safe to get in a car with a man you don't know.

4.

JOUMANA: I would very much want to help this woman. Um, she looks like such a nice mom, but having been brought up in a, in a city, I still couldn't get myself to do it. I would help her by, um, telling her that I'll go down the road and phone a local locksmith's for her, or go to the nearest police station and tell them to come help her, but I wouldn't physically help her.

LORELEI: Yes, if this woman asked for help, I probably would. I mean, I look at her – well, frankly, it's like looking in a mirror, and, um, I trust myself, so I think I would trust her and help her, yes.

5.

JOUMANA: Erm, I would be extremely suspicious, and I would question him again and again. I'd probably keep saying, 'OK, but what do I have to do?' And if he was terribly persistent, I'd just take it and walk away.

LORELEI: If this man came up to me and offered me $100, I'd say something like, 'Take a hike, Buddy' or 'Why don't you use it and get yourself a haircut?'

REVIEW AND DEVELOPMENT

REVIEW OF UNIT 17

Exercise 1B

BARRIE: Have you ever seen a man who looks like a dog?

BOB: Yes, I saw a bus driver who looked like a greyhound once.

REBECCA: No, I haven't but I know a woman who looks exactly like a cat.

BARRIE: Have you ever seen a woman who looks like a bird?

JACQUI: Yes, I've got a friend who looks like a bird because she's got an extremely long nose.

BARRIE: Have you ever seen a photo that looks like a painting?

REBECCA: Yes, my father took a beautiful photograph in Italy that looked just like a painting. I wish I'd taken it.

BARRIE: Have you ever seen a house that looks like a museum?

REBECCA: Yes, my grandmother bought all her furniture and pictures in the 1930s, so the house looked like a 1930s museum.

BARRIE: Have you ever seen a vegetable that looks like a person's face?

JACQUI: No, I haven't, but I have seen, um, a potato that looked like somebody's bottom.

BARRIE: Have you ever seen a telephone that looks like a statue?

REBECCA: Yes, I saw one in a shop. It was horrible.

BARRIE: Have you ever seen a hat that looks like a fruit basket?

JACQUI: Yes, I have … at the racing at Ascot last year. I saw a wonderful hat covered in fruit that looked just like a fruit basket.

BARRIE: Have you seen a, a cigarette lighter that looks like a gun?

BOB: Yes, I own a cigarette lighter that looks like a gun.

BARRIE: How about … have you ever seen a child who looks like an adult?

JACQUI: Yes. About two weeks ago on television on one of the interview programmes. A child was interviewed, and he looked like an adult and he even sounded like an adult, but he was only eight years old.

REVIEW AND DEVELOPMENT

REVIEW OF UNIT 18

Exercise 3

The answers are:
among and *stomach*
borrow and *shopping*
average and *busy*
noun and *crowd*
height and *crime*
Greece and *at least*
own and *notebook*
champagne and *neighbour*
solution and *arrange*
corkscrew and *organise*

UNIT 20 THE SENSES

SOUNDS OF THE TWENTIETH CENTURY

Exercise 1

1. someone opening a can of fizzy drink
2. a washing machine on fast spin
3. a digital wrist watch
4. the hiss of a fellow passenger's personal stereo
5. the ping of an oven or microwave when it's ready
6. a video machine ejecting a cassette
7. a computer keyboard
8. the zoom lens on a camera
9. a doorbell

Exercise 3

A: Excuse me.
B: (*no reply*)
A: Excuse me.
B: (*no reply*)
A: Excuse me.
B: Yes?
A: Could you turn that thing down a bit. It's making a horrible noise.
B: But I'm using headphones.
A: Yes, I know, but I can still hear it, and it's very irritating.
B: Right, OK. Is that better?
A: Yes. Thank you.

CHOOSING PERFUMES AND EAU DE COLOGNE

Exercise 3

Version 1
Perfume comes in different concentrations, with *perfume* being the strongest and longest lasting: it has about 20% perfume and 80% alcohol. *Eau de toilette* contains about 5-12% perfume, while *eau de cologne* contains only 2-6%. There is a fairly new product called *eau de parfum* which contains up to 15% pure perfume. *After-shave*, which is of course for men, is similar to eau de toilette, but has more alcohol in it to clean the skin, and less smell.

If you're planning to buy perfume, the best time is later in the day when your sense of smell is better than in the morning. It's best not to test more than two at a time (one on each wrist) or your nose will become confused. You often see people rubbing it, which isn't a good idea. You should really wait for about 30 minutes for the perfume to develop on your skin. And then it should last for a few hours after that.

Perfumes smell different on different people with different skins. Other things can affect it too: smoking, for one. If you're taking any medication, it can affect the skin, and certain strong foods like garlic and spices can change the smell of a perfume.

Don't try to save perfume for special occasions because it evaporates, or goes darker. Use it within six months of opening it, and keep it in a cool, dark place, like a drawer or a box.

Version 2

MAN: So tell me, I've always been confused. Perfume, after-shave, eau de toilette, eau de parfum and eau de cologne – how are they different?

WOMAN: Oh, it's about the, the different concentrations of perfume, the balance between perfume and alcohol.

MAN: I see.

WOMAN: Uh, so the strongest is, is perfume, which has about 20% perfume to 80% alcohol, and of course that means that it lasts longer. Um, and then you come to the eau de toilette, which is about 5–12% perfume, um, and then you're down to the eau de cologne, which is about 2–6% perfume, and of course doesn't last as long.

MAN: I see.

WOMAN: Um, now after-shave, which is of course for men, um, is similar to eau de toilette, but it has a bit more alcohol and that's to clean the skin.

MAN: Oh.

WOMAN: Now the new product, the one that people might not be quite so familiar with, is eau de parfum, and that comes in between perfume and eau de toilette. It's got about 15% perfume. So that's the scale of all those things.

MAN: So when is the best time of the day to test perfume or after-shave?

WOMAN: Oh, the best time is, is the end of the day.

MAN: Really?

WOMAN: Well, that's because, um, the end of the day your sense of smell is, is better, which is why, um, it's quite possible to, to buy something when your sense of smell is not good, and you get it home, and you don't like it. So you need to buy it when your sense of smell is, is strong which is at the end of the day.

MAN: I see, yes. So what's the maximum number of types then you can test at one time?

WOMAN: Well, really you should you should only test two. I mean we're all tempted to try them all, but, um, your nose will get confused by more than two smells. You can have one on each hand and then it's quite easy to separate them. If you've got more than one on one hand, they start to, the smells start to mix, of course.

MAN: How long should it last on your skin, then?

WOMAN: Well, obviously this depends on the strength, whether it's perfume or eau de cologne, etc.

MAN: Yeah.

WOMAN: Um, and on your skin because we all have different reactions, but it should last a few hours.

MAN: So, well what affects it, you know, when you're wearing it?

WOMAN: Um, well the skin obviously. Um, and people react differently, so a perfume that might smell, you might recognise a perfume on someone and think it's really wonderful, you go and try it, and it smells different because your skin is different. And so, of course, that will change how the perfume smells. But there are … anything that can change your skin will affect it, so if you smoke, that can change how the perfume reacts on your skin. And certain things you eat, of course, coming from the outside …

MAN: Of course.

WOMAN: … from the inside out, um, very strong spicy food can, can affect perfume. Also any, any medicine, because that's affecting you from the inside, and affecting your skin can change perfume, so it doesn't always stay the same.

MAN: So, after you've opened a bottle of perfume, how long can you keep it?

WOMAN: Um, well, I suppose about six months before it starts to change. We've all done it, we've all kept perfume at the back of the drawer, and we think it's our favourite one, so we save it up, but actually that's a very bad idea because your favourite perfume, which you've carefully hoarded, does start to change and so it doesn't smell the same, so if possible it's best to use it before that time.

REVIEW AND DEVELOPMENT

REVIEW OF UNIT 18

Exercise 1

1. Do beards grow on trees?
2. If a man escapes, does he get away?
3. If a shop is crowded, is it full of people?
4. Is *empty* the opposite of *full*?
5. If you complain about something, are you happy?
6. Can you feed a cat?
7. Can you take trousers to a dry cleaner's?
8. Can you put trousers in a diary?
9. Does a meeting often have an agenda?
10. Does a credit card have a number?
11. If you go on foot, do you walk?
12. If you cancel a meeting, does it take place?
13. If you are on your own, are you with other people?
14. If you punch someone, are they happy?
15. Do you open wine bottles with a corkscrew?

UNIT 21 TIME

A NEW WORLD CALENDAR

Exercise 1

January February March April May June July
August September October November December

1st 2nd 3rd 4th 5th 6th 7th 8th 9th 10th
11th 12th 13th 14th 15th 16th 17th 18th 19th
20th
21st 22nd 23rd 24th 25th 26th 27th 28th 29th
30th 31st

SOME TIME IN MY PAST

Exercise 4

1. Jack
I've retired now, and there's a lot I like about being retired. I've got plenty of time to do the things *I* want, not what everyone else wants me to do. For instance, I used to have my

own business, and I had to work every weekend. That's a thing of the past, thank goodness. Nowadays I'm out in the garden all the time or I go for long walks, which I never used to do.

I find my tastes have changed a bit too. I spend a lot of time listening to classical music, and I know that this will surprise you but, er, I also like loud rock music. I used to love punk music in the 70s. I think it's because I'm a bit of an anarchist – I never really enjoyed wearing a suit, being a businessman, all that kind of thing. And I used to have long hair when I was younger. It always embarrassed my children!

2. Val

Well, I teach little children and I don't have a family myself, so I think of my pupils as 'my' children. I used to have a lot of problems with them but, well, I've got a lot more experience now and I can handle them better. I think all children fight – I used to have fights with my sister, but we get on OK now. I think it's just part of learning to live with each other.

Teaching children is *really* hard work. At first I used to get home and just, well I just used to fall asleep on the sofa, often in front of the TV. And then I remember thinking, 'Oh, this is stupid. What a waste of time!' So I joined a book club. I never used to read much, but these days I *really* enjoy it. It makes me forget about work, and well, it makes me forget about work in the nicest possible way.

3. Don

INTERVIEWER: How old are you, Don?

DON: 16.

INTERVIEWER: Right, well, I want to know a bit about your spare time, I mean, what do you do in your free time?

DON: Well, I go to concerts a lot with my friends, and we go to lots of discos and parties.

INTERVIEWER: Hmm. And what about sport? Do you get any exercise?

DON: No, nothing much apart from dancing. I don't have time for it. I used to play tennis, but I'm too old now.

INTERVIEWER: What?

DON: Well, I mean, all my friends have stopped playing. We used to play when I was about 10 or 12, but …

INTERVIEWER: Right. OK, well, how about when you're at home?

DON: What, with my family?

INTERVIEWER: Yes.

DON: Well, I don't spend much time at home. I suppose we have dinner together, watch the news, that kind of thing. I used to play a lot of computer games, but my dad got worried because I did it for five hours a day, so one day he gave me some money to go to a concert, and that was it. I bet he's sorry now!

REVIEW AND DEVELOPMENT

REVIEW OF UNIT 20

Exercise 2

BOB: I like the smell of lemons.

REBECCA: Mmm, so do I.

BOB: I can speak Swedish.

REBECCA: So can I.

BOB: I don't like black coffee very much.

REBECCA: No, neither do I.

BOB: I'm not very interested in sport.

REBECCA: Oh, really? I am.

BOB: I'm British.

REBECCA: I'm not.

BOB: I can't stand noisy neighbours.

REBECCA: No, neither can I.

BOB: I live in a flat.

REBECCA: So do I.

BOB: I can swim.

REBECCA: Oh, really? I can't.

BOB: I don't eat meat.

REBECCA: No, neither do I.

BOB: I'm going to the theatre next week.

REBECCA: Oh, really? I'm not.

UNIT 22 A SENSE OF HISTORY

HISTORICAL EVENTS

Exercise 1

First of all, in 1947, India became an independent country. Then in 1960, Theodore Maiman was one of the men responsible for the invention and development of lasers. Fourteen years later, after a huge scandal known as *Watergate*, President Richard Nixon was forced to resign, and in the following year General Franco died after thirty-six years in power.

The nineteen eighties didn't start very well. In 1980, John Lennon was murdered in front of his own apartment block by a man called Mark Chapman, and then the next year, Anwar Sadat was assassinated in Egypt by rebel soldiers during a ceremony.

Seven years on, a dreadful earthquake in Armenia killed 45,000 people, and in the same year as that, Carl Lewis won the 100 metres gold medal at the Seoul Olympics. In actual fact, he came second in the race to Ben Johnson of Canada, but Johnson lost his gold medal because he had been taking illegal drugs.

In 1991, Boris Yeltsin was elected President of Russia. And it was in the following year that part of Windsor Castle, which is one of Queen Elizabeth's official residences, was destroyed by fire … and the damage was estimated at over £40 million.

REWRITING HISTORY

Exercise 2

Version 1

1.

I remember learning that life began in the sea, and I also remember our teacher telling us about all the wives of King Henry the Eighth. Oh, and I remember seeing pictures of all of them in my history book.

When we were about 16, we studied the history of America, and I remember learning a lot about the Wall Street Crash which started the Depression in the 1930s, but not much before that – and I don't remember learning anything about the American Civil War, or George Washington and all that.

Oh, and I can remember studying the history of Ancient Greece and the Romans, but I couldn't tell you now anything that I learnt – except that I think the Romans invented some kind of central heating system under the floor!

2.

Uh, I remember, er, when I was about ten years old doing, er, a project on the Roman Empire. And I was about ten years old, and I was very proud of it, er, cos I'd written six pages – but I'd actually copied a lot of it from an encyclopaedia.

3.

I don't remember much history from, from senior school. Er, the history I learnt at junior school made a much stronger impression. I can, I can remember studying the Vikings. I, I thought they were wonderful. I can remember making a model of a Viking longboat from straws.

4.

I wasn't really very good at history. We had a succession of rather bad history teachers at my convent. But I remember once our history teacher was ill and another teacher took the lesson, and it was marvellous. It was all about the Russian Revolution and Rasputin, and it was so exciting … and, um, from then onwards I, I enjoyed it much more.

Version 2

1.

I remember learning about the Aztecs in Mexico, and I do remember studying King Henry the Eighth and all of his wives. I don't remember learning anything about, er, modern history and the things that have directly affected my life now.

2.

I remember learning a lot about acts of parliament and kings and queens and famous English personalities. But I don't remember learning anything about the history of other countries, apart from occasionally something in French or German history, but nothing about the rest of the world what we might call …

3.

I don't really remember any details about, um, the history that I learnt. Certainly not dates or political events, but there are certain periods that interested me very much; like I remember, um, Ancient Egypt and, er, I was always fascinated by the, the gods that were like animals, like Osiris and, um, and Isis, and, uh, those, those things. And, er, also Stone Age Britain I was, I was always fascinated by. But the thing I enjoyed most really in all those things were doing the drawings and, and the details and what people wore and things like that.

4.

I remember learning a great deal about the social and economic history of England, and being very upset over the little boys working down the mines. But I don't really remember learning very much about, um, foreign history at all. A little bit of French history, perhaps, but, um, nothing really about anywhere else in the world.

REVIEW AND DEVELOPMENT

REVIEW OF UNIT 20
Exercise 1A

The smell of burning wood always reminds me of going camping when I was a child and being outdoors and my parents.

The smell of cigar smoke always reminds me of an uncle who used to visit us every year, and he was rich, so I associate cigar smoke with being given pocket money.

The smell of leather reminds me of my first car which had leather seats and I remember the thrill of driving away for the first time.

The feel of snakeskin reminds me of a briefcase I was given once as a gift.

The taste of mouthwash reminds me of the dentist and makes me feel very uncomfortable.

The taste of cream reminds me of when I was a child and it was a treat on Sundays.

The feel of marble always reminds me of Spain and cold marble floors in all the houses.

UNIT 23 WHOSE LIFE IS IT ANYWAY?

CHOOSING A NAME

Exercise 4

Here, according to Jo-Ann, are some mistakes that people make:

First of all, it isn't a good idea to give your child the same name as his father, because the child always feels that he is smaller as a person. Even if he's really tall! Boxer George Foreman has named five sons after himself. Those children will always be George Foreman.

And another thing you should never do is to give a child a, um, a 'joke' name like Lloyd Boyd, for instance. Or giving a child the name of a character from, from a nursery rhyme.

You also have to be very careful about names that seem strange to other people. In the hippie days, people used names like Seagull, America and, er, and Free. For some reason, famous people tend to use unusual names. The singer and actress Cher named her children Chastity and Elijah Blue. *Rambo* star Sylvester Stallone has a son called Sage Moonblood. These are not the greatest names to give kids.

But if your surname is common like Smith or Jones, avoid a plain first name like Jane or John. Choose something distinctive. For instance, the film star Sigourney Weaver's real first name is Susan. She felt the name didn't fit her, so she chose the name Sigourney. That really is quite distinctive.

Finally, don't choose funny little names like Bitsy, Buffy and Fifi. These belong to cats and dogs – not people. A silly name can cause lots of problems when a child grows up and starts to make a career.

CHOOSING A PARTNER

Exercise 3

Version 1

Joumana

I think it's very important that, erm, a partner has the same interests and hobbies, because if you are working all day every day and you just have a bit of free time in the evenings and on weekends, you should at least be able to spend the time together, doing things you both enjoy doing.

I don't think it's terribly important to have a similar financial situation. Erm, it's OK to help each other out when you need to; if someone's earning more than another, that's OK.

What I think is very important is that you have, er, similar education, so that you are basically on the same level, you can speak to each other on the same level.

Coming from different countries, er, might be exciting, but it can cause a lot of problems culturally, and, erm, you can end up quite confused, not knowing exactly where you stand, so … coming from the same country as your partner is quite important.

TRUE TO LIFE PRE-INTERMEDIATE © Cambridge University Press 1995

Version 2
Nick

Choosing a partner, I think one of the most important things is that you share the same interests, and likes and dislikes about how you like to fill your time. That's very important to me, that you can … I like going to the theatre, to the cinema, erm, and I would like somebody that would come along with me to share those experiences. And that I think is the most important thing that leads towards you being partners for life.

Er, something that is important to me, but I don't think would be important for the partner would be the sort of food we eat. Um, I'm a vegetarian, but I don't, erm, try and push that onto anybody else, and in fact, I, I feed meat to my cats, so … I mean, I still support the meat industry. So, er, and I think you can, you can sort of eat quite separately if, if that was necessary.

It is quite important that whoever was going to be my partner had similar political views. I don't think I have very entrenched views, but if I meet somebody who is radically different from me, I find it difficult. It gets in the way of everything else, so they have to be somewhere close politically to me.

I don't think it's important, erm, the education you've had, because, er, well, I feel that most of your education comes after you've left school anyway, um, so that shouldn't be an issue. As long as you're the same sort of people, if you're on the same wavelength, I think that's the most important thing.

REVIEW AND DEVELOPMENT

REVIEW OF UNIT 21

Exercise 1

1. What do they do when they get home from school?
2. The play lasted over three and a half hours.
3. I'll ring her when I've got the money for her.
4. He's going to get married in a fortnight's time.
5. When I was younger, I never used to like the taste of garlic.
6. She used to listen to music a lot, but these days she prefers gardening.

UNIT 24 CINEMA AND THE ARTS

CREATIVE PEOPLE

Exercise 3

INTERVIEWER: You chose to be a costume designer, but with the kind of skills that you have, maybe you could've been other things. I mean, do you think you could be, um, a fashion designer, for example?
NICKIE: I think I definitely could be a fashion designer.
INTERVIEWER: Really?
NICKIE: Yes, because I design clothes in my job, and very often I do have to design modern clothes.
INTERVIEWER: Right. How about a photographer?
NICKIE: I don't think I could be a photographer. I think it's a bit too technical for me, too many gadgets to work with.
INTERVIEWER: I see. OK. And, er, an architect. Is that very different?
NICKIE: I think possibly I could've been an architect because in my training … I trained to design sets as well, so that entails a lot of technical drawings which I could do if I wanted to.
INTERVIEWER: So you did a lot of drawing. So how about being a painter?

NICKIE: I could be a painter. I don't think I'd be a very good painter, though.
INTERVIEWER: OK.

INTERVIEWER: So Martin, you're a holographer, but I'm going to ask you about some other jobs. Uh … do you think, for example, an architect, could you … could you be an architect with your skills?
MARTIN: No, I, I don't think I could be an architect. Um … architecture requires skills about precision, and I think a great understanding of how things are put together, and I, and I think my skills are more about, um, understanding *why* things work and maybe not how.
INTERVIEWER: OK. And could you be a, a photographer?
MARTIN: Yes, I could be a photographer. My, my own discipline of holography and photography is very closely inter-related.
INTERVIEWER: Um, what about a fashion designer? Could you be a fashion designer?
MARTIN: No, I could never be a fashion designer. Um, I, I love clothes very much, um, but, um, I don't understand fabrics well enough and, you know, how clothes are made to, to be a successful fashion designer.
INTERVIEWER: And how about a painter?
MARTIN: Um, like Nickie, I think I could be a painter, but not a good painter.
INTERVIEWER: A better holographer?
MARTIN: A better holographer, I think so, yes.

THE OSCARS

Exercise 3

1. The Oscar awards began in a. 1927 b. 1931 or c. 1937.
2. The Oscar got its name when a secretary thought it looked like a. her father b. her brother or c. her uncle.
3. An Oscar is a. 24cm high b. 34cm high, or c. 44cm high.
4. Each year members of the Academy choose the winners from a. four films b. five films c. six films.
5. The ceremony was postponed in 1968 because of the death of a. Ronald Reagan b. Louis B Mayer or c. Martin Luther King.
6. *Ben Hur* won a. nine Oscars b. ten Oscars or c. eleven Oscars.
7. Woody Allen has won a. two Oscars b. three Oscars or c. five Oscars.
8. When she won her award Shirley Temple was a. five b. seven or c. nine.
9. Jessica Tandy won her award in a. 1989 b. 1990 or c.1991.
10. An Oscar will probably increase the earnings of a film by more than a. $10m b. $20m or c. $200m.